Machine Learning with Python Cookbook

Practical Solutions from Preprocessing to Deep Learning

Chris Albon

Beijing · Boston · Farnham · Sebastopol · Tokyo

Machine Learning with Python Cookbook

by Chris Albon

Published by O'Reilly Media, Inc., 1005 Gravenstein Highway North, Sebastopol, CA 95472.

O'Reilly books may be purchased for educational, business, or sales promotional use. Online editions are also available for most titles (*http://oreilly.com/safari*). For more information, contact our corporate/institutional sales department: 800-998-9938 or *corporate@oreilly.com*.

Editors: Rachel Roumeliotis and Jeff Bleiel
Production Editor: Melanie Yarbrough
Copyeditor: Kim Cofer
Proofreader: Rachel Monaghan

Indexer: Wendy Catalano
Interior Designer: David Futato
Cover Designer: Karen Montgomery
Illustrator: Rebecca Demarest

April 2018:   First Edition

Revision History for the First Edition

2018-03-09:   First Release

See *http://oreilly.com/catalog/errata.csp?isbn=9781491989388* for release details.

978-1-491-98938-8

[LSI]

Table of Contents

Preface

Over the last few years machine learning has become embedded in a wide variety of day-to-day business, nonprofit, and government operations. As the popularity of machine learning increased, a cottage industry of high-quality literature that taught applied machine learning to practitioners developed. This literature has been highly successful in training an entire generation of data scientists and machine learning engineers. This literature also approached the topic of machine learning from the perspective of providing a learning resource to teach an individual what machine learning is and how it works. However, while fruitful, this approach left out a different perspective on the topic: the nuts and bolts of doing machine learning day to day. That is the motivation of this book—not as a tome of machine learning knowledge for the student but as a wrench for the professional, to sit with dog-eared pages on desks ready to solve the practical day-to-day problems of a machine learning practitioner.

More specifically, the book takes a task-based approach to machine learning, with almost 200 self-contained solutions (you can copy and paste the code and it'll run) for the most common tasks a data scientist or machine learning engineer building a model will run into.

The ultimate goal is for the book to be a reference for people building real machine learning systems. For example, imagine a reader has a JSON file containing 1,000 categorical and numerical features with missing data and categorical target vectors with imbalanced classes, and wants an interpretable model. The motivation for this book is to provide recipes to help the reader learn processes such as:

- 2.5 Loading a JSON file
- 4.2 Standardizing a Feature
- 5.3 Encoding Dictionaries of Features
- 5.4 Imputing Missing Class Values

- 9.1 Reducing Features Using Principal Components
- 12.2 Selecting Best Models Using Randomized Search
- 14.4 Training a Random Forest Classifier
- 14.7 Selecting Random Features in Random Forests

The goal is for the reader to be able to:

1. Copy/paste the code and gain confidence that it actually works with the included toy dataset.
2. Read the discussion to gain an understanding of the theory behind the technique the code is executing and learn which parameters are important to consider.
3. Insert/combine/adapt the code from the recipes to construct the actual application.

Who This Book Is For

This book is not an introduction to machine learning. If you are not comfortable with the basic concepts of machine learning or have never spent time learning machine learning, do not buy this book. Instead, this book is for the machine learning practitioner who, while comfortable with the theory and concepts of machine learning, would benefit from a quick reference containing code to solve challenges he runs into working on machine learning on an everyday basis.

This book assumes the reader is comfortable with the Python programming language and package management.

Who This Book Is Not For

As stated previously, this book is not an introduction to machine learning. This book should not be your first. If you are unfamiliar with concepts like cross-validation, random forest, and gradient descent, you will likely not benefit from this book as much as one of the many high-quality texts specifically designed to introduce you to the topic. I recommend reading one of those books and then coming back to this book to learn working, practical solutions for machine learning.

Terminology Used in This Book

Machine learning draws upon techniques from a wide range of fields, including computer science, statistics, and mathematics. For this reason, there is significant variation in the terminology used in the discussions of machine learning:

Observation
    A single unit in our level of observation—for example, a person, a sale, or a record.

Learning algorithms
    An algorithm used to learn the best parameters of a model—for example, linear regression, naive Bayes, or decision trees.

Models
    An output of a learning algorithm's training. Learning algorithms train models, which we then use to make predictions.

Parameters
    The weights or coefficients of a model learned through training.

Hyperparameters
    The settings of a learning algorithm that need to be set before training.

Performance
    A metric used to evaluate a model.

Loss
    A metric to maximize or minimize through training.

Train
    Applying a learning algorithm to data using numerical approaches like gradient descent.

Fit
    Applying a learning algorithm to data using analytical approaches.

Data
    A collection of observations.

Acknowledgments

This book would not have been possible without the kind help of a number of friends and strangers. Listing everyone who lent a hand to this project would be impossible, but I wanted to at least mention: Angela Bassa, Teresa Borcuch, Justin Bozonier, Andre deBruin, Numa Dhamani, Dan Friedman, Joel Grus, Sarah Guido, Bill Kambouroglou, Mat Kelcey, Lizzie Kumar, Hilary Parker, Niti Paudyal, Sebastian Raschka, and Shreya Shankar.

I owe them all a beer or five.

## CHAPTER 1

Vectors, Matrices, and Arrays

1.0 Introduction

NumPy is the foundation of the Python machine learning stack. NumPy allows for efficient operations on the data structures often used in machine learning: vectors, matrices, and tensors. While NumPy is not the focus of this book, it will show up frequently throughout the following chapters. This chapter covers the most common NumPy operations we are likely to run into while working on machine learning workflows.

1.1 Creating a Vector

Problem

You need to create a vector.

Solution

Use NumPy to create a one-dimensional array:

```
# Load library
import numpy as np

# Create a vector as a row
vector_row = np.array([1, 2, 3])

# Create a vector as a column
vector_column = np.array([[1],
                          [2],
                          [3]])
```

Discussion

NumPy's main data structure is the multidimensional array. To create a vector, we simply create a one-dimensional array. Just like vectors, these arrays can be represented horizontally (i.e., rows) or vertically (i.e., columns).

See Also

- Vectors, Math Is Fun (*http://bit.ly/2FB5q1v*)
- Euclidean vector, Wikipedia (*http://bit.ly/2FtnRoL*)

1.2 Creating a Matrix

Problem

You need to create a matrix.

Solution

Use NumPy to create a two-dimensional array:

```
# Load library
import numpy as np

# Create a matrix
matrix = np.array([[1, 2],
                   [1, 2],
                   [1, 2]])
```

Discussion

To create a matrix we can use a NumPy two-dimensional array. In our solution, the matrix contains three rows and two columns (a column of 1s and a column of 2s).

NumPy actually has a dedicated matrix data structure:

```
matrix_object = np.mat([[1, 2],
                        [1, 2],
                        [1, 2]])

matrix([[1, 2],
        [1, 2],
        [1, 2]])
```

However, the matrix data structure is not recommended for two reasons. First, arrays are the de facto standard data structure of NumPy. Second, the vast majority of NumPy operations return arrays, not matrix objects.

See Also

- Matrix, Wikipedia (*http://bit.ly/2Ftnevp*)
- Matrix, Wolfram MathWorld (*http://bit.ly/2Fut7IJ*)

1.3 Creating a Sparse Matrix

Problem

Given data with very few nonzero values, you want to efficiently represent it.

Solution

Create a sparse matrix:

```
# Load libraries
import numpy as np
from scipy import sparse

# Create a matrix
matrix = np.array([[0, 0],
                   [0, 1],
                   [3, 0]])

# Create compressed sparse row (CSR) matrix
matrix_sparse = sparse.csr_matrix(matrix)
```

Discussion

A frequent situation in machine learning is having a huge amount of data; however, most of the elements in the data are zeros. For example, imagine a matrix where the columns are every movie on Netflix, the rows are every Netflix user, and the values are how many times a user has watched that particular movie. This matrix would have tens of thousands of columns and millions of rows! However, since most users do not watch most movies, the vast majority of elements would be zero.

Sparse matrices only store nonzero elements and assume all other values will be zero, leading to significant computational savings. In our solution, we created a NumPy array with two nonzero values, then converted it into a sparse matrix. If we view the sparse matrix we can see that only the nonzero values are stored:

```
# View sparse matrix
print(matrix_sparse)

  (1, 1)    1
  (2, 0)    3
```

There are a number of types of sparse matrices. However, in *compressed sparse row* (CSR) matrices, (1, 1) and (2, 0) represent the (zero-indexed) indices of the non-zero values 1 and 3, respectively. For example, the element 1 is in the second row and second column. We can see the advantage of sparse matrices if we create a much larger matrix with many more zero elements and then compare this larger matrix with our original sparse matrix:

```
# Create larger matrix
matrix_large = np.array([[0, 0, 0, 0, 0, 0, 0, 0, 0, 0],
                         [0, 1, 0, 0, 0, 0, 0, 0, 0, 0],
                         [3, 0, 0, 0, 0, 0, 0, 0, 0, 0]])

# Create compressed sparse row (CSR) matrix
matrix_large_sparse = sparse.csr_matrix(matrix_large)

# View original sparse matrix
print(matrix_sparse)

  (1, 1)    1
  (2, 0)    3

# View larger sparse matrix
print(matrix_large_sparse)

  (1, 1)    1
  (2, 0)    3
```

As we can see, despite the fact that we added many more zero elements in the larger matrix, its sparse representation is exactly the same as our original sparse matrix. That is, the addition of zero elements did not change the size of the sparse matrix.

As mentioned, there are many different types of sparse matrices, such as compressed sparse column, list of lists, and dictionary of keys. While an explanation of the different types and their implications is outside the scope of this book, it is worth noting that while there is no "best" sparse matrix type, there are meaningful differences between them and we should be conscious about why we are choosing one type over another.

See Also

- Sparse matrices, SciPy documentation (*http://bit.ly/2HReBZR*)
- 101 Ways to Store a Sparse Matrix (*http://bit.ly/2HS43cI*)

1.4 Selecting Elements

Problem

You need to select one or more elements in a vector or matrix.

Solution

NumPy's arrays make that easy:

```
# Load library
import numpy as np

# Create row vector
vector = np.array([1, 2, 3, 4, 5, 6])

# Create matrix
matrix = np.array([[1, 2, 3],
                   [4, 5, 6],
                   [7, 8, 9]])

# Select third element of vector
vector[2]

3

# Select second row, second column
matrix[1,1]

5
```

Discussion

Like most things in Python, NumPy arrays are zero-indexed, meaning that the index of the first element is 0, not 1. With that caveat, NumPy offers a wide variety of methods for selecting (i.e., indexing and slicing) elements or groups of elements in arrays:

```
# Select all elements of a vector
vector[:]

array([1, 2, 3, 4, 5, 6])

# Select everything up to and including the third element
vector[:3]

array([1, 2, 3])

# Select everything after the third element
vector[3:]

array([4, 5, 6])

# Select the last element
vector[-1]

6

# Select the first two rows and all columns of a matrix
matrix[:2,:]

array([[1, 2, 3],
       [4, 5, 6]])
```

```
# Select all rows and the second column
matrix[:,1:2]

array([[2],
       [5],
       [8]])
```

1.5 Describing a Matrix

Problem

You want to describe the shape, size, and dimensions of the matrix.

Solution

Use shape, size, and ndim:

```
# Load library
import numpy as np

# Create matrix
matrix = np.array([[1, 2, 3, 4],
                   [5, 6, 7, 8],
                   [9, 10, 11, 12]])

# View number of rows and columns
matrix.shape

(3, 4)

# View number of elements (rows * columns)
matrix.size

12

# View number of dimensions
matrix.ndim

2
```

Discussion

This might seem basic (and it is); however, time and again it will be valuable to check the shape and size of an array both for further calculations and simply as a gut check after some operation.

1.6 Applying Operations to Elements

Problem

You want to apply some function to multiple elements in an array.

Solution

Use NumPy's vectorize:

```python
# Load library
import numpy as np

# Create matrix
matrix = np.array([[1, 2, 3],
                   [4, 5, 6],
                   [7, 8, 9]])

# Create function that adds 100 to something
add_100 = lambda i: i + 100

# Create vectorized function
vectorized_add_100 = np.vectorize(add_100)

# Apply function to all elements in matrix
vectorized_add_100(matrix)

array([[101, 102, 103],
       [104, 105, 106],
       [107, 108, 109]])
```

Discussion

NumPy's vectorize class converts a function into a function that can apply to all elements in an array or slice of an array. It's worth noting that vectorize is essentially a for loop over the elements and does not increase performance. Furthermore, NumPy arrays allow us to perform operations between arrays even if their dimensions are not the same (a process called *broadcasting*). For example, we can create a much simpler version of our solution using broadcasting:

```python
# Add 100 to all elements
matrix + 100

array([[101, 102, 103],
       [104, 105, 106],
       [107, 108, 109]])
```

1.7 Finding the Maximum and Minimum Values

Problem

You need to find the maximum or minimum value in an array.

Solution

Use NumPy's max and min:

```
# Load library
import numpy as np

# Create matrix
matrix = np.array([[1, 2, 3],
                   [4, 5, 6],
                   [7, 8, 9]])

# Return maximum element
np.max(matrix)
```

```
9
```

```
# Return minimum element
np.min(matrix)
```

```
1
```

Discussion

Often we want to know the maximum and minimum value in an array or subset of an array. This can be accomplished with the max and min methods. Using the axis parameter we can also apply the operation along a certain axis:

```
# Find maximum element in each column
np.max(matrix, axis=0)
```

```
array([7, 8, 9])
```

```
# Find maximum element in each row
np.max(matrix, axis=1)
```

```
array([3, 6, 9])
```

1.8 Calculating the Average, Variance, and Standard Deviation

Problem

You want to calculate some descriptive statistics about an array.

Solution

Use NumPy's mean, var, and std:

```
# Load library
import numpy as np

# Create matrix
matrix = np.array([[1, 2, 3],
                   [4, 5, 6],
                   [7, 8, 9]])
```

```
# Return mean
np.mean(matrix)

5.0

# Return variance
np.var(matrix)

6.666666666666667

# Return standard deviation
np.std(matrix)

2.5819888974716112
```

Discussion

Just like with max and min, we can easily get descriptive statistics about the whole matrix or do calculations along a single axis:

```
# Find the mean value in each column
np.mean(matrix, axis=0)

array([ 4.,  5.,  6.])
```

1.9 Reshaping Arrays

Problem

You want to change the shape (number of rows and columns) of an array without changing the element values.

Solution

Use NumPy's reshape:

```
# Load library
import numpy as np

# Create 4x3 matrix
matrix = np.array([[1, 2, 3],
                   [4, 5, 6],
                   [7, 8, 9],
                   [10, 11, 12]])

# Reshape matrix into 2x6 matrix
matrix.reshape(2, 6)

array([[ 1,  2,  3,  4,  5,  6],
       [ 7,  8,  9, 10, 11, 12]])
```

Discussion

reshape allows us to restructure an array so that we maintain the same data but it is organized as a different number of rows and columns. The only requirement is that the shape of the original and new matrix contain the same number of elements (i.e., the same size). We can see the size of a matrix using size:

```
matrix.size
```

```
12
```

One useful argument in reshape is -1, which effectively means "as many as needed," so reshape(-1, 1) means one row and as many columns as needed:

```
matrix.reshape(1, -1)
```

```
array([[ 1,  2,  3,  4,  5,  6,  7,  8,  9, 10, 11, 12]])
```

Finally, if we provide one integer, reshape will return a 1D array of that length:

```
matrix.reshape(12)
```

```
array([ 1,  2,  3,  4,  5,  6,  7,  8,  9, 10, 11, 12])
```

1.10 Transposing a Vector or Matrix

Problem

You need to transpose a vector or matrix.

Solution

Use the T method:

```
# Load library
import numpy as np

# Create matrix
matrix = np.array([[1, 2, 3],
                   [4, 5, 6],
                   [7, 8, 9]])

# Transpose matrix
matrix.T
```

```
array([[1, 4, 7],
       [2, 5, 8],
       [3, 6, 9]])
```

Discussion

Transposing is a common operation in linear algebra where the column and row indices of each element are swapped. One nuanced point that is typically overlooked outside of a linear algebra class is that, technically, a vector cannot be transposed because it is just a collection of values:

```
# Transpose vector
np.array([1, 2, 3, 4, 5, 6]).T

array([1, 2, 3, 4, 5, 6])
```

However, it is common to refer to transposing a vector as converting a row vector to a column vector (notice the second pair of brackets) or vice versa:

```
# Tranpose row vector
np.array([[1, 2, 3, 4, 5, 6]]).T

array([[1],
       [2],
       [3],
       [4],
       [5],
       [6]])
```

1.11 Flattening a Matrix

Problem

You need to transform a matrix into a one-dimensional array.

Solution

Use flatten:

```
# Load library
import numpy as np

# Create matrix
matrix = np.array([[1, 2, 3],
                   [4, 5, 6],
                   [7, 8, 9]])

# Flatten matrix
matrix.flatten()

array([1, 2, 3, 4, 5, 6, 7, 8, 9])
```

Discussion

flatten is a simple method to transform a matrix into a one-dimensional array. Alternatively, we can use reshape to create a row vector:

```
matrix.reshape(1, -1)

array([[1, 2, 3, 4, 5, 6, 7, 8, 9]])
```

1.12 Finding the Rank of a Matrix

Problem

You need to know the rank of a matrix.

Solution

Use NumPy's linear algebra method matrix_rank:

```
# Load library
import numpy as np

# Create matrix
matrix = np.array([[1, 1, 1],
                   [1, 1, 10],
                   [1, 1, 15]])

# Return matrix rank
np.linalg.matrix_rank(matrix)

2
```

Discussion

The rank of a matrix is the dimensions of the vector space spanned by its columns or rows. Finding the rank of a matrix is easy in NumPy thanks to matrix_rank.

See Also

- The Rank of a Matrix, CliffsNotes (*http://bit.ly/2HUzkMs*)

1.13 Calculating the Determinant

Problem

You need to know the determinant of a matrix.

Solution

Use NumPy's linear algebra method det:

```
# Load library
import numpy as np

# Create matrix
matrix = np.array([[1, 2, 3],
                   [2, 4, 6],
                   [3, 8, 9]])

# Return determinant of matrix
np.linalg.det(matrix)

0.0
```

Discussion

It can sometimes be useful to calculate the determinant of a matrix. NumPy makes this easy with det.

See Also

- The determinant | Essence of linear algebra, chapter 5, 3Blue1Brown (*http://bit.ly/2FA6ToM*)
- Determinant, Wolfram MathWorld (*http://bit.ly/2FxSUzC*)

1.14 Getting the Diagonal of a Matrix

Problem

You need to get the diagonal elements of a matrix.

Solution

Use diagonal:

```
# Load library
import numpy as np

# Create matrix
matrix = np.array([[1, 2, 3],
                   [2, 4, 6],
                   [3, 8, 9]])

# Return diagonal elements
matrix.diagonal()
```

```
array([1, 4, 9])
```

Discussion

NumPy makes getting the diagonal elements of a matrix easy with `diagonal`. It is also possible to get a diagonal off from the main diagonal by using the `offset` parameter:

```
# Return diagonal one above the main diagonal
matrix.diagonal(offset=1)

array([2, 6])

# Return diagonal one below the main diagonal
matrix.diagonal(offset=-1)

array([2, 8])
```

1.15 Calculating the Trace of a Matrix

Problem

You need to calculate the trace of a matrix.

Solution

Use `trace`:

```
# Load library
import numpy as np

# Create matrix
matrix = np.array([[1, 2, 3],
                   [2, 4, 6],
                   [3, 8, 9]])

# Return trace
matrix.trace()

14
```

Discussion

The trace of a matrix is the sum of the diagonal elements and is often used under the hood in machine learning methods. Given a NumPy multidimensional array, we can calculate the trace using `trace`. We can also return the diagonal of a matrix and calculate its sum:

```
# Return diagonal and sum elements
sum(matrix.diagonal())

14
```

See Also

- The Trace of a Square Matrix (*http://bit.ly/2FunM45*)

1.16 Finding Eigenvalues and Eigenvectors

Problem

You need to find the eigenvalues and eigenvectors of a square matrix.

Solution

Use NumPy's `linalg.eig`:

```
# Load library
import numpy as np

# Create matrix
matrix = np.array([[1, -1, 3],
                   [1, 1, 6],
                   [3, 8, 9]])

# Calculate eigenvalues and eigenvectors
eigenvalues, eigenvectors = np.linalg.eig(matrix)

# View eigenvalues
eigenvalues

array([ 13.55075847,   0.74003145,  -3.29078992])

# View eigenvectors
eigenvectors

array([[-0.17622017, -0.96677403, -0.53373322],
       [-0.435951  ,  0.2053623 , -0.64324848],
       [-0.88254925,  0.15223105,  0.54896288]])
```

Discussion

Eigenvectors are widely used in machine learning libraries. Intuitively, given a linear transformation represented by a matrix, *A*, eigenvectors are vectors that, when that transformation is applied, change only in scale (not direction). More formally:

$$A\mathbf{v} = \lambda\mathbf{v}$$

where *A* is a square matrix, λ contains the eigenvalues and *v* contains the eigenvectors. In NumPy's linear algebra toolset, `eig` lets us calculate the eigenvalues, and eigenvectors of any square matrix.

See Also

- Eigenvectors and Eigenvalues Explained Visually, Setosa.io (*http://bit.ly/2Hb32LV*)
- Eigenvectors and eigenvalues | Essence of linear algebra, Chapter 10, 3Blue1Brown (*http://bit.ly/2HeGppK*)

1.17 Calculating Dot Products

Problem

You need to calculate the dot product of two vectors.

Solution

Use NumPy's dot:

```
# Load library
import numpy as np

# Create two vectors
vector_a = np.array([1,2,3])
vector_b = np.array([4,5,6])

# Calculate dot product
np.dot(vector_a, vector_b)

32
```

Discussion

The dot product of two vectors, *a* and *b*, is defined as:

$$\sum_{i=1}^{n} a_i b_i$$

where a_i is the *i*th element of vector *a*. We can use NumPy's dot class to calculate the dot product. Alternatively, in Python 3.5+ we can use the new @ operator:

```
# Calculate dot product
vector_a @ vector_b

32
```

See Also

- Vector dot product and vector length, Khan Academy (*http://bit.ly/2Fr0AUe*)
- Dot Product, Paul's Online Math Notes (*http://bit.ly/2HgZHLp*)

1.18 Adding and Subtracting Matrices

Problem

You want to add or subtract two matrices.

Solution

Use NumPy's add and subtract:

```
# Load library
import numpy as np

# Create matrix
matrix_a = np.array([[1, 1, 1],
                     [1, 1, 1],
                     [1, 1, 2]])

# Create matrix
matrix_b = np.array([[1, 3, 1],
                     [1, 3, 1],
                     [1, 3, 8]])

# Add two matrices
np.add(matrix_a, matrix_b)

array([[ 2,  4,  2],
       [ 2,  4,  2],
       [ 2,  4, 10]])

# Subtract two matrices
np.subtract(matrix_a, matrix_b)

array([[ 0, -2,  0],
       [ 0, -2,  0],
       [ 0, -2, -6]])
```

Discussion

Alternatively, we can simply use the + and - operators:

```
# Add two matrices
matrix_a + matrix_b
```

```
array([[ 2,  4,  2],
       [ 2,  4,  2],
       [ 2,  4, 10]])
```

1.19 Multiplying Matrices

Problem

You want to multiply two matrices.

Solution

Use NumPy's dot:

```
# Load library
import numpy as np

# Create matrix
matrix_a = np.array([[1, 1],
                     [1, 2]])

# Create matrix
matrix_b = np.array([[1, 3],
                     [1, 2]])

# Multiply two matrices
np.dot(matrix_a, matrix_b)

array([[2, 5],
       [3, 7]])
```

Discussion

Alternatively, in Python 3.5+ we can use the @ operator:

```
# Multiply two matrices
matrix_a @ matrix_b

array([[2, 5],
       [3, 7]])
```

If we want to do element-wise multiplication, we can use the * operator:

```
# Multiply two matrices element-wise
matrix_a * matrix_b

array([[1, 3],
       [1, 4]])
```

See Also

- Array vs. Matrix Operations, MathWorks (*http://bit.ly/2FtpXVr*)

1.20 Inverting a Matrix

Problem

You want to calculate the inverse of a square matrix.

Solution

Use NumPy's linear algebra `inv` method:

```
# Load library
import numpy as np

# Create matrix
matrix = np.array([[1, 4],
                   [2, 5]])

# Calculate inverse of matrix
np.linalg.inv(matrix)

array([[-1.66666667,  1.33333333],
       [ 0.66666667, -0.33333333]])
```

Discussion

The inverse of a square matrix, **A**, is a second matrix $\mathbf{A}^{-1}$, such that:

$$\mathbf{A}\mathbf{A}^{-1} = \mathbf{I}$$

where **I** is the identity matrix. In NumPy we can use `linalg.inv` to calculate $\mathbf{A}^{-1}$ if it exists. To see this in action, we can multiply a matrix by its inverse and the result is the identity matrix:

```
# Multiply matrix and its inverse
matrix @ np.linalg.inv(matrix)

array([[ 1.,  0.],
       [ 0.,  1.]])
```

See Also

- Inverse of a Matrix (*http://bit.ly/2Fzf0BS*)

1.21 Generating Random Values

Problem

You want to generate pseudorandom values.

Solution

Use NumPy's random:

```
# Load library
import numpy as np

# Set seed
np.random.seed(0)

# Generate three random floats between 0.0 and 1.0
np.random.random(3)

array([ 0.5488135 ,  0.71518937,  0.60276338])
```

Discussion

NumPy offers a wide variety of means to generate random numbers, many more than can be covered here. In our solution we generated floats; however, it is also common to generate integers:

```
# Generate three random integers between 1 and 10
np.random.randint(0, 11, 3)

array([3, 7, 9])
```

Alternatively, we can generate numbers by drawing them from a distribution:

```
# Draw three numbers from a normal distribution with mean 0.0
# and standard deviation of 1.0
np.random.normal(0.0, 1.0, 3)

array([-1.42232584,  1.52006949, -0.29139398])

# Draw three numbers from a logistic distribution with mean 0.0 and scale of 1.0
np.random.logistic(0.0, 1.0, 3)

array([-0.98118713, -0.08939902,  1.46416405])

# Draw three numbers greater than or equal to 1.0 and less than 2.0
np.random.uniform(1.0, 2.0, 3)

array([ 1.47997717,  1.3927848 ,  1.83607876])
```

Finally, it can sometimes be useful to return the same random numbers multiple times to get predictable, repeatable results. We can do this by setting the "seed" (an integer) of the pseudorandom generator. Random processes with the same seed will always produce the same output. We will use seeds throughout this book so that the code you see in the book and the code you run on your computer produces the same results.

## CHAPTER 2

Loading Data

2.0 Introduction

The first step in any machine learning endeavor is to get the raw data into our system. The raw data might be a logfile, dataset file, or database. Furthermore, often we will want to retrieve data from multiple sources. The recipes in this chapter look at methods of loading data from a variety of sources, including CSV files and SQL databases. We also cover methods of generating simulated data with desirable properties for experimentation. Finally, while there are many ways to load data in the Python ecosystem, we will focus on using the pandas library's extensive set of methods for loading external data, and using scikit-learn—an open source machine learning library in Python—for generating simulated data.

2.1 Loading a Sample Dataset

Problem

You want to load a preexisting sample dataset.

Solution

scikit-learn comes with a number of popular datasets for you to use:

```
# Load scikit-learn's datasets
from sklearn import datasets

# Load digits dataset
digits = datasets.load_digits()

# Create features matrix
features = digits.data
```

```
# Create target vector
target = digits.target

# View first observation
features[0]
array([  0.,   0.,   5.,  13.,   9.,   1.,   0.,   0.,   0.,   0.,  13.,
        15.,  10.,  15.,   5.,   0.,   0.,   3.,  15.,   2.,   0.,  11.,
         8.,   0.,   0.,   4.,  12.,   0.,   0.,   8.,   8.,   0.,   0.,
         5.,   8.,   0.,   0.,   9.,   8.,   0.,   0.,   4.,  11.,   0.,
         1.,  12.,   7.,   0.,   0.,   2.,  14.,   5.,  10.,  12.,   0.,
         0.,   0.,   0.,   6.,  13.,  10.,   0.,   0.,   0.])
```

Discussion

Often we do not want to go through the work of loading, transforming, and cleaning a real-world dataset before we can explore some machine learning algorithm or method. Luckily, scikit-learn comes with some common datasets we can quickly load. These datasets are often called "toy" datasets because they are far smaller and cleaner than a dataset we would see in the real world. Some popular sample datasets in scikit-learn are:

load_boston
: Contains 503 observations on Boston housing prices. It is a good dataset for exploring regression algorithms.

load_iris
: Contains 150 observations on the measurements of Iris flowers. It is a good dataset for exploring classification algorithms.

load_digits
: Contains 1,797 observations from images of handwritten digits. It is a good dataset for teaching image classification.

See Also

- scikit-learn toy datasets (*http://bit.ly/2HS6Dzq*)
- The Digit Dataset (*http://bit.ly/2mNSEBZ*)

2.2 Creating a Simulated Dataset

Problem

You need to generate a dataset of simulated data.

Solution

scikit-learn offers many methods for creating simulated data. Of those, three methods are particularly useful.

When we want a dataset designed to be used with linear regression, make_regression is a good choice:

```
# Load library
from sklearn.datasets import make_regression

# Generate features matrix, target vector, and the true coefficients
features, target, coefficients = make_regression(n_samples = 100,
                                                 n_features = 3,
                                                 n_informative = 3,
                                                 n_targets = 1,
                                                 noise = 0.0,
                                                 coef = True,
                                                 random_state = 1)

# View feature matrix and target vector
print('Feature Matrix\n', features[:3])
print('Target Vector\n', target[:3])

Feature Matrix
 [[ 1.29322588 -0.61736206 -0.11044703]
 [-2.793085    0.36633201  1.93752881]
 [ 0.80186103 -0.18656977  0.0465673 ]]
Target Vector
 [-10.37865986  25.5124503   19.67705609]
```

If we are interested in creating a simulated dataset for classification, we can use make_classification:

```
# Load library
from sklearn.datasets import make_classification

# Generate features matrix and target vector
features, target = make_classification(n_samples = 100,
                                       n_features = 3,
                                       n_informative = 3,
                                       n_redundant = 0,
                                       n_classes = 2,
                                       weights = [.25, .75],
                                       random_state = 1)

# View feature matrix and target vector
print('Feature Matrix\n', features[:3])
print('Target Vector\n', target[:3])

Feature Matrix
 [[ 1.06354768 -1.42632219  1.02163151]
 [ 0.23156977  1.49535261  0.33251578]
```

```
[ 0.15972951  0.83533515 -0.40869554]]
Target Vector
[1 0 0]
```

Finally, if we want a dataset designed to work well with clustering techniques, scikit-learn offers make_blobs:

```
# Load library
from sklearn.datasets import make_blobs

# Generate feature matrix and target vector
features, target = make_blobs(n_samples = 100,
                              n_features = 2,
                              centers = 3,
                              cluster_std = 0.5,
                              shuffle = True,
                              random_state = 1)

# View feature matrix and target vector
print('Feature Matrix\n', features[:3])
print('Target Vector\n', target[:3])

Feature Matrix
 [[ -1.22685609   3.25572052]
 [ -9.57463218  -4.38310652]
 [-10.71976941  -4.20558148]]
Target Vector
 [0 1 1]
```

Discussion

As might be apparent from the solutions, make_regression returns a feature matrix of float values and a target vector of float values, while make_classification and make_blobs return a feature matrix of float values and a target vector of integers representing membership in a class.

scikit-learn's simulated datasets offer extensive options to control the type of data generated. scikit-learn's documentation contains a full description of all the parameters, but a few are worth noting.

In make_regression and make_classification, n_informative determines the number of features that are used to generate the target vector. If n_informative is less than the total number of features (n_features), the resulting dataset will have redundant features that can be identified through feature selection techniques.

In addition, make_classification contains a weights parameter that allows us to simulate datasets with imbalanced classes. For example, weights = [.25, .75] would return a dataset with 25% of observations belonging to one class and 75% of observations belonging to a second class.

For make_blobs, the centers parameter determines the number of clusters generated. Using the matplotlib visualization library, we can visualize the clusters generated by make_blobs:

```
# Load library
import matplotlib.pyplot as plt

# View scatterplot
plt.scatter(features[:,0], features[:,1], c=target)
plt.show()
```

See Also

- make_regression documentation (*http://bit.ly/2FtIBwo*)
- make_classification documentation (*http://bit.ly/2FtIKzW*)
- make_blobs documentation (*http://bit.ly/2FqKMAZ*)

2.3 Loading a CSV File

Problem

You need to import a comma-separated values (CSV) file.

Solution

Use the pandas library's `read_csv` to load a local or hosted CSV file:

```
# Load library
import pandas as pd

# Create URL
url = 'https://tinyurl.com/simulated_data'

# Load dataset
dataframe = pd.read_csv(url)

# View first two rows
dataframe.head(2)
```

	integer	datetime	category
0	5	2015-01-01 00:00:00	0
1	5	2015-01-01 00:00:01	0

Discussion

There are two things to note about loading CSV files. First, it is often useful to take a quick look at the contents of the file before loading. It can be very helpful to see how a dataset is structured beforehand and what parameters we need to set to load in the file. Second, `read_csv` has over 30 parameters and therefore the documentation can be daunting. Fortunately, those parameters are mostly there to allow it to handle a wide variety of CSV formats. For example, CSV files get their names from the fact that the values are literally separated by commas (e.g., one row might be `2,"2015-01-01 00:00:00",0`); however, it is common for "CSV" files to use other characters as separators, like tabs. pandas' `sep` parameter allows us to define the delimiter used in the file. Although it is not always the case, a common formatting issue with CSV files is that the first line of the file is used to define column headers (e.g., `integer`, `datetime`, `category` in our solution). The `header` parameter allows us to specify if or where a header row exists. If a header row does not exist, we set `header=None`.

2.4 Loading an Excel File

Problem

You need to import an Excel spreadsheet.

Solution

Use the pandas library's `read_excel` to load an Excel spreadsheet:

```
# Load library
import pandas as pd

# Create URL
url = 'https://tinyurl.com/simulated_excel'

# Load data
dataframe = pd.read_excel(url, sheetname=0, header=1)

# View the first two rows
dataframe.head(2)
```

	5	2015-01-01 00:00:00	0
0	5	2015-01-01 00:00:01	0
1	9	2015-01-01 00:00:02	0

Discussion

This solution is similar to our solution for reading CSV files. The main difference is the additional parameter, sheetname, that specifies which sheet in the Excel file we wish to load. sheetname can accept both strings containing the name of the sheet and integers pointing to sheet positions (zero-indexed). If we need to load multiple sheets, include them as a list. For example, sheetname=[0,1,2, "Monthly Sales"] will return a dictionary of pandas DataFrames containing the first, second, and third sheets and the sheet named Monthly Sales.

2.5 Loading a JSON File

Problem

You need to load a JSON file for data preprocessing.

Solution

The pandas library provides read_json to convert a JSON file into a pandas object:

```
# Load library
import pandas as pd

# Create URL
url = 'https://tinyurl.com/simulated_json'

# Load data
dataframe = pd.read_json(url, orient='columns')

# View the first two rows
dataframe.head(2)
```

```
category
datetime
integer
0
0
2015-01-01 00:00:00
5
1
0
2015-01-01 00:00:01
5
```

Discussion

Importing JSON files into pandas is similar to the last few recipes we have seen. The key difference is the `orient` parameter, which indicates to pandas how the JSON file is structured. However, it might take some experimenting to figure out which argument (`split`, `records`, `index`, `columns`, and `values`) is the right one. Another helpful tool pandas offers is `json_normalize`, which can help convert semistructured JSON data into a pandas DataFrame.

See Also

- `json_normalize` documentation (*http://bit.ly/2HQqwaa*)

2.6 Querying a SQL Database

Problem

You need to load data from a database using the structured query language (SQL).

Solution

pandas' `read_sql_query` allows us to make a SQL query to a database and load it:

```
# Load libraries
import pandas as pd
from sqlalchemy import create_engine

# Create a connection to the database
database_connection = create_engine('sqlite:///sample.db')

# Load data
dataframe = pd.read_sql_query('SELECT * FROM data', database_connection)

# View first two rows
dataframe.head(2)
```

	first_name	last_name	age	preTestScore	postTestScore
0	Jason	Miller	42	4	25
1	Molly	Jacobson	52	24	94

Discussion

Out of all of the recipes presented in this chapter, this recipe is probably the one we will use most in the real world. SQL is the lingua franca for pulling data from databases. In this recipe we first use `create_engine` to define a connection to a SQL database engine called SQLite. Next we use pandas' `read_sql_query` to query that database using SQL and put the results in a DataFrame.

SQL is a language in its own right and, while beyond the scope of this book, it is certainly worth knowing for anyone wanting to learn machine learning. Our SQL query, `SELECT * FROM data`, asks the database to give us all columns (`*`) from the table called `data`.

See Also

- SQLite (*https://www.sqlite.org*)
- W3Schools SQL Tutorial (*https://www.w3schools.com/sql*)

## CHAPTER 3

Data Wrangling

3.0 Introduction

Data wrangling is a broad term used, often informally, to describe the process of transforming raw data to a clean and organized format ready for use. For us, data wrangling is only one step in preprocessing our data, but it is an important step.

The most common data structure used to "wrangle" data is the data frame, which can be both intuitive and incredibly versatile. Data frames are tabular, meaning that they are based on rows and columns like you would see in a spreadsheet. Here is a data frame created from data about passengers on the *Titanic*:

```
# Load library
import pandas as pd

# Create URL
url = 'https://tinyurl.com/titanic-csv'

# Load data as a dataframe
dataframe = pd.read_csv(url)

# Show first 5 rows
dataframe.head(5)
```

	Name	PClass	Age	Sex	Survived	SexCode
0	Allen, Miss Elisabeth Walton	1st	29.00	female	1	1
1	Allison, Miss Helen Loraine	1st	2.00	female	0	1
2	Allison, Mr Hudson Joshua Creighton	1st	30.00	male	0	0
3	Allison, Mrs Hudson JC (Bessie Waldo Daniels)	1st	25.00	female	0	1
4	Allison, Master Hudson Trevor	1st	0.92	male	1	0

There are three important things to notice in this data frame.

First, in a data frame each row corresponds to one observation (e.g., a passenger) and each column corresponds to one feature (gender, age, etc.). For example, by looking at the first observation we can see that Miss Elisabeth Walton Allen stayed in first class, was 29 years old, was female, and survived the disaster.

Second, each column contains a name (e.g., Name, PClass, Age) and each row contains an index number (e.g., 0 for the lucky Miss Elisabeth Walton Allen). We will use these to select and manipulate observations and features.

Third, two columns, Sex and SexCode, contain the same information in different formats. In Sex, a woman is indicated by the string female, while in SexCode, a woman is indicated by using the integer 1. We will want all our features to be unique, and therefore we will need to remove one of these columns.

In this chapter, we will cover a wide variety of techniques to manipulate data frames using the pandas library with the goal of creating a clean, well-structured set of observations for further preprocessing.

3.1 Creating a Data Frame

Problem

You want to create a new data frame.

Solution

pandas has many methods of creating a new DataFrame object. One easy method is to create an empty data frame using DataFrame and then define each column separately:

```
# Load library
import pandas as pd

# Create DataFrame
dataframe = pd.DataFrame()

# Add columns
dataframe['Name'] = ['Jacky Jackson', 'Steven Stevenson']
dataframe['Age'] = [38, 25]
dataframe['Driver'] = [True, False]

# Show DataFrame
dataframe
```

	Name	Age	Driver
0	Jacky Jackson	38	True
1	Steven Stevenson	25	False

Alternatively, once we have created a DataFrame object, we can append new rows to the bottom:

```
# Create row
new_person = pd.Series(['Molly Mooney', 40, True], index=['Name','Age','Driver'])

# Append row
dataframe.append(new_person, ignore_index=True)
```

	Name	Age	Driver
0	Jacky Jackson	38	True
1	Steven Stevenson	25	False
2	Molly Mooney	40	True

Discussion

pandas offers what can feel like an infinite number of ways to create a DataFrame. In the real world, creating an empty DataFrame and then populating it will almost never happen. Instead, our DataFrames will be created from real data we have loading from other sources (e.g., a CSV file or database).

3.2 Describing the Data

Problem

You want to view some characteristics of a DataFrame.

Solution

One of the easiest things we can do after loading the data is view the first few rows using head:

```
# Load library
import pandas as pd

# Create URL
url = 'https://tinyurl.com/titanic-csv'

# Load data
dataframe = pd.read_csv(url)

# Show two rows
dataframe.head(2)
```

	Name	PClass	Age	Sex	Survived	SexCode
0	Allen, Miss Elisabeth Walton	1st	29.0	female	1	1
1	Allison, Miss Helen Loraine	1st	2.0	female	0	1

We can also take a look at the number of rows and columns:

```
# Show dimensions
dataframe.shape
```

```
(1313, 6)
```

Additionally, we can get descriptive statistics for any numeric columns using describe:

```
# Show statistics
dataframe.describe()
```

	Age	Survived	SexCode
count	756.000000	1313.000000	1313.000000
mean	30.397989	0.342727	0.351866
std	14.259049	0.474802	0.477734
min	0.170000	0.000000	0.000000
25%	21.000000	0.000000	0.000000
50%	28.000000	0.000000	0.000000
75%	39.000000	1.000000	1.000000
max	71.000000	1.000000	1.000000

Discussion

After we load some data, it is a good idea to understand how it is structured and what kind of information it contains. Ideally, we would view the full data directly. But with most real-world cases, the data could have thousands to hundreds of thousands to millions of rows and columns. Instead, we have to rely on pulling samples to view small slices and calculating summary statistics of the data.

In our solution, we are using a toy dataset of the passengers of the *Titanic* on her last voyage. Using head we can take a look at the first few rows (five by default) of the data. Alternatively, we can use tail to view the last few rows. With shape we can see how many rows and columns our DataFrame contains. And finally, with describe we can see some basic descriptive statistics for any numerical column.

It is worth noting that summary statistics do not always tell the full story. For example, pandas treats the columns Survived and SexCode as numeric columns because they contain 1s and 0s. However, in this case the numerical values represent categories. For example, if Survived equals 1, it indicates that the passenger survived the disaster. For this reason, some of the summary statistics provided don't make sense, such as the standard deviation of the SexCode column (an indicator of the passenger's gender).

3.3 Navigating DataFrames

Problem

You need to select individual data or slices of a DataFrame.

Solution

Use loc or iloc to select one or more rows or values:

```
# Load library
import pandas as pd

# Create URL
url = 'https://tinyurl.com//titanic-csv'

# Load data
dataframe = pd.read_csv(url)

# Select first row
dataframe.iloc[0]

Name          Allen, Miss Elisabeth Walton
PClass                                 1st
Age                                     29
Sex                                 female
Survived                                 1
SexCode                                  1
Name: 0, dtype: object
```

We can use : to define a slice of rows we want, such as selecting the second, third, and fourth rows:

```
# Select three rows
dataframe.iloc[1:4]
```

	Name	PClass	Age	Sex	Survived	SexCode
1	Allison, Miss Helen Loraine	1st	2.0	female	0	1
2	Allison, Mr Hudson Joshua Creighton	1st	30.0	male	0	0
3	Allison, Mrs Hudson JC (Bessie Waldo Daniels)	1st	25.0	female	0	1

We can even use it to get all rows up to a point, such as all rows up to and including the fourth row:

```
# Select three rows
dataframe.iloc[:4]
```

	Name	PClass	Age	Sex	Survived	SexCode
0	Allen, Miss Elisabeth Walton	1st	29.0	female	1	1
1	Allison, Miss Helen Loraine	1st	2.0	female	0	1
2	Allison, Mr Hudson Joshua Creighton	1st	30.0	male	0	0
3	Allison, Mrs Hudson JC (Bessie Waldo Daniels)	1st	25.0	female	0	1

DataFrames do not need to be numerically indexed. We can set the index of a Data-Frame to any value where the value is unique to each row. For example, we can set the index to be passenger names and then select rows using a name:

```
# Set index
dataframe = dataframe.set_index(dataframe['Name'])

# Show row
dataframe.loc['Allen, Miss Elisabeth Walton']

Name           Allen, Miss Elisabeth Walton
PClass                                  1st
Age                                      29
Sex                                  female
Survived                                  1
SexCode                                   1
Name: Allen, Miss Elisabeth Walton, dtype: object
```

Discussion

All rows in a pandas DataFrame have a unique index value. By default, this index is an integer indicating the row position in the DataFrame; however, it does not have to be. DataFrame indexes can be set to be unique alphanumeric strings or customer numbers. To select individual rows and slices of rows, pandas provides two methods:

- loc is useful when the index of the DataFrame is a label (e.g., a string).
- iloc works by looking for the position in the DataFrame. For example, iloc[0] will return the first row regardless of whether the index is an integer or a label.

It is useful to be comfortable with both loc and iloc since they will come up a lot during data cleaning.

3.4 Selecting Rows Based on Conditionals

Problem

You want to select DataFrame rows based on some condition.

Solution

This can be easily done in pandas. For example, if we wanted to select all the women on the *Titanic*:

```
# Load library
import pandas as pd

# Create URL
url = 'https://tinyurl.com/titanic-csv'

# Load data
dataframe = pd.read_csv(url)

# Show top two rows where column 'sex' is 'female'
dataframe[dataframe['Sex'] == 'female'].head(2)
```

	Name	PClass	Age	Sex	Survived	SexCode
0	Allen, Miss Elisabeth Walton	1st	29.0	female	1	1
1	Allison, Miss Helen Loraine	1st	2.0	female	0	1

Take a second and look at the format of this solution. `dataframe['Sex'] == 'female'` is our conditional statement; by wrapping that in `dataframe[]` we are telling pandas to "select all the rows in the DataFrame where the value of `dataframe['Sex']` is `'female'`.

Multiple conditions are easy as well. For example, here we select all the rows where the passenger is a female 65 or older:

```
# Filter rows
dataframe[(dataframe['Sex'] == 'female') & (dataframe['Age'] >= 65)]
```

	Name	PClass	Age	Sex	Survived	SexCode
73	Crosby, Mrs Edward Gifford (Catherine Elizabet...	1st	69.0	female	1	1

Discussion

Conditionally selecting and filtering data is one of the most common tasks in data wrangling. You rarely want all the raw data from the source; instead, you are interested in only some subsection of it. For example, you might only be interested in stores in certain states or the records of patients over a certain age.

3.5 Replacing Values

Problem

You need to replace values in a DataFrame.

Solution

pandas' `replace` is an easy way to find and replace values. For example, we can replace any instance of `"female"` in the Sex column with `"Woman"`:

```
# Load library
import pandas as pd

# Create URL
url = 'https://tinyurl.com/titanic-csv'

# Load data
dataframe = pd.read_csv(url)

# Replace values, show two rows
dataframe['Sex'].replace("female", "Woman").head(2)

0    Woman
1    Woman
Name: Sex, dtype: object
```

We can also replace multiple values at the same time:

```
# Replace "female" and "male with "Woman" and "Man"
dataframe['Sex'].replace(["female", "male"], ["Woman", "Man"]).head(5)

0    Woman
1    Woman
2      Man
3    Woman
4      Man
Name: Sex, dtype: object
```

We can also find and replace across the entire `DataFrame` object by specifying the whole data frame instead of a single column:

```
# Replace values, show two rows
dataframe.replace(1, "One").head(2)
```

	Name	PClass	Age	Sex	Survived	SexCode
0	Allen, Miss Elisabeth Walton	1st	29	female	One	One
1	Allison, Miss Helen Loraine	1st	2	female	0	One

`replace` also accepts regular expressions:

```
# Replace values, show two rows
dataframe.replace(r"1st", "First", regex=True).head(2)
```

	Name	PClass	Age	Sex	Survived	SexCode
0	Allen, Miss Elisabeth Walton	First	29.0	female	1	1
1	Allison, Miss Helen Loraine	First	2.0	female	0	1

Discussion

`replace` is a tool we use to replace values that is simple and yet has the powerful ability to accept regular expressions.

3.6 Renaming Columns

Problem

You want to rename a column in a pandas DataFrame.

Solution

Rename columns using the `rename` method:

```
# Load library
import pandas as pd

# Create URL
url = 'https://tinyurl.com/titanic-csv'

# Load data
dataframe = pd.read_csv(url)

# Rename column, show two rows
dataframe.rename(columns={'PClass': 'Passenger Class'}).head(2)
```

	Name	Passenger Class	Age	Sex	Survived	SexCode
0	Allen, Miss Elisabeth Walton	1st	29.0	female	1	1
1	Allison, Miss Helen Loraine	1st	2.0	female	0	1

Notice that the `rename` method can accept a dictionary as a parameter. We can use the dictionary to change multiple column names at once:

```
# Rename columns, show two rows
dataframe.rename(columns={'PClass': 'Passenger Class', 'Sex': 'Gender'}).head(2)
```

	Name	Passenger Class	Age	Gender	Survived	SexCode
0	Allen, Miss Elisabeth Walton	1st	29.0	female	1	1
1	Allison, Miss Helen Loraine	1st	2.0	female	0	1

Discussion

Using `rename` with a dictionary as an argument to the `columns` parameter is my preferred way to rename columns because it works with any number of columns. If we want to rename all columns at once, this helpful snippet of code creates a dictionary with the old column names as keys and empty strings as values:

```
# Load library
import collections

# Create dictionary
column_names = collections.defaultdict(str)

# Create keys
for name in dataframe.columns:
    column_names[name]

# Show dictionary
column_names

defaultdict(str,
            {'Age': '',
             'Name': '',
             'PClass': '',
             'Sex': '',
             'SexCode': '',
             'Survived': ''})
```

3.7 Finding the Minimum, Maximum, Sum, Average, and Count

Problem

You want to find the min, max, sum, average, or count of a numeric column.

Solution

pandas comes with some built-in methods for commonly used descriptive statistics:

```
# Load library
import pandas as pd

# Create URL
url = 'https://tinyurl.com/titanic-csv'

# Load data
dataframe = pd.read_csv(url)

# Calculate statistics
print('Maximum:', dataframe['Age'].max())
print('Minimum:', dataframe['Age'].min())
print('Mean:', dataframe['Age'].mean())
print('Sum:', dataframe['Age'].sum())
print('Count:', dataframe['Age'].count())

Maximum: 71.0
Minimum: 0.17
Mean: 30.397989417989415
```

```
Sum: 22980.879999999997
Count: 756
```

Discussion

In addition to the statistics used in the solution, pandas offers variance (`var`), standard deviation (`std`), kurtosis (`kurt`), skewness (`skew`), standard error of the mean (`sem`), mode (`mode`), median (`median`), and a number of others.

Furthermore, we can also apply these methods to the whole DataFrame:

```
# Show counts
dataframe.count()

Name        1313
PClass      1313
Age          756
Sex         1313
Survived    1313
SexCode     1313
dtype: int64
```

3.8 Finding Unique Values

Problem

You want to select all unique values in a column.

Solution

Use `unique` to view an array of all unique values in a column:

```
# Load library
import pandas as pd

# Create URL
url = 'https://tinyurl.com/titanic-csv'

# Load data
dataframe = pd.read_csv(url)

# Select unique values
dataframe['Sex'].unique()

array(['female', 'male'], dtype=object)
```

Alternatively, `value_counts` will display all unique values with the number of times each value appears:

```
# Show counts
dataframe['Sex'].value_counts()
```

```
male      851
female    462
Name: Sex, dtype: int64
```

Discussion

Both `unique` and `value_counts` are useful for manipulating and exploring categorical columns. Very often in categorical columns there will be classes that need to be handled in the data wrangling phase. For example, in the *Titanic* dataset, `PClass` is a column indicating the class of a passenger's ticket. There were three classes on the *Titanic*; however, if we use `value_counts` we can see a problem:

```
# Show counts
dataframe['PClass'].value_counts()

3rd    711
1st    322
2nd    279
*        1
Name: PClass, dtype: int64
```

While almost all passengers belong to one of three classes as expected, a single passenger has the class `*`. There are a number of strategies for handling this type of issue, which we will address in Chapter 5, but for now just realize that "extra" classes are common in categorical data and should not be ignored.

Finally, if we simply want to count the number of unique values, we can use `nunique`:

```
# Show number of unique values
dataframe['PClass'].nunique()

4
```

3.9 Handling Missing Values

Problem

You want to select missing values in a DataFrame.

Solution

`isnull` and `notnull` return booleans indicating whether a value is missing:

```
# Load library
import pandas as pd

# Create URL
url = 'https://tinyurl.com/titanic-csv'

# Load data
```

```
dataframe = pd.read_csv(url)

## Select missing values, show two rows
dataframe[dataframe['Age'].isnull()].head(2)
```

	Name	PClass	Age	Sex	Survived	SexCode
12	Aubert, Mrs Leontine Pauline	1st	NaN	female	1	1
13	Barkworth, Mr Algernon H	1st	NaN	male	1	0

Discussion

Missing values are a ubiquitous problem in data wrangling, yet many underestimate the difficulty of working with missing data. pandas uses NumPy's NaN ("Not A Number") value to denote missing values, but it is important to note that NaN is not fully implemented natively in pandas. For example, if we wanted to replace all strings containing male with missing values, we return an error:

```
# Attempt to replace values with NaN
dataframe['Sex'] = dataframe['Sex'].replace('male', NaN)

-------------------------------------------------------------------------

NameError                                 Traceback (most recent call last)

<ipython-input-7-5682d714f87d> in <module>()
      1 # Attempt to replace values with NaN
----> 2 dataframe['Sex'] = dataframe['Sex'].replace('male', NaN)


NameError: name 'NaN' is not defined
-------------------------------------------------------------------------
```

To have full functionality with NaN we need to import the NumPy library first:

```
# Load library
import numpy as np

# Replace values with NaN
dataframe['Sex'] = dataframe['Sex'].replace('male', np.nan)
```

Oftentimes a dataset uses a specific value to denote a missing observation, such as NONE, -999, or .. pandas' read_csv includes a parameter allowing us to specify the values used to indicate missing values:

```
# Load data, set missing values
dataframe = pd.read_csv(url, na_values=[np.nan, 'NONE', -999])
```

3.10 Deleting a Column

Problem

You want to delete a column from your DataFrame.

Solution

The best way to delete a column is to use `drop` with the parameter `axis=1` (i.e., the column axis):

```
# Load library
import pandas as pd

# Create URL
url = 'https://tinyurl.com/titanic-csv'

# Load data
dataframe = pd.read_csv(url)

# Delete column
dataframe.drop('Age', axis=1).head(2)
```

	Name	PClass	Sex	Survived	SexCode
0	Allen, Miss Elisabeth Walton	1st	female	1	1
1	Allison, Miss Helen Loraine	1st	female	0	1

You can also use a list of column names as the main argument to drop multiple columns at once:

```
# Drop columns
dataframe.drop(['Age', 'Sex'], axis=1).head(2)
```

	Name	PClass	Survived	SexCode
0	Allen, Miss Elisabeth Walton	1st	1	1
1	Allison, Miss Helen Loraine	1st	0	1

If a column does not have a name (which can sometimes happen), you can drop it by its column index using `dataframe.columns`:

```
# Drop column
dataframe.drop(dataframe.columns[1], axis=1).head(2)
```

	Name	Age	Sex	Survived	SexCode
0	Allen, Miss Elisabeth Walton	29.0	female	1	1
1	Allison, Miss Helen Loraine	2.0	female	0	1

Discussion

`drop` is the idiomatic method of deleting a column. An alternative method is `del dataframe['Age']`, which works most of the time but is not recommended because of how it is called within pandas (the details of which are outside the scope of this book).

One habit I recommend learning is to never use pandas' `inplace=True` argument. Many pandas methods include an `inplace` parameter, which when `True` edits the DataFrame directly. This can lead to problems in more complex data processing pipelines because we are treating the DataFrames as mutable objects (which they technically are). I recommend treating DataFrames as immutable objects. For example:

```
# Create a new DataFrame
dataframe_name_dropped = dataframe.drop(dataframe.columns[0], axis=1)
```

In this example, we are not mutating the DataFrame `dataframe` but instead are making a new DataFrame that is an altered version of `dataframe` called `data frame_name_dropped`. If you treat your DataFrames as immutable objects, you will save yourself a lot of headaches down the road.

3.11 Deleting a Row

Problem

You want to delete one or more rows from a DataFrame.

Solution

Use a boolean condition to create a new DataFrame excluding the rows you want to delete:

```
# Load library
import pandas as pd

# Create URL
url = 'https://tinyurl.com/titanic-csv'

# Load data
dataframe = pd.read_csv(url)

# Delete rows, show first two rows of output
dataframe[dataframe['Sex'] != 'male'].head(2)
```

	Name	PClass	Age	Sex	Survived	SexCode
0	Allen, Miss Elisabeth Walton	1st	29.0	female	1	1
1	Allison, Miss Helen Loraine	1st	2.0	female	0	1

Discussion

While technically you can use the drop method (for example, `df.drop([0, 1],`
`axis=0)` to drop the first two rows), a more practical method is simply to wrap a
boolean condition inside `df[]`. The reason is because we can use the power of conditionals to delete either a single row or (far more likely) many rows at once.

We can use boolean conditions to easily delete single rows by matching a unique
value:

```
# Delete row, show first two rows of output
dataframe[dataframe['Name'] != 'Allison, Miss Helen Loraine'].head(2)
```

	Name	PClass	Age	Sex	Survived	SexCode
0	Allen, Miss Elisabeth Walton	1st	29.0	female	1	1
2	Allison, Mr Hudson Joshua Creighton	1st	30.0	male	0	0

And we can even use it to delete a single row by row index:

```
# Delete row, show first two rows of output
dataframe[dataframe.index != 0].head(2)
```

	Name	PClass	Age	Sex	Survived	SexCode
1	Allison, Miss Helen Loraine	1st	2.0	female	0	1
2	Allison, Mr Hudson Joshua Creighton	1st	30.0	male	0	0

3.12 Dropping Duplicate Rows

Problem

You want to drop duplicate rows from your DataFrame.

Solution

Use `drop_duplicates`, but be mindful of the parameters:

```
# Load library
import pandas as pd

# Create URL
url = 'https://tinyurl.com/titanic-csv'

# Load data
dataframe = pd.read_csv(url)

# Drop duplicates, show first two rows of output
dataframe.drop_duplicates().head(2)
```

	Name	PClass	Age	Sex	Survived	SexCode
0	Allen, Miss Elisabeth Walton	1st	29.0	female	1	1
1	Allison, Miss Helen Loraine	1st	2.0	female	0	1

Discussion

A keen reader will notice that the solution didn't actually drop any rows:

```
# Show number of rows
print("Number Of Rows In The Original DataFrame:", len(dataframe))
print("Number Of Rows After Deduping:", len(dataframe.drop_duplicates()))

Number Of Rows In The Original DataFrame: 1313
Number Of Rows After Deduping: 1313
```

The reason is because `drop_duplicates` defaults to only dropping rows that match perfectly across all columns. Under this condition, every row in our DataFrame, `dataframe`, is actually unique. However, often we want to consider only a subset of columns to check for duplicate rows. We can accomplish this using the `subset` parameter:

```
# Drop duplicates
dataframe.drop_duplicates(subset=['Sex'])
```

	Name	PClass	Age	Sex	Survived	SexCode
0	Allen, Miss Elisabeth Walton	1st	29.0	female	1	1
2	Allison, Mr Hudson Joshua Creighton	1st	30.0	male	0	0

Take a close look at the preceding output: we told `drop_duplicates` to only consider any two rows with the same value for `Sex` to be duplicates and to drop them. Now we are left with a DataFrame of only two rows: one man and one woman. You might be asking why `drop_duplicates` decided to keep these two rows instead of two different rows. The answer is that `drop_duplicates` defaults to keeping the first occurrence of a duplicated row and dropping the rest. We can control this behavior using the `keep` parameter:

```
# Drop duplicates
dataframe.drop_duplicates(subset=['Sex'], keep='last')
```

	Name	PClass	Age	Sex	Survived	SexCode
1307	Zabour, Miss Tamini	3rd	NaN	female	0	1
1312	Zimmerman, Leo	3rd	29.0	male	0	0

A related method is `duplicated`, which returns a boolean series denoting if a row is a duplicate or not. This is a good option if you don't want to simply drop duplicates.

3.13 Grouping Rows by Values

Problem

You want to group individual rows according to some shared value.

Solution

groupby is one of the most powerful features in pandas:

```
# Load library
import pandas as pd

# Create URL
url = 'https://tinyurl.com/titanic-csv'

# Load data
dataframe = pd.read_csv(url)

# Group rows by the values of the column 'Sex', calculate mean
# of each group
dataframe.groupby('Sex').mean()
```

Sex	Age	Survived	SexCode
female	29.396424	0.666667	1.0
male	31.014338	0.166863	0.0

Discussion

groupby is where data wrangling really starts to take shape. It is very common to have a DataFrame where each row is a person or an event and we want to group them according to some criterion and then calculate a statistic. For example, you can imagine a DataFrame where each row is an individual sale at a national restaurant chain and we want the total sales per restaurant. We can accomplish this by grouping rows by individual resturants and then calculating the sum of each group.

Users new to groupby often write a line like this and are confused by what is returned:

```
# Group rows
dataframe.groupby('Sex')

<pandas.core.groupby.DataFrameGroupBy object at 0x10efacf28>
```

Why didn't it return something more useful? The reason is because groupby needs to be paired with some operation we want to apply to each group, such as calculating an aggregate statistic (e.g., mean, median, sum). When talking about grouping we often use shorthand and say "group by gender," but that is incomplete. For grouping to be useful, we need to group by something and then apply a function to each of those groups:

```
# Group rows, count rows
dataframe.groupby('Survived')['Name'].count()

Survived
0    863
1    450
Name: Name, dtype: int64
```

Notice Name added after the groupby? That is because particular summary statistics are only meaningful to certain types of data. For example, while calculating the average age by gender makes sense, calculating the total age by gender does not. In this case we group the data into survived or not, then count the number of names (i.e., passengers) in each group.

We can also group by a first column, then group that grouping by a second column:

```
# Group rows, calculate mean
dataframe.groupby(['Sex','Survived'])['Age'].mean()

Sex     Survived
female  0           24.901408
        1           30.867143
male    0           32.320780
        1           25.951875
Name: Age, dtype: float64
```

3.14 Grouping Rows by Time

Problem

You need to group individual rows by time periods.

Solution

Use resample to group rows by chunks of time:

```
# Load libraries
import pandas as pd
import numpy as np

# Create date range
time_index = pd.date_range('06/06/2017', periods=100000, freq='30S')

# Create DataFrame
dataframe = pd.DataFrame(index=time_index)

# Create column of random values
dataframe['Sale_Amount'] = np.random.randint(1, 10, 100000)
```

```
# Group rows by week, calculate sum per week
dataframe.resample('W').sum()
```

	Sale_Amount
2017-06-11	86423
2017-06-18	101045
2017-06-25	100867
2017-07-02	100894
2017-07-09	100438
2017-07-16	10297

Discussion

Our standard *Titanic* dataset does not contain a datetime column, so for this recipe we have generated a simple DataFrame where each row is an individual sale. For each sale we know its date and time and its dollar amount (this data isn't realistic because every sale takes place precisely 30 seconds apart and is an exact dollar amount, but for the sake of simplicity let us pretend).

The raw data looks like this:

```
# Show three rows
dataframe.head(3)
```

	Sale_Amount
2017-06-06 00:00:00	7
2017-06-06 00:00:30	2
2017-06-06 00:01:00	7

Notice that the date and time of each sale is the index of the DataFrame; this is because `resample` requires the index to be datetime-like values.

Using `resample` we can group the rows by a wide array of time periods (offsets) and then we can calculate some statistic on each time group:

```
# Group by two weeks, calculate mean
dataframe.resample('2W').mean()
```

	Sale_Amount
2017-06-11	5.001331
2017-06-25	5.007738
2017-07-09	4.993353
2017-07-23	4.950481

```
# Group by month, count rows
dataframe.resample('M').count()
```

	Sale_Amount
2017-06-30	72000
2017-07-31	28000

You might notice that in the two outputs the datetime index is a date despite the fact that we are grouping by weeks and months, respectively. The reason is because by default `resample` returns the label of the right "edge" (the last label) of the time group. We can control this behavior using the `label` parameter:

```
# Group by month, count rows
dataframe.resample('M', label='left').count()
```

	Sale_Amount
2017-05-31	72000
2017-06-30	28000

See Also

- List of pandas time offset aliases (*http://bit.ly/2FxfTe4*)

3.15 Looping Over a Column

Problem

You want to iterate over every element in a column and apply some action.

Solution

You can treat a pandas column like any other sequence in Python:

```
# Load library
import pandas as pd

# Create URL
url = 'https://tinyurl.com/titanic-csv'

# Load data
dataframe = pd.read_csv(url)

# Print first two names uppercased
for name in dataframe['Name'][0:2]:
    print(name.upper())
```

```
ALLEN, MISS ELISABETH WALTON
ALLISON, MISS HELEN LORAINE
```

Discussion

In addition to loops (often called for loops), we can also use list comprehensions:

```
# Show first two names uppercased
[name.upper() for name in dataframe['Name'][0:2]]
```

```
['ALLEN, MISS ELISABETH WALTON', 'ALLISON, MISS HELEN LORAINE']
```

Despite the temptation to fall back on for loops, a more Pythonic solution would use pandas' apply method, described in the next recipe.

3.16 Applying a Function Over All Elements in a Column

Problem

You want to apply some function over all elements in a column.

Solution

Use apply to apply a built-in or custom function on every element in a column:

```
# Load library
import pandas as pd

# Create URL
url = 'https://tinyurl.com/titanic-csv'

# Load data
dataframe = pd.read_csv(url)

# Create function
def uppercase(x):
    return x.upper()

# Apply function, show two rows
dataframe['Name'].apply(uppercase)[0:2]

0      ALLEN, MISS ELISABETH WALTON
1       ALLISON, MISS HELEN LORAINE
Name: Name, dtype: object
```

Discussion

apply is a great way to do data cleaning and wrangling. It is common to write a function to perform some useful operation (separate first and last names, convert strings to floats, etc.) and then map that function to every element in a column.

3.17 Applying a Function to Groups

Problem

You have grouped rows using `groupby` and want to apply a function to each group.

Solution

Combine `groupby` and `apply`:

```
# Load library
import pandas as pd

# Create URL
url = 'https://tinyurl.com/titanic-csv'

# Load data
dataframe = pd.read_csv(url)

# Group rows, apply function to groups
dataframe.groupby('Sex').apply(lambda x: x.count())
```

Sex	Name	PClass	Age	Sex	Survived	SexCode
female	462	462	288	462	462	462
male	851	851	468	851	851	851

Discussion

In Recipe 3.16 I mentioned `apply`. `apply` is particularly useful when you want to apply a function to groups. By combining `groupby` and `apply` we can calculate custom statistics or apply any function to each group separately.

3.18 Concatenating DataFrames

Problem

You want to concatenate two DataFrames.

Solution

Use `concat` with `axis=0` to concatenate along the row axis:

```
# Load library
import pandas as pd

# Create DataFrame
```

```
data_a = {'id': ['1', '2', '3'],
          'first': ['Alex', 'Amy', 'Allen'],
          'last': ['Anderson', 'Ackerman', 'Ali']}
dataframe_a = pd.DataFrame(data_a, columns = ['id', 'first', 'last'])

# Create DataFrame
data_b = {'id': ['4', '5', '6'],
          'first': ['Billy', 'Brian', 'Bran'],
          'last': ['Bonder', 'Black', 'Balwner']}
dataframe_b = pd.DataFrame(data_b, columns = ['id', 'first', 'last'])

# Concatenate DataFrames by rows
pd.concat([dataframe_a, dataframe_b], axis=0)
```

	id	first	last
0	1	Alex	Anderson
1	2	Amy	Ackerman
2	3	Allen	Ali
0	4	Billy	Bonder
1	5	Brian	Black
2	6	Bran	Balwner

You can use `axis=1` to concatenate along the column axis:

```
# Concatenate DataFrames by columns
pd.concat([dataframe_a, dataframe_b], axis=1)
```

	id	first	last	id	first	last
0	1	Alex	Anderson	4	Billy	Bonder
1	2	Amy	Ackerman	5	Brian	Black
2	3	Allen	Ali	6	Bran	Balwner

Discussion

Concatenating is not a word you hear much outside of computer science and programming, so if you have not heard it before, do not worry. The informal definition of *concatenate* is to glue two objects together. In the solution we glued together two small DataFrames using the `axis` parameter to indicate whether we wanted to stack the two DataFrames on top of each other or place them side by side.

Alternatively we can use `append` to add a new row to a DataFrame:

```
# Create row
row = pd.Series([10, 'Chris', 'Chillon'], index=['id', 'first', 'last'])

# Append row
dataframe_a.append(row, ignore_index=True)
```

	id	first	last
0	1	Alex	Anderson
1	2	Amy	Ackerman
2	3	Allen	Ali
3	10	Chris	Chillon

3.19 Merging DataFrames

Problem

You want to merge two DataFrames.

Solution

To inner join, use merge with the on parameter to specify the column to merge on:

```
# Load library
import pandas as pd

# Create DataFrame
employee_data = {'employee_id': ['1', '2', '3', '4'],
                 'name': ['Amy Jones', 'Allen Keys', 'Alice Bees',
                 'Tim Horton']}
dataframe_employees = pd.DataFrame(employee_data, columns = ['employee_id',
                                                             'name'])

# Create DataFrame
sales_data = {'employee_id': ['3', '4', '5', '6'],
              'total_sales': [23456, 2512, 2345, 1455]}
dataframe_sales = pd.DataFrame(sales_data, columns = ['employee_id',
                                                      'total_sales'])

# Merge DataFrames
pd.merge(dataframe_employees, dataframe_sales, on='employee_id')
```

	employee_id	name	total_sales
0	3	Alice Bees	23456
1	4	Tim Horton	2512

merge defaults to inner joins. If we want to do an outer join, we can specify that with the how parameter:

```
# Merge DataFrames
pd.merge(dataframe_employees, dataframe_sales, on='employee_id', how='outer')
```

	employee_id	name	total_sales
0	1	Amy Jones	NaN
1	2	Allen Keys	NaN
2	3	Alice Bees	23456.0
3	4	Tim Horton	2512.0
4	5	NaN	2345.0
5	6	NaN	1455.0

The same parameter can be used to specify left and right joins:

```
# Merge DataFrames
pd.merge(dataframe_employees, dataframe_sales, on='employee_id', how='left')
```

	employee_id	name	total_sales
0	1	Amy Jones	NaN
1	2	Allen Keys	NaN
2	3	Alice Bees	23456.0
3	4	Tim Horton	2512.0

We can also specify the column name in each DataFrame to merge on:

```
# Merge DataFrames
pd.merge(dataframe_employees,
         dataframe_sales,
         left_on='employee_id',
         right_on='employee_id')
```

	employee_id	name	total_sales
0	3	Alice Bees	23456
1	4	Tim Horton	2512

If instead of merging on two columns we want to merge on the indexes of each Data-Frame, we can replace the left_on and right_on parameters with right_index=True and left_index=True.

Discussion

Oftentimes, the data we need to use is complex; it doesn't always come in one piece. Instead in the real world, we're usually faced with disparate datasets, from multiple database queries or files. To get all that data into one place, we can load each data query or data file into pandas as individual DataFrames and then merge them together into a single DataFrame.

This process might be familiar to anyone who has used SQL, a popular language for doing merging operations (called *joins*). While the exact parameters used by pandas will be different, they follow the same general patterns used by other software languages and tools.

There are three aspects to specify with any `merge` operation. First, we have to specify the two DataFrames we want to merge together. In the solution we named them `data frame_employees` and `dataframe_sales`. Second, we have to specify the name(s) of the columns to merge on—that is, the columns whose values are shared between the two DataFrames. For example, in our solution both DataFrames have a column named `employee_id`. To merge the two DataFrames we will match up the values in each DataFrame's `employee_id` column with each other. If these two columns use the same name, we can use the `on` parameter. However, if they have different names we can use `left_on` and `right_on`.

What is the left and right DataFrame? The simple answer is that the left DataFrame is the first one we specified in `merge` and the right DataFrame is the second one. This language comes up again in the next sets of parameters we will need.

The last aspect, and most difficult for some people to grasp, is the type of merge operation we want to conduct. This is specified by the `how` parameter. `merge` supports the four main types of joins:

Inner
> Return only the rows that match in both DataFrames (e.g., return any row with an `employee_id` value appearing in both `dataframe_employees` and `data frame_sales`).

Outer
> Return all rows in both DataFrames. If a row exists in one DataFrame but not in the other DataFrame, fill NaN values for the missing values (e.g., return all rows in both `employee_id` and `dataframe_sales`).

Left
> Return all rows from the left DataFrame but only rows from the right DataFrame that matched with the left DataFrame. Fill NaN values for the missing values (e.g., return all rows from `dataframe_employees` but only rows from `data frame_sales` that have a value for `employee_id` that appears in `data frame_employees`).

Right
> Return all rows from the right DataFrame but only rows from the left DataFrame that matched with the right DataFrame. Fill NaN values for the missing values (e.g., return all rows from `dataframe_sales` but only rows from `data`

`frame_employees` that have a value for `employee_id` that appears in `data
frame_sales`).

If you did not understand all of that right now, I encourage you to play around with the how parameter in your code and see how it affects what `merge` returns.

See Also

- A Visual Explanation of SQL Joins (*http://bit.ly/2Fxgcpe*)
- pandas documentation on merging (*http://bit.ly/2Fuo4rH*)

## CHAPTER 4

Handling Numerical Data

4.0 Introduction

Quantitative data is the measurement of something—whether class size, monthly sales, or student scores. The natural way to represent these quantities is numerically (e.g., 29 students, $529,392 in sales). In this chapter, we will cover numerous strategies for transforming raw numerical data into features purpose-built for machine learning algorithms.

4.1 Rescaling a Feature

Problem

You need to rescale the values of a numerical feature to be between two values.

Solution

Use scikit-learn's `MinMaxScaler` to rescale a feature array:

```
# Load libraries
import numpy as np
from sklearn import preprocessing

# Create feature
feature = np.array([[-500.5],
                    [-100.1],
                    [0],
                    [100.1],
                    [900.9]])

# Create scaler
minmax_scale = preprocessing.MinMaxScaler(feature_range=(0, 1))
```

```
# Scale feature
scaled_feature = minmax_scale.fit_transform(feature)

# Show feature
scaled_feature

array([[ 0.        ],
       [ 0.28571429],
       [ 0.35714286],
       [ 0.42857143],
       [ 1.        ]])
```

Discussion

Rescaling is a common preprocessing task in machine learning. Many of the algorithms described later in this book will assume all features are on the same scale, typically 0 to 1 or –1 to 1. There are a number of rescaling techniques, but one of the simplest is called *min-max scaling*. Min-max scaling uses the minimum and maximum values of a feature to rescale values to within a range. Specifically, min-max calculates:

$$x'_i = \frac{x_i - \min(x)}{\max(x) - \min(x)}$$

where x is the feature vector, x'_i is an individual element of feature x, and x'_i is the rescaled element. In our example, we can see from the outputted array that the feature has been successfully rescaled to between 0 and 1:

```
array([[ 0.        ],
       [ 0.28571429],
       [ 0.35714286],
       [ 0.42857143],
       [ 1.        ]])
```

scikit-learn's `MinMaxScaler` offers two options to rescale a feature. One option is to use `fit` to calculate the minimum and maximum values of the feature, then use `trans form` to rescale the feature. The second option is to use `fit_transform` to do both operations at once. There is no mathematical difference between the two options, but there is sometimes a practical benefit to keeping the operations separate because it allows us to apply the same transformation to different *sets* of the data.

See Also

- Feature scaling, Wikipedia (*http://bit.ly/2Fuug2Z*)

- About Feature Scaling and Normalization, Sebastian Raschka (*http://bit.ly/ 2FwwRcM*)

4.2 Standardizing a Feature

Problem

You want to transform a feature to have a mean of 0 and a standard deviation of 1.

Solution

scikit-learn's `StandardScaler` performs both transformations:

```
# Load libraries
import numpy as np
from sklearn import preprocessing

# Create feature
x = np.array([[-1000.1],
              [-200.2],
              [500.5],
              [600.6],
              [9000.9]])

# Create scaler
scaler = preprocessing.StandardScaler()

# Transform the feature
standardized = scaler.fit_transform(x)

# Show feature
standardized

array([[-0.76058269],
       [-0.54177196],
       [-0.35009716],
       [-0.32271504],
       [ 1.97516685]])
```

Discussion

A common alternative to min-max scaling discussed in Recipe 4.1 is rescaling of features to be approximately standard normally distributed. To achieve this, we use standardization to transform the data such that it has a mean, x̄, of 0 and a standard deviation, σ, of 1. Specifically, each element in the feature is transformed so that:

$$x_i' = \frac{x_i - \bar{x}}{\sigma}$$

where x'_i is our standardized form of x_i. The transformed feature represents the number of standard deviations the original value is away from the feature's mean value (also called a *z-score* in statistics).

Standardization is a common go-to scaling method for machine learning preprocessing and in my experience is used more than min-max scaling. However, it depends on the learning algorithm. For example, principal component analysis often works better using standardization, while min-max scaling is often recommended for neural networks (both algorithms are discussed later in this book). As a general rule, I'd recommend defaulting to standardization unless you have a specific reason to use an alternative.

We can see the effect of standardization by looking at the mean and standard deviation of our solution's output:

```
# Print mean and standard deviation
print("Mean:", round(standardized.mean()))
print("Standard deviation:", standardized.std())

Mean: 0.0
Standard deviation: 1.0
```

If our data has significant outliers, it can negatively impact our standardization by affecting the feature's mean and variance. In this scenario, it is often helpful to instead rescale the feature using the median and quartile range. In scikit-learn, we do this using the `RobustScaler` method:

```
# Create scaler
robust_scaler = preprocessing.RobustScaler()

# Transform feature
robust_scaler.fit_transform(x)

array([[ -1.87387612],
       [ -0.875     ],
       [  0.        ],
       [  0.125     ],
       [ 10.61488511]])
```

4.3 Normalizing Observations

Problem

You want to rescale the feature values of observations to have unit norm (a total length of 1).

Solution

Use `Normalizer` with a `norm` argument:

```
# Load libraries
import numpy as np
from sklearn.preprocessing import Normalizer

# Create feature matrix
features = np.array([[0.5, 0.5],
                     [1.1, 3.4],
                     [1.5, 20.2],
                     [1.63, 34.4],
                     [10.9, 3.3]])

# Create normalizer
normalizer = Normalizer(norm="l2")

# Transform feature matrix
normalizer.transform(features)

array([[ 0.70710678,  0.70710678],
       [ 0.30782029,  0.95144452],
       [ 0.07405353,  0.99725427],
       [ 0.04733062,  0.99887928],
       [ 0.95709822,  0.28976368]])
```

Discussion

Many rescaling methods (e.g., min-max scaling and standardization) operate on features; however, we can also rescale across individual observations. `Normalizer` rescales the values on individual observations to have unit norm (the sum of their lengths is 1). This type of rescaling is often used when we have many equivalent features (e.g., text classification when every word or n-word group is a feature).

`Normalizer` provides three norm options with Euclidean norm (often called L2) being the default argument:

$$\| x \|_2 = \sqrt{x_1^2 + x_2^2 + \cdots + x_n^2}$$

where x is an individual observation and x_n is that observation's value for the nth feature.

```
# Transform feature matrix
features_l2_norm = Normalizer(norm="l2").transform(features)

# Show feature matrix
features_l2_norm

array([[ 0.70710678,  0.70710678],
       [ 0.30782029,  0.95144452],
       [ 0.07405353,  0.99725427],
       [ 0.04733062,  0.99887928],
       [ 0.95709822,  0.28976368]])
```

Alternatively, we can specify Manhattan norm (L1):

$$\| x \|_1 = \sum_{i=1}^{n} |x_i| .$$

```
# Transform feature matrix
features_l1_norm = Normalizer(norm="l1").transform(features)

# Show feature matrix
features_l1_norm
array([[ 0.5       ,  0.5       ],
       [ 0.24444444,  0.75555556],
       [ 0.06912442,  0.93087558],
       [ 0.04524008,  0.95475992],
       [ 0.76760563,  0.23239437]])
```

Intuitively, L2 norm can be thought of as the distance between two points in New York for a bird (i.e., a straight line), while L1 can be thought of as the distance for a human walking on the street (walk north one block, east one block, north one block, east one block, etc.), which is why it is called "Manhattan norm" or "Taxicab norm."

Practically, notice that `norm='l1'` rescales an observation's values so they sum to 1, which can sometimes be a desirable quality:

```
# Print sum
print("Sum of the first observation\'s values:",
    features_l1_norm[0, 0] + features_l1_norm[0, 1])

Sum of the first observation's values: 1.0
```

4.4 Generating Polynomial and Interaction Features

Problem

You want to create polynominal and interaction features.

Solution

Even though some choose to create polynomial and interaction features manually, scikit-learn offers a built-in method:

```
# Load libraries
import numpy as np
from sklearn.preprocessing import PolynomialFeatures

# Create feature matrix
features = np.array([[2, 3],
                     [2, 3],
```

```
                 [2, 3]])

# Create PolynomialFeatures object
polynomial_interaction = PolynomialFeatures(degree=2, include_bias=False)

# Create polynomial features
polynomial_interaction.fit_transform(features)
array([[ 2.,   3.,   4.,   6.,   9.],
       [ 2.,   3.,   4.,   6.,   9.],
       [ 2.,   3.,   4.,   6.,   9.]])
```

The degree parameter determines the maximum degree of the polynomial. For example, degree=2 will create new features raised to the second power:

$$x_1, x_2, x_1^2, x_2^2$$

while degree=3 will create new features raised to the second and third power:

$$x_1, x_2, x_1^2, x_2^2, x_1^3, x_2^3$$

Furthermore, by default PolynomialFeatures includes interaction features:

$$x_1 x_2$$

We can restrict the features created to only interaction features by setting interaction_only to True:

```
interaction = PolynomialFeatures(degree=2,
            interaction_only=True, include_bias=False)
            interaction.fit_transform(features)
array([[ 2.,   3.,   6.],
       [ 2.,   3.,   6.],
       [ 2.,   3.,   6.]])
```

Discussion

Polynomial features are often created when we want to include the notion that there exists a nonlinear relationship between the features and the target. For example, we might suspect that the effect of age on the probability of having a major medical condition is not constant over time but increases as age increases. We can encode that nonconstant effect in a feature, x, by generating that feature's higher-order forms (x^2, x^3, etc.).

Additionally, often we run into situations where the effect of one feature is dependent on another feature. A simple example would be if we were trying to predict whether or not our coffee was sweet and we had two features: 1) whether or not the coffee was stirred and 2) if we added sugar. Individually, each feature does not predict coffee sweetness, but the combination of their effects does. That is, a coffee would only be sweet if the coffee had sugar and was stirred. The effects of each feature on the target (sweetness) are dependent on each other. We can encode that relationship by including an interaction feature that is the product of the individual features.

4.5 Transforming Features

Problem

You want to make a custom transformation to one or more features.

Solution

In scikit-learn, use FunctionTransformer to apply a function to a set of features:

```
# Load libraries
import numpy as np
from sklearn.preprocessing import FunctionTransformer

# Create feature matrix
features = np.array([[2, 3],
                     [2, 3],
                     [2, 3]])

# Define a simple function
def add_ten(x):
    return x + 10

# Create transformer
ten_transformer = FunctionTransformer(add_ten)

# Transform feature matrix
ten_transformer.transform(features)

array([[12, 13],
       [12, 13],
       [12, 13]])
```

We can create the same transformation in pandas using apply:

```
# Load library
import pandas as pd

# Create DataFrame
df = pd.DataFrame(features, columns=["feature_1", "feature_2"])
```

```
# Apply function
df.apply(add_ten)
```

	feature_1	feature_2
0	12	13
1	12	13
2	12	13

Discussion

It is common to want to make some custom transformations to one or more features. For example, we might want to create a feature that is the natural log of the values of the different feature. We can do this by creating a function and then mapping it to features using either scikit-learn's `FunctionTransformer` or pandas' `apply`. In the solution we created a very simple function, `add_ten`, which added 10 to each input, but there is no reason we could not define a much more complex function.

4.6 Detecting Outliers

Problem

You want to identify extreme observations.

Solution

Detecting outliers is unfortunately more of an art than a science. However, a common method is to assume the data is normally distributed and based on that assumption "draw" an ellipse around the data, classifying any observation inside the ellipse as an inlier (labeled as 1) and any observation outside the ellipse as an outlier (labeled as -1):

```
# Load libraries
import numpy as np
from sklearn.covariance import EllipticEnvelope
from sklearn.datasets import make_blobs

# Create simulated data
features, _ = make_blobs(n_samples = 10,
                         n_features = 2,
                         centers = 1,
                         random_state = 1)

# Replace the first observation's values with extreme values
features[0,0] = 10000
features[0,1] = 10000

# Create detector
```

```
outlier_detector = EllipticEnvelope(contamination=.1)

# Fit detector
outlier_detector.fit(features)

# Predict outliers
outlier_detector.predict(features)

array([-1,  1,  1,  1,  1,  1,  1,  1,  1,  1])
```

A major limitation of this approach is the need to specify a contamination parameter, which is the proportion of observations that are outliers—a value that we don't know. Think of contamination as our estimate of the cleanliness of our data. If we expect our data to have few outliers, we can set contamination to something small. However, if we believe that the data is very likely to have outliers, we can set it to a higher value.

Instead of looking at observations as a whole, we can instead look at individual features and identify extreme values in those features using interquartile range (IQR):

```
# Create one feature
feature = features[:,0]

# Create a function to return index of outliers
def indicies_of_outliers(x):
    q1, q3 = np.percentile(x, [25, 75])
    iqr = q3 - q1
    lower_bound = q1 - (iqr * 1.5)
    upper_bound = q3 + (iqr * 1.5)
    return np.where((x > upper_bound) | (x < lower_bound))

# Run function
indicies_of_outliers(feature)

(array([0]),)
```

IQR is the difference between the first and third quartile of a set of data. You can think of IQR as the spread of the bulk of the data, with outliers being observations far from the main concentration of data. Outliers are commonly defined as any value 1.5 IQRs less than the first quartile or 1.5 IQRs greater than the third quartile.

Discussion

There is no single best technique for detecting outliers. Instead, we have a collection of techniques all with their own advantages and disadvantages. Our best strategy is often trying multiple techniques (e.g., both EllipticEnvelope and IQR-based detection) and looking at the results as a whole.

If at all possible, we should take a look at observations we detect as outliers and try to understand them. For example, if we have a dataset of houses and one feature is number of rooms, is an outlier with 100 rooms really a house or is it actually a hotel that has been misclassified?

See Also

- Three ways to detect outliers (and the source of the IQR function used in this recipe) (*http://bit.ly/2FzMC2k*)

4.7 Handling Outliers

Problem

You have outliers.

Solution

Typically we have three strategies we can use to handle outliers. First, we can drop them:

```
# Load library
import pandas as pd

# Create DataFrame
houses = pd.DataFrame()
houses['Price'] = [534433, 392333, 293222, 4322032]
houses['Bathrooms'] = [2, 3.5, 2, 116]
houses['Square_Feet'] = [1500, 2500, 1500, 48000]

# Filter observations
houses[houses['Bathrooms'] < 20]
```

	Price	Bathrooms	Square_Feet
0	534433	2.0	1500
1	392333	3.5	2500
2	293222	2.0	1500

Second, we can mark them as outliers and include it as a feature:

```
# Load library
import numpy as np

# Create feature based on boolean condition
houses["Outlier"] = np.where(houses["Bathrooms"] < 20, 0, 1)

# Show data
houses
```

	Price	Bathrooms	Square_Feet	Outlier
0	534433	2.0	1500	0
1	392333	3.5	2500	0
2	293222	2.0	1500	0
3	4322032	116.0	48000	1

Finally, we can transform the feature to dampen the effect of the outlier:

```
# Log feature
houses["Log_Of_Square_Feet"] = [np.log(x) for x in houses["Square_Feet"]]

# Show data
houses
```

	Price	Bathrooms	Square_Feet	Outlier	Log_Of_Square_Feet
0	534433	2.0	1500	0	7.313220
1	392333	3.5	2500	0	7.824046
2	293222	2.0	1500	0	7.313220
3	4322032	116.0	48000	1	10.778956

Discussion

Similar to detecting outliers, there is no hard-and-fast rule for handling them. How we handle them should be based on two aspects. First, we should consider what makes them an outlier. If we believe they are errors in the data such as from a broken sensor or a miscoded value, then we might drop the observation or replace outlier values with NaN since we can't believe those values. However, if we believe the outliers are genuine extreme values (e.g., a house [mansion] with 200 bathrooms), then marking them as outliers or transforming their values is more appropriate.

Second, how we handle outliers should be based on our goal for machine learning. For example, if we want to predict house prices based on features of the house, we might reasonably assume the price for mansions with over 100 bathrooms is driven by a different dynamic than regular family homes. Furthermore, if we are training a model to use as part of an online home loan web application, we might assume that our potential users will not include billionaires looking to buy a mansion.

So what should we do if we have outliers? Think about why they are outliers, have an end goal in mind for the data, and, most importantly, remember that not making a decision to address outliers is itself a decision with implications.

One additional point: if you do have outliers standardization might not be appropriate because the mean and variance might be highly influenced by the outliers. In this case, use a rescaling method more robust against outliers like RobustScaler.

See Also

- RobustScaler documentation (*http://bit.ly/2DcgyNT*)

4.8 Discretizating Features

Problem

You have a numerical feature and want to break it up into discrete bins.

Solution

Depending on how we want to break up the data, there are two techniques we can use. First, we can binarize the feature according to some threshold:

```
# Load libraries
import numpy as np
from sklearn.preprocessing import Binarizer

# Create feature
age = np.array([[6],
                [12],
                [20],
                [36],
                [65]])

# Create binarizer
binarizer = Binarizer(18)

# Transform feature
binarizer.fit_transform(age)

array([[0],
       [0],
       [1],
       [1],
       [1]])
```

Second, we can break up numerical features according to multiple thresholds:

```
# Bin feature
np.digitize(age, bins=[20,30,64])

array([[0],
       [0],
       [1],
       [2],
       [3]])
```

Note that the arguments for the bins parameter denote the left edge of each bin. For example, the 20 argument does not include the element with the value of 20, only the two values smaller than 20. We can switch this behavior by setting the parameter right to True:

```
# Bin feature
np.digitize(age, bins=[20,30,64], right=True)

array([[0],
       [0],
       [0],
       [2],
       [3]])
```

Discussion

Discretization can be a fruitful strategy when we have reason to believe that a numerical feature should behave more like a categorical feature. For example, we might believe there is very little difference in the spending habits of 19- and 20-year-olds, but a significant difference between 20- and 21-year-olds (the age in the United States when young adults can consume alcohol). In that example, it could be useful to break up individuals in our data into those who can drink alcohol and those who cannot. Similarly, in other cases it might be useful to discretize our data into three or more bins.

In the solution, we saw two methods of discretization—scikit-learn's Binarizer for two bins and NumPy's digitize for three or more bins—however, we can also use digitize to binarize features like Binarizer by only specifying a single threshold:

```
# Bin feature
np.digitize(age, bins=[18])

array([[0],
       [0],
       [1],
       [1],
       [1]])
```

See Also

- digitize documentation (*http://bit.ly/2HSciFP*)

4.9 Grouping Observations Using Clustering

Problem

You want to cluster observations so that similar observations are grouped together.

Solution

If you know that you have *k* groups, you can use k-means clustering to group similar observations and output a new feature containing each observation's group membership:

```
# Load libraries
import pandas as pd
from sklearn.datasets import make_blobs
from sklearn.cluster import KMeans

# Make simulated feature matrix
features, _ = make_blobs(n_samples = 50,
                         n_features = 2,
                         centers = 3,
                         random_state = 1)

# Create DataFrame
dataframe = pd.DataFrame(features, columns=["feature_1", "feature_2"])

# Make k-means clusterer
clusterer = KMeans(3, random_state=0)

# Fit clusterer
clusterer.fit(features)

# Predict values
dataframe["group"] = clusterer.predict(features)

# View first few observations
dataframe.head(5)
```

	feature_1	feature_2	group
0	−9.877554	−3.336145	0
1	−7.287210	−8.353986	2
2	−6.943061	−7.023744	2
3	−7.440167	−8.791959	2
4	−6.641388	−8.075888	2

Discussion

We are jumping ahead of ourselves a bit and will go much more in depth about clustering algorithms later in the book. However, I wanted to point out that we can use clustering as a preprocessing step. Specifically, we use unsupervised learning algorithms like k-means to cluster observations into groups. The end result is a categorical feature with similar observations being members of the same group.

Don't worry if you did not understand all of that right now: just file away the idea that clustering can be used in preprocessing. And if you really can't wait, feel free to flip to Chapter 19 now.

4.10 Deleting Observations with Missing Values

Problem

You need to delete observations containing missing values.

Solution

Deleting observations with missing values is easy with a clever line of NumPy:

```
# Load library
import numpy as np

# Create feature matrix
features = np.array([[1.1, 11.1],
                     [2.2, 22.2],
                     [3.3, 33.3],
                     [4.4, 44.4],
                     [np.nan, 55]])

# Keep only observations that are not (denoted by ~) missing
features[~np.isnan(features).any(axis=1)]

array([[ 1.1,  11.1],
       [ 2.2,  22.2],
       [ 3.3,  33.3],
       [ 4.4,  44.4]])
```

Alternatively, we can drop missing observations using pandas:

```
# Load library
import pandas as pd

# Load data
dataframe = pd.DataFrame(features, columns=["feature_1", "feature_2"])

# Remove observations with missing values
dataframe.dropna()
```

	feature_1	feature_2
0	1.1	11.1
1	2.2	22.2
2	3.3	33.3
3	4.4	44.4

Discussion

Most machine learning algorithms cannot handle any missing values in the target and feature arrays. For this reason, we cannot ignore missing values in our data and must address the issue during preprocessing.

The simplest solution is to delete every observation that contains one or more missing values, a task quickly and easily accomplished using NumPy or pandas.

That said, we should be very reluctant to delete observations with missing values. Deleting them is the nuclear option, since our algorithm loses access to the information contained in the observation's non-missing values.

Just as important, depending on the cause of the missing values, deleting observations can introduce bias into our data. There are three types of missing data:

Missing Completely At Random (MCAR)
> The probability that a value is missing is independent of everything. For example, a survey respondent rolls a die before answering a question: if she rolls a six, she skips that question.

Missing At Random (MAR)
> The probability that a value is missing is not completely random, but depends on the information captured in other features. For example, a survey asks about gender identity and annual salary and women are more likely to skip the salary question; however, their nonresponse depends only on information we have captured in our gender identity feature.

Missing Not At Random (MNAR)
> The probability that a value is missing is not random and depends on information not captured in our features. For example, a survey asks about gender identity and women are more likely to skip the salary question, and we do not have a gender identity feature in our data.

It is sometimes acceptable to delete observations if they are MCAR or MAR. However, if the value is MNAR, the fact that a value is missing is itself information. Deleting MNAR observations can inject bias into our data because we are removing observations produced by some unobserved systematic effect.

See Also

- Identifying the Three Types of Missing Data (*http://bit.ly/2Fto4bx*)
- Missing-Data Imputation (*http://bit.ly/2FAkKLI*)

4.11 Imputing Missing Values

Problem

You have missing values in your data and want to fill in or predict their values.

Solution

If you have a small amount of data, predict the missing values using k-nearest neighbors (KNN):

```
# Load libraries
import numpy as np
from fancyimpute import KNN
from sklearn.preprocessing import StandardScaler
from sklearn.datasets import make_blobs

# Make a simulated feature matrix
features, _ = make_blobs(n_samples = 1000,
                         n_features = 2,
                         random_state = 1)

# Standardize the features
scaler = StandardScaler()
standardized_features = scaler.fit_transform(features)

# Replace the first feature's first value with a missing value
true_value = standardized_features[0,0]
standardized_features[0,0] = np.nan

# Predict the missing values in the feature matrix
features_knn_imputed = KNN(k=5, verbose=0).complete(standardized_features)

# Compare true and imputed values
print("True Value:", true_value)
print("Imputed Value:", features_knn_imputed[0,0])
```

```
True Value: 0.8730186114
Imputed Value: 1.09553327131
```

Alternatively, we can use scikit-learn's `Imputer` module to fill in missing values with the feature's mean, median, or most frequent value. However, we will typically get worse results than KNN:

```
# Load library
from sklearn.preprocessing import Imputer

# Create imputer
mean_imputer = Imputer(strategy="mean", axis=0)

# Impute values
```

```
features_mean_imputed = mean_imputer.fit_transform(features)

# Compare true and imputed values
print("True Value:", true_value)
print("Imputed Value:", features_mean_imputed[0,0])

True Value: 0.8730186114
Imputed Value: -3.05837272461
```

Discussion

There are two main strategies for replacing missing data with substitute values, each of which has strengths and weaknesses. First, we can use machine learning to predict the values of the missing data. To do this we treat the feature with missing values as a target vector and use the remaining subset of features to predict missing values. While we can use a wide range of machine learning algorithms to impute values, a popular choice is KNN. KNN is addressed in depth later in Chapter 14, but the short explanation is that the algorithm uses the k nearest observations (according to some distance metric) to predict the missing value. In our solution we predicted the missing value using the five closest observations.

The downside to KNN is that in order to know which observations are the closest to the missing value, it needs to calculate the distance between the missing value and every single observation. This is reasonable in smaller datasets, but quickly becomes problematic if a dataset has millions of observations.

An alternative and more scalable strategy is to fill in all missing values with some average value. For example, in our solution we used scikit-learn to fill in missing values with a feature's mean value. The imputed value is often not as close to the true value as when we used KNN, but we can scale mean-filling to data containing millions of observations easily.

If we use imputation, it is a good idea to create a binary feature indicating whether or not the observation contains an imputed value.

See Also

- A Study of K-Nearest Neighbour as an Imputation Method (*http://bit.ly/2HS9sAT*)

## CHAPTER 5

Handling Categorical Data

5.0 Introduction

It is often useful to measure objects not in terms of their quantity but in terms of some quality. We frequently represent this qualitative information as an observation's membership in a discrete category such as gender, colors, or brand of car. However, not all categorical data is the same. Sets of categories with no intrinsic ordering is called *nominal*. Examples of nominal categories include:

- Blue, Red, Green
- Man, Woman
- Banana, Strawberry, Apple

In contrast, when a set of categories has some natural ordering we refer to it as *ordinal*. For example:

- Low, Medium, High
- Young, Old
- Agree, Neutral, Disagree

Furthermore, categorical information is often represented in data as a vector or column of strings (e.g., `"Maine"`, `"Texas"`, `"Delaware"`). The problem is that most machine learning algorithms require inputs be numerical values.

The k-nearest neighbor algorithm provides a simple example. One step in the algorithm is calculating the distances between observations—often using Euclidean distance:

$$\sqrt{\sum_{i=1}^{n} (x_i - y_i)^2}$$

where x and y are two observations and subscript i denotes the value for the observations' ith feature. However, the distance calculation obviously is impossible if the value of x_i is a string (e.g., `"Texas"`). Instead, we need to convert the string into some numerical format so that it can be inputted into the Euclidean distance equation. Our goal is to make a transformation that properly conveys the information in the categories (ordinality, relative intervals between categories, etc.). In this chapter we will cover techniques for making this transformation as well as overcoming other challenges often encountered when handling categorical data.

5.1 Encoding Nominal Categorical Features

Problem

You have a feature with nominal classes that has no intrinsic ordering (e.g., apple, pear, banana).

Solution

One-hot encode the feature using scikit-learn's `LabelBinarizer`:

```
# Import libraries
import numpy as np
from sklearn.preprocessing import LabelBinarizer, MultiLabelBinarizer

# Create feature
feature = np.array([["Texas"],
                    ["California"],
                    ["Texas"],
                    ["Delaware"],
                    ["Texas"]])

# Create one-hot encoder
one_hot = LabelBinarizer()

# One-hot encode feature
one_hot.fit_transform(feature)

array([[0, 0, 1],
       [1, 0, 0],
       [0, 0, 1],
       [0, 1, 0],
       [0, 0, 1]])
```

We can use the `classes_` method to output the classes:

```
# View feature classes
one_hot.classes_
```

```
array(['California', 'Delaware', 'Texas'],
      dtype='<U10')
```

If we want to reverse the one-hot encoding, we can use `inverse_transform`:

```
# Reverse one-hot encoding
one_hot.inverse_transform(one_hot.transform(feature))
```

```
array(['Texas', 'California', 'Texas', 'Delaware', 'Texas'],
      dtype='<U10')
```

We can even use pandas to one-hot encode the feature:

```
# Import library
import pandas as pd
```

```
# Create dummy variables from feature
pd.get_dummies(feature[:,0])
```

	California	Delaware	Texas
0	0	0	1
1	1	0	0
2	0	0	1
3	0	1	0
4	0	0	1

One helpful ability of scikit-learn is to handle a situation where each observation lists multiple classes:

```
# Create multiclass feature
multiclass_feature = [("Texas", "Florida"),
                      ("California", "Alabama"),
                      ("Texas", "Florida"),
                      ("Delware", "Florida"),
                      ("Texas", "Alabama")]
```

```
# Create multiclass one-hot encoder
one_hot_multiclass = MultiLabelBinarizer()
```

```
# One-hot encode multiclass feature
one_hot_multiclass.fit_transform(multiclass_feature)
```

```
array([[0, 0, 0, 1, 1],
       [1, 1, 0, 0, 0],
       [0, 0, 0, 1, 1],
       [0, 0, 1, 1, 0],
       [1, 0, 0, 0, 1]])
```

Once again, we can see the classes with the `classes_` method:

```
# View classes
one_hot_multiclass.classes_

array(['Alabama', 'California', 'Delware', 'Florida', 'Texas'], dtype=object)
```

Discussion

We might think the proper strategy is to assign each class a numerical value (e.g., Texas = 1, California = 2). However, when our classes have no intrinsic ordering (e.g., Texas isn't "less" than California), our numerical values erroneously create an ordering that is not present.

The proper strategy is to create a binary feature for each class in the original feature. This is often called *one-hot encoding* (in machine learning literature) or *dummying* (in statistical and research literature). Our solution's feature was a vector containing three classes (i.e., Texas, California, and Delaware). In one-hot encoding, each class becomes its own feature with 1s when the class appears and 0s otherwise. Because our feature had three classes, one-hot encoding returned three binary features (one for each class). By using one-hot encoding we can capture the membership of an observation in a class while preserving the notion that the class lacks any sort of hierarchy.

Finally, it is worthwhile to note that it is often recommended that after one-hot encoding a feature, we drop one of the one-hot encoded features in the resulting matrix to avoid linear dependence.

See Also

- Dummy Variable Trap, Algosome (*http://bit.ly/2FvVJkC*)
- Dropping one of the columns when using one-hot encoding, CrossValidated (*http://bit.ly/2FwrxG0*)

5.2 Encoding Ordinal Categorical Features

Problem

You have an ordinal categorical feature (e.g., high, medium, low).

Solution

Use pandas DataFrame's `replace` method to transform string labels to numerical equivalents:

```
# Load library
import pandas as pd
```

```
# Create features
dataframe = pd.DataFrame({"Score": ["Low", "Low", "Medium", "Medium", "High"]})

# Create mapper
scale_mapper = {"Low":1,
                "Medium":2,
                "High":3}

# Replace feature values with scale
dataframe["Score"].replace(scale_mapper)

0    1
1    1
2    2
3    2
4    3
Name: Score, dtype: int64
```

Discussion

Often we have a feature with classes that have some kind of natural ordering. A famous example is the Likert scale:

- Strongly Agree
- Agree
- Neutral
- Disagree
- Strongly Disagree

When encoding the feature for use in machine learning, we need to transform the ordinal classes into numerical values that maintain the notion of ordering. The most common approach is to create a dictionary that maps the string label of the class to a number and then apply that map to the feature.

It is important that our choice of numeric values is based on our prior information on the ordinal classes. In our solution, high is literally three times larger than low. This is fine in any instances, but can break down if the assumed intervals between the classes are not equal:

```
dataframe = pd.DataFrame({"Score": ["Low",
                                    "Low",
                                    "Medium",
                                    "Medium",
                                    "High",
                                    "Barely More Than Medium"]})

scale_mapper = {"Low":1,
                "Medium":2,
```

```
                    "Barely More Than Medium": 3,
                    "High":4}

dataframe["Score"].replace(scale_mapper)

0    1
1    1
2    2
3    2
4    4
5    3
Name: Score, dtype: int64
```

In this example, the distance between Low and Medium is the same as the distance between Medium and Barely More Than Medium, which is almost certainly not accurate. The best approach is to be conscious about the numerical values mapped to classes:

```
scale_mapper = {"Low":1,
                "Medium":2,
                "Barely More Than Medium": 2.1,
                "High":3}

dataframe["Score"].replace(scale_mapper)

0    1.0
1    1.0
2    2.0
3    2.0
4    3.0
5    2.1
Name: Score, dtype: float64
```

5.3 Encoding Dictionaries of Features

Problem

You have a dictionary and want to convert it into a feature matrix.

Solution

Use DictVectorizer:

```
# Import library
from sklearn.feature_extraction import DictVectorizer

# Create dictionary
data_dict = [{"Red": 2, "Blue": 4},
             {"Red": 4, "Blue": 3},
             {"Red": 1, "Yellow": 2},
             {"Red": 2, "Yellow": 2}]
```

```
# Create dictionary vectorizer
dictvectorizer = DictVectorizer(sparse=False)

# Convert dictionary to feature matrix
features = dictvectorizer.fit_transform(data_dict)

# View feature matrix
features

array([[ 4.,  2.,  0.],
       [ 3.,  4.,  0.],
       [ 0.,  1.,  2.],
       [ 0.,  2.,  2.]])
```

By default `DictVectorizer` outputs a sparse matrix that only stores elements with a value other than 0. This can be very helpful when we have massive matrices (often encountered in natural language processing) and want to minimize the memory requirements. We can force `DictVectorizer` to output a dense matrix using `sparse=False`.

We can get the names of each generated feature using the `get_feature_names` method:

```
# Get feature names
feature_names = dictvectorizer.get_feature_names()

# View feature names
feature_names

['Blue', 'Red', 'Yellow']
```

While not necessary, for the sake of illustration we can create a pandas DataFrame to view the output better:

```
# Import library
import pandas as pd

# Create dataframe from features
pd.DataFrame(features, columns=feature_names)
```

	Blue	Red	Yellow
0	4.0	2.0	0.0
1	3.0	4.0	0.0
2	0.0	1.0	2.0
3	0.0	2.0	2.0

Discussion

A dictionary is a popular data structure used by many programming languages; however, machine learning algorithms expect the data to be in the form of a matrix. We can accomplish this using scikit-learn's `dictvectorizer`.

This is a common situation when working with natural language processing. For example, we might have a collection of documents and for each document we have a dictionary containing the number of times every word appears in the document. Using `dictvectorizer`, we can easily create a feature matrix where every feature is the number of times a word appears in each document:

```
# Create word counts dictionaries for four documents
doc_1_word_count = {"Red": 2, "Blue": 4}
doc_2_word_count = {"Red": 4, "Blue": 3}
doc_3_word_count = {"Red": 1, "Yellow": 2}
doc_4_word_count = {"Red": 2, "Yellow": 2}

# Create list
doc_word_counts = [doc_1_word_count,
                   doc_2_word_count,
                   doc_3_word_count,
                   doc_4_word_count]

# Convert list of word count dictionaries into feature matrix
dictvectorizer.fit_transform(doc_word_counts)

array([[ 4.,  2.,  0.],
       [ 3.,  4.,  0.],
       [ 0.,  1.,  2.],
       [ 0.,  2.,  2.]])
```

In our toy example there are only three unique words (Red, Yellow, Blue) so there are only three features in our matrix; however, you can imagine that if each document was actually a book in a university library our feature matrix would be very large (and then we would want to set `spare` to `True`).

See Also

- How to use dictionaries in Python (*http://bit.ly/2HReoWz*)
- SciPy Sparse Matrices (*http://bit.ly/2HReBZR*)

5.4 Imputing Missing Class Values

Problem

You have a categorical feature containing missing values that you want to replace with predicted values.

Solution

The ideal solution is to train a machine learning classifier algorithm to predict the missing values, commonly a k-nearest neighbors (KNN) classifier:

```python
# Load libraries
import numpy as np
from sklearn.neighbors import KNeighborsClassifier

# Create feature matrix with categorical feature
X = np.array([[0, 2.10, 1.45],
              [1, 1.18, 1.33],
              [0, 1.22, 1.27],
              [1, -0.21, -1.19]])

# Create feature matrix with missing values in the categorical feature
X_with_nan = np.array([[np.nan, 0.87, 1.31],
                       [np.nan, -0.67, -0.22]])

# Train KNN learner
clf = KNeighborsClassifier(3, weights='distance')
trained_model = clf.fit(X[:,1:], X[:,0])

# Predict missing values' class
imputed_values = trained_model.predict(X_with_nan[:,1:])

# Join column of predicted class with their other features
X_with_imputed = np.hstack((imputed_values.reshape(-1,1), X_with_nan[:,1:]))

# Join two feature matrices
np.vstack((X_with_imputed, X))

array([[ 0.  ,  0.87,  1.31],
       [ 1.  , -0.67, -0.22],
       [ 0.  ,  2.1 ,  1.45],
       [ 1.  ,  1.18,  1.33],
       [ 0.  ,  1.22,  1.27],
       [ 1.  , -0.21, -1.19]])
```

An alternative solution is to fill in missing values with the feature's most frequent value:

```python
from sklearn.preprocessing import Imputer
```

```
# Join the two feature matrices
X_complete = np.vstack((X_with_nan, X))

imputer = Imputer(strategy='most_frequent', axis=0)

imputer.fit_transform(X_complete)
array([[ 0.  ,  0.87,  1.31],
       [ 0.  , -0.67, -0.22],
       [ 0.  ,  2.1 ,  1.45],
       [ 1.  ,  1.18,  1.33],
       [ 0.  ,  1.22,  1.27],
       [ 1.  , -0.21, -1.19]])
```

Discussion

When we have missing values in a categorical feature, our best solution is to open our toolbox of machine learning algorithms to predict the values of the missing observations. We can accomplish this by treating the feature with the missing values as the target vector and the other features as the feature matrix. A commonly used algorithm is KNN (discussed in depth later in this book), which assigns to the missing value the median class of the k nearest observations.

Alternatively, we can fill in missing values with the most frequent class of the feature. While less sophisticated than KNN, it is much more scalable to larger data. In either case, it is advisable to include a binary feature indicating which observations contain imputed values.

See Also

- Overcoming Missing Values in a Random Forest Classifier (*http://bit.ly/ 2HSsNBF*)
- A Study of K-Nearest Neighbour as an Imputation Method (*http://bit.ly/ 2HS9sAT*)

5.5 Handling Imbalanced Classes

Problem

You have a target vector with highly imbalanced classes.

Solution

Collect more data. If that isn't possible, change the metrics used to evaluate your model. If that doesn't work, consider using a model's built-in class weight parameters (if available), downsampling, or upsampling. We cover evaluation metrics in a later chapter, so for now let us focus on class weight parameters, downsampling, and upsampling.

To demonstrate our solutions, we need to create some data with imbalanced classes. Fisher's Iris dataset contains three balanced classes of 50 observations, each indicating the species of flower (*Iris setosa*, *Iris virginica*, and *Iris versicolor*). To unbalance the dataset, we remove 40 of the 50 *Iris setosa* observations and then merge the *Iris virginica* and *Iris versicolor* classes. The end result is a binary target vector indicating if an observation is an *Iris setosa* flower or not. The result is 10 observations of *Iris setosa* (class 0) and 100 observations of not Iris setosa (class 1):

```
# Load libraries
import numpy as np
from sklearn.ensemble import RandomForestClassifier
from sklearn.datasets import load_iris

# Load iris data
iris = load_iris()

# Create feature matrix
features = iris.data

# Create target vector
target = iris.target

# Remove first 40 observations
features = features[40:,:]
target = target[40:]

# Create binary target vector indicating if class 0
target = np.where((target == 0), 0, 1)

# Look at the imbalanced target vector
target
array([0, 0, 0, 0, 0, 0, 0, 0, 0, 0, 1, 1, 1, 1, 1, 1, 1, 1, 1, 1, 1, 1, 1,
       1, 1, 1, 1, 1, 1, 1, 1, 1, 1, 1, 1, 1, 1, 1, 1, 1, 1, 1, 1, 1, 1, 1,
       1, 1, 1, 1, 1, 1, 1, 1, 1, 1, 1, 1, 1, 1, 1, 1, 1, 1, 1, 1, 1, 1, 1,
       1, 1, 1, 1, 1, 1, 1, 1, 1, 1, 1, 1, 1, 1, 1, 1, 1, 1, 1, 1, 1, 1, 1,
       1, 1, 1, 1, 1, 1, 1, 1, 1, 1, 1, 1, 1, 1, 1, 1, 1, 1, 1, 1])
```

Many algorithms in scikit-learn offer a parameter to weight classes during training to counteract the effect of their imbalance. While we have not covered it yet, `RandomFor estClassifier` is a popular classification algorithm and includes a `class_weight` parameter. You can pass an argument specifying the desired class weights explicitly:

```
# Create weights
weights = {0: .9, 1: 0.1}
```

```
# Create random forest classifier with weights
RandomForestClassifier(class_weight=weights)

RandomForestClassifier(bootstrap=True, class_weight={0: 0.9, 1: 0.1},
          criterion='gini', max_depth=None, max_features='auto',
          max_leaf_nodes=None, min_impurity_decrease=0.0,
          min_impurity_split=None, min_samples_leaf=1,
          min_samples_split=2, min_weight_fraction_leaf=0.0,
          n_estimators=10, n_jobs=1, oob_score=False, random_state=None,
          verbose=0, warm_start=False)
```

Or you can pass balanced, which automatically creates weights inversely proportional to class frequencies:

```
# Train a random forest with balanced class weights
RandomForestClassifier(class_weight="balanced")

RandomForestClassifier(bootstrap=True, class_weight='balanced',
          criterion='gini', max_depth=None, max_features='auto',
          max_leaf_nodes=None, min_impurity_decrease=0.0,
          min_impurity_split=None, min_samples_leaf=1,
          min_samples_split=2, min_weight_fraction_leaf=0.0,
          n_estimators=10, n_jobs=1, oob_score=False, random_state=None,
          verbose=0, warm_start=False)
```

Alternatively, we can downsample the majority class or upsample the minority class. In downsampling, we randomly sample without replacement from the majority class (i.e., the class with more observations) to create a new subset of observations equal in size to the minority class. For example, if the minority class has 10 observations, we will randomly select 10 observations from the majority class and use those 20 observations as our data. Here we do exactly that using our unbalanced Iris data:

```
# Indicies of each class' observations
i_class0 = np.where(target == 0)[0]
i_class1 = np.where(target == 1)[0]

# Number of observations in each class
n_class0 = len(i_class0)
n_class1 = len(i_class1)

# For every observation of class 0, randomly sample
# from class 1 without replacement
i_class1_downsampled = np.random.choice(i_class1, size=n_class0, replace=False)

# Join together class 0's target vector with the
# downsampled class 1's target vector
np.hstack((target[i_class0], target[i_class1_downsampled]))

array([0, 0, 0, 0, 0, 0, 0, 0, 0, 0, 1, 1, 1, 1, 1, 1, 1, 1, 1, 1])

# Join together class 0's feature matrix with the
# downsampled class 1's feature matrix
np.vstack((features[i_class0,:], features[i_class1_downsampled,:]))[0:5]
```

```
array([[ 5. ,  3.5,  1.3,  0.3],
       [ 4.5,  2.3,  1.3,  0.3],
       [ 4.4,  3.2,  1.3,  0.2],
       [ 5. ,  3.5,  1.6,  0.6],
       [ 5.1,  3.8,  1.9,  0.4]])
```

Our other option is to upsample the minority class. In upsampling, for every observation in the majority class, we randomly select an observation from the minority class with replacement. The end result is the same number of observations from the minority and majority classes. Upsampling is implemented very similarly to downsampling, just in reverse:

```
# For every observation in class 1, randomly sample from class 0 with replacement
i_class0_upsampled = np.random.choice(i_class0, size=n_class1, replace=True)

# Join together class 0's upsampled target vector with class 1's target vector
np.concatenate((target[i_class0_upsampled], target[i_class1]))
```

```
array([0, 0, 0, 0, 0, 0, 0, 0, 0, 0, 0, 0, 0, 0, 0, 0, 0, 0, 0, 0, 0, 0,
       0, 0, 0, 0, 0, 0, 0, 0, 0, 0, 0, 0, 0, 0, 0, 0, 0, 0, 0, 0, 0, 0,
       0, 0, 0, 0, 0, 0, 0, 0, 0, 0, 0, 0, 0, 0, 0, 0, 0, 0, 0, 0, 0, 0,
       0, 0, 0, 0, 0, 0, 0, 0, 0, 0, 0, 0, 0, 0, 0, 0, 0, 0, 0, 0, 0, 0,
       0, 0, 0, 0, 0, 0, 0, 0, 1, 1, 1, 1, 1, 1, 1, 1, 1, 1, 1, 1, 1, 1,
       1, 1, 1, 1, 1, 1, 1, 1, 1, 1, 1, 1, 1, 1, 1, 1, 1, 1, 1, 1, 1, 1,
       1, 1, 1, 1, 1, 1, 1, 1, 1, 1, 1, 1, 1, 1, 1, 1, 1, 1, 1, 1, 1, 1,
       1, 1, 1, 1, 1, 1, 1, 1, 1, 1, 1, 1, 1, 1, 1, 1, 1, 1, 1, 1, 1, 1,
       1, 1, 1, 1, 1, 1, 1, 1, 1, 1, 1, 1, 1, 1, 1])
```

```
# Join together class 0's upsampled feature matrix with class 1's feature matrix
np.vstack((features[i_class0_upsampled,:], features[i_class1,:]))[0:5]
```

```
array([[ 5. ,  3.5,  1.6,  0.6],
       [ 5. ,  3.5,  1.6,  0.6],
       [ 5. ,  3.3,  1.4,  0.2],
       [ 4.5,  2.3,  1.3,  0.3],
       [ 4.8,  3. ,  1.4,  0.3]])
```

Discussion

In the real world, imbalanced classes are everywhere—most visitors don't click the buy button and many types of cancer are thankfully rare. For this reason, handling imbalanced classes is a common activity in machine learning.

Our best strategy is simply to collect more observations—especially observations from the minority class. However, this is often just not possible, so we have to resort to other options.

A second strategy is to use a model evaluation metric better suited to imbalanced classes. Accuracy is often used as a metric for evaluating the performance of a model, but when imbalanced classes are present accuracy can be ill suited. For example, if only 0.5% of observations have some rare cancer, then even a naive model that predicts nobody has cancer will be 99.5% accurate. Clearly this is not ideal. Some better metrics we discuss in later chapters are confusion matrices, precision, recall, F1 scores, and ROC curves.

A third strategy is to use the class weighing parameters included in implementations of some models. This allows us to have the algorithm adjust for imbalanced classes. Fortunately, many scikit-learn classifiers have a `class_weight` parameter, making it a good option.

The fourth and fifth strategies are related: downsampling and upsampling. In downsampling we create a random subset of the majority class of equal size to the minority class. In upsampling we repeatedly sample with replacement from the minority class to make it of equal size as the majority class. The decision between using downsampling and upsampling is context-specific, and in general we should try both to see which produces better results.

## CHAPTER 6

Handling Text

6.0 Introduction

Unstructured text data, like the contents of a book or a tweet, is both one of the most interesting sources of features and one of the most complex to handle. In this chapter, we will cover strategies for transforming text into information-rich features. This is not to say that the recipes covered here are comprehensive. There exist entire academic disciplines focused on handling this and similar types of data, and the contents of all their techniques would fill a small library. Despite this, there are some commonly used techniques, and a knowledge of these will add valuable tools to our preprocessing toolbox.

6.1 Cleaning Text

Problem

You have some unstructured text data and want to complete some basic cleaning.

Solution

Most basic text cleaning operations should only replace Python's core string operations, in particular `strip`, `replace`, and `split`:

```
# Create text
text_data = ["   Interrobang. By Aishwarya Henriette     ",
             "Parking And Going. By Karl Gautier",
             "    Today Is The night. By Jarek Prakash   "]

# Strip whitespaces
strip_whitespace = [string.strip() for string in text_data]
```

```
# Show text
strip_whitespace

['Interrobang. By Aishwarya Henriette',
 'Parking And Going. By Karl Gautier',
 'Today Is The night. By Jarek Prakash']

# Remove periods
remove_periods = [string.replace(".", "") for string in strip_whitespace]

# Show text
remove_periods

['Interrobang By Aishwarya Henriette',
 'Parking And Going By Karl Gautier',
 'Today Is The night By Jarek Prakash']
```

We also create and apply a custom transformation function:

```
# Create function
def capitalizer(string: str) -> str:
    return string.upper()

# Apply function
[capitalizer(string) for string in remove_periods]

['INTERROBANG BY AISHWARYA HENRIETTE',
 'PARKING AND GOING BY KARL GAUTIER',
 'TODAY IS THE NIGHT BY JAREK PRAKASH']
```

Finally, we can use regular expressions to make powerful string operations:

```
# Import library
import re

# Create function
def replace_letters_with_X(string: str) -> str:
    return re.sub(r"[a-zA-Z]", "X", string)

# Apply function
[replace_letters_with_X(string) for string in remove_periods]

['XXXXXXXXXXX XX XXXXXXXXX XXXXXXXXX',
 'XXXXXXX XXX XXXXX XX XXXX XXXXXXX',
 'XXXXX XX XXX XXXXX XX XXXXX XXXXXXX']
```

Discussion

Most text data will need to be cleaned before we can use it to build features. Most basic text cleaning can be completed using Python's standard string operations. In the real world we will most likely define a custom cleaning function (e.g., `capitalizer`) combining some cleaning tasks and apply that to the text data.

- Beginners Tutorial for Regular Expressions in Python (*http://bit.ly/2HTGZuu*)

6.2 Parsing and Cleaning HTML

Problem

You have text data with HTML elements and want to extract just the text.

Solution

Use Beautiful Soup's extensive set of options to parse and extract from HTML:

```
# Load library
from bs4 import BeautifulSoup

# Create some HTML code
html = """
        <div class='full_name'><span style='font-weight:bold'>
        Masego</span> Azra</div>"
        """

# Parse html
soup = BeautifulSoup(html, "lxml")

# Find the div with the class "full_name", show text
soup.find("div", { "class" : "full_name" }).text

'Masego Azra'
```

Discussion

Despite the strange name, Beautiful Soup is a powerful Python library designed for scraping HTML. Typically Beautiful Soup is used scrape live websites, but we can just as easily use it to extract text data embedded in HTML. The full range of Beautiful Soup operations is beyond the scope of this book, but even the few methods used in our solution show how easily we can parse HTML code to extract the data we want.

See Also

- Beautiful Soup (*http://bit.ly/2pwZcYs*)

6.3 Removing Punctuation

Problem

You have a feature of text data and want to remove punctuation.

Solution

Define a function that uses `translate` with a dictionary of punctuation characters:

```
# Load libraries
import unicodedata
import sys

# Create text
text_data = ['Hi!!!! I. Love. This. Song....',
             '10000% Agree!!!! #LoveIT',
             'Right?!?!']

# Create a dictionary of punctuation characters
punctuation = dict.fromkeys(i for i in range(sys.maxunicode)
                            if unicodedata.category(chr(i)).startswith('P'))

# For each string, remove any punctuation characters
[string.translate(punctuation) for string in text_data]

['Hi I Love This Song', '10000 Agree LoveIT', 'Right']
```

Discussion

`translate` is a Python method popular due to its blazing speed. In our solution, first we created a dictionary, `punctuation`, with all punctuation characters according to Unicode as its keys and `None` as its values. Next we translated all characters in the string that are in `punctuation` into `None`, effectively removing them. There are more readable ways to remove punctuation, but this somewhat hacky solution has the advantage of being far faster than alternatives.

It is important to be conscious of the fact that punctuation contains information (e.g., "Right?" versus "Right!"). Removing punctuation is often a necessary evil to create features; however, if the punctuation is important we should make sure to take that into account.

6.4 Tokenizing Text

Problem

You have text and want to break it up into individual words.

Solution

Natural Language Toolkit for Python (NLTK) has a powerful set of text manipulation operations, including word tokenizing:

```
# Load library
from nltk.tokenize import word_tokenize

# Create text
string = "The science of today is the technology of tomorrow"

# Tokenize words
word_tokenize(string)

['The', 'science', 'of', 'today', 'is', 'the', 'technology', 'of', 'tomorrow']
```

We can also tokenize into sentences:

```
# Load library
from nltk.tokenize import sent_tokenize

# Create text
string = "The science of today is the technology of tomorrow. Tomorrow is today."

# Tokenize sentences
sent_tokenize(string)

['The science of today is the technology of tomorrow.', 'Tomorrow is today.']
```

Discussion

Tokenization, especially word tokenization, is a common task after cleaning text data because it is the first step in the process of turning the text into data we will use to construct useful features.

6.5 Removing Stop Words

Problem

Given tokenized text data, you want to remove extremely common words (e.g., *a*, *is*, *of*, *on*) that contain little informational value.

Solution

Use NLTK's stopwords:

```
# Load library
from nltk.corpus import stopwords

# You will have to download the set of stop words the first time
# import nltk
```

```
# nltk.download('stopwords')

# Create word tokens
tokenized_words = ['i',
                   'am',
                   'going',
                   'to',
                   'go',
                   'to',
                   'the',
                   'store',
                   'and',
                   'park']

# Load stop words
stop_words = stopwords.words('english')

# Remove stop words
[word for word in tokenized_words if word not in stop_words]

['going', 'go', 'store', 'park']
```

Discussion

While "stop words" can refer to any set of words we want to remove before process‐
ing, frequently the term refers to extremely common words that themselves contain
little information value. NLTK has a list of common stop words that we can use to
find and remove stop words in our tokenized words:

```
# Show stop words
stop_words[:5]

['i', 'me', 'my', 'myself', 'we']
```

Note that NLTK's stopwords assumes the tokenized words are all lowercased.

6.6 Stemming Words

Problem

You have tokenized words and want to convert them into their root forms.

Solution

Use NLTK's PorterStemmer:

```
# Load library
from nltk.stem.porter import PorterStemmer

# Create word tokens
tokenized_words = ['i', 'am', 'humbled', 'by', 'this', 'traditional', 'meeting']
```

```
# Create stemmer
porter = PorterStemmer()

# Apply stemmer
[porter.stem(word) for word in tokenized_words]

['i', 'am', 'humbl', 'by', 'thi', 'tradit', 'meet']
```

Discussion

Stemming reduces a word to its stem by identifying and removing affixes (e.g., gerunds) while keeping the root meaning of the word. For example, both "tradition" and "traditional" have "tradit" as their stem, indicating that while they are different words they represent the same general concept. By stemming our text data, we transform it to something less readable, but closer to its base meaning and thus more suitable for comparison across observations. NLTK's `PorterStemmer` implements the widely used Porter stemming algorithm to remove or replace common suffixes to produce the word stem.

See Also

- Porter Stemming Algorithm (*http://bit.ly/2FB5ZZb*)

6.7 Tagging Parts of Speech

Problem

You have text data and want to tag each word or character with its part of speech.

Solution

Use NLTK's pre-trained parts-of-speech tagger:

```
# Load libraries
from nltk import pos_tag
from nltk import word_tokenize

# Create text
text_data = "Chris loved outdoor running"

# Use pre-trained part of speech tagger
text_tagged = pos_tag(word_tokenize(text_data))

# Show parts of speech
text_tagged

[('Chris', 'NNP'), ('loved', 'VBD'), ('outdoor', 'RP'), ('running', 'VBG')]
```

The output is a list of tuples with the word and the tag of the part of speech. NLTK uses the Penn Treebank parts for speech tags. Some examples of the Penn Treebank tags are:

Tag	Part of speech
NNP	Proper noun, singular
NN	Noun, singular or mass
RB	Adverb
VBD	Verb, past tense
VBG	Verb, gerund or present participle
JJ	Adjective
PRP	Personal pronoun

Once the text has been tagged, we can use the tags to find certain parts of speech. For example, here are all nouns:

```
# Filter words
[word for word, tag in text_tagged if tag in ['NN','NNS','NNP','NNPS'] ]

['Chris']
```

A more realistic situation would be that we have data where every observation contains a tweet and we want to convert those sentences into features for individual parts of speech (e.g., a feature with 1 if a proper noun is present, and 0 otherwise):

```
# Create text
tweets = ["I am eating a burrito for breakfast",
          "Political science is an amazing field",
          "San Francisco is an awesome city"]

# Create list
tagged_tweets = []

# Tag each word and each tweet
for tweet in tweets:
    tweet_tag = nltk.pos_tag(word_tokenize(tweet))
    tagged_tweets.append([tag for word, tag in tweet_tag])

# Use one-hot encoding to convert the tags into features
one_hot_multi = MultiLabelBinarizer()
one_hot_multi.fit_transform(tagged_tweets)

array([[1, 1, 0, 1, 0, 1, 1, 1, 0],
       [1, 0, 1, 1, 0, 0, 0, 0, 1],
       [1, 0, 1, 1, 1, 0, 0, 0, 1]])
```

Using classes_ we can see that each feature is a part-of-speech tag:

```
# Show feature names
one_hot_multi.classes_
```

```
array(['DT', 'IN', 'JJ', 'NN', 'NNP', 'PRP', 'VBG', 'VBP', 'VBZ'], dtype=object)
```

Discussion

If our text is English and not on a specialized topic (e.g., medicine) the simplest solution is to use NLTK's pre-trained parts-of-speech tagger. However, if `pos_tag` is not very accurate, NLTK also gives us the ability to train our own tagger. The major downside of training a tagger is that we need a large corpus of text where the tag of each word is known. Constructing this tagged corpus is obviously labor intensive and is probably going to be a last resort.

All that said, if we had a tagged corpus and wanted to train a tagger, the following is an example of how we could do it. The corpus we are using is the Brown Corpus, one of the most popular sources of tagged text. Here we use a backoff *n*-gram tagger, where *n* is the number of previous words we take into account when predicting a word's part-of-speech tag. First we take into account the previous two words using `TrigramTagger`; if two words are not present, we "back off" and take into account the tag of the previous one word using `BigramTagger`, and finally if that fails we only look at the word itself using `UnigramTagger`. To examine the accuracy of our tagger, we split our text data into two parts, train our tagger on one part, and test how well it predicts the tags of the second part:

```
# Load library
from nltk.corpus import brown
from nltk.tag import UnigramTagger
from nltk.tag import BigramTagger
from nltk.tag import TrigramTagger

# Get some text from the Brown Corpus, broken into sentences
sentences = brown.tagged_sents(categories='news')

# Split into 4000 sentences for training and 623 for testing
train = sentences[:4000]
test = sentences[4000:]

# Create backoff tagger
unigram = UnigramTagger(train)
bigram = BigramTagger(train, backoff=unigram)
trigram = TrigramTagger(train, backoff=bigram)

# Show accuracy
trigram.evaluate(test)

0.8179229731754832
```

See Also

- Penn Treebank (*http://bit.ly/2HROPo5*)

- Brown Corpus (*http://bit.ly/2FzgMTx*)

6.8 Encoding Text as a Bag of Words

Problem

You have text data and want to create a set of features indicating the number of times an observation's text contains a particular word.

Solution

Use scikit-learn's `CountVectorizer`:

```
# Load library
import numpy as np
from sklearn.feature_extraction.text import CountVectorizer

# Create text
text_data = np.array(['I love Brazil. Brazil!',
                      'Sweden is best',
                      'Germany beats both'])



# Create the bag of words feature matrix
count = CountVectorizer()
bag_of_words = count.fit_transform(text_data)

# Show feature matrix
bag_of_words

<3x8 sparse matrix of type '<class 'numpy.int64'>'
    with 8 stored elements in Compressed Sparse Row format>
```

This output is a sparse array, which is often necessary when we have a large amount of text. However, in our toy example we can use `toarray` to view a matrix of word counts for each observation:

```
bag_of_words.toarray()

array([[0, 0, 0, 2, 0, 0, 1, 0],
       [0, 1, 0, 0, 0, 1, 0, 1],
       [1, 0, 1, 0, 1, 0, 0, 0]], dtype=int64)
```

We can use the `vocabulary_` method to view the word associated with each feature:

```
# Show feature names
count.get_feature_names()

['beats', 'best', 'both', 'brazil', 'germany', 'is', 'love', 'sweden']
```

This might be confusing, so for the sake of clarity here is what the feature matrix looks like with the words as column names (each row is one observation):

beats	best	both	brazil	germany	is	love	sweden
0	0	0	2	0	0	1	0
0	1	0	0	0	1	0	1
1	0	1	0	1	0	0	0

Discussion

One of the most common methods of transforming text into features is by using a bag-of-words model. Bag-of-words models output a feature for every unique word in text data, with each feature containing a count of occurrences in observations. For example, in our solution the sentence I love Brazil. Brazil! has a value of 2 in the "brazil" feature because the word *brazil* appears two times.

The text data in our solution was purposely small. In the real world, a single observation of text data could be the contents of an entire book! Since our bag-of-words model creates a feature for every unique word in the data, the resulting matrix can contain thousands of features. This means that the size of the matrix can sometimes become very large in memory. However, luckily we can exploit a common characteristic of bag-of-words feature matrices to reduce the amount of data we need to store.

Most words likely do not occur in most observations, and therefore bag-of-words feature matrices will contain mostly 0s as values. We call these types of matrices "sparse." Instead of storing all values of the matrix, we can only store nonzero values and then assume all other values are 0. This will save us memory when we have large feature matrices. One of the nice features of CountVectorizer is that the output is a sparse matrix by default.

CountVectorizer comes with a number of useful parameters to make creating bag-of-words feature matrices easy. First, while by default every feature is a word, that does not have to be the case. Instead we can set every feature to be the combination of two words (called a 2-gram) or even three words (3-gram). ngram_range sets the minimum and maximum size of our *n*-grams. For example, (2,3) will return all 2-grams and 3-grams. Second, we can easily remove low-information filler words using stop_words either with a built-in list or a custom list. Finally, we can restrict the words or phrases we want to consider to a certain list of words using vocabulary. For example, we could create a bag-of-words feature matrix for only occurrences of country names:

```
# Create feature matrix with arguments
count_2gram = CountVectorizer(ngram_range=(1,2),
                              stop_words="english",
                              vocabulary=['brazil'])
```

```
bag = count_2gram.fit_transform(text_data)

# View feature matrix
bag.toarray()

array([[2],
       [0],
       [0]])
# View the 1-grams and 2-grams
count_2gram.vocabulary_

{'brazil': 0}
```

See Also

- *n*-gram (*https://en.wikipedia.org/wiki/N-gram*)
- Bag of Words Meets Bags of Popcorn (*http://bit.ly/2HRba5v*)

6.9 Weighting Word Importance

Problem

You want a bag of words, but with words weighted by their importance to an observation.

Solution

Compare the frequency of the word in a document (a tweet, movie review, speech transcript, etc.) with the frequency of the word in all other documents using term frequency-inverse document frequency (tf-idf). scikit-learn makes this easy with TfidfVectorizer:

```
# Load libraries
import numpy as np
from sklearn.feature_extraction.text import TfidfVectorizer

# Create text
text_data = np.array(['I love Brazil. Brazil!',
                      'Sweden is best',
                      'Germany beats both'])

# Create the tf-idf feature matrix
tfidf = TfidfVectorizer()
feature_matrix = tfidf.fit_transform(text_data)

# Show tf-idf feature matrix
feature_matrix
```

```
<3x8 sparse matrix of type '<class 'numpy.float64'>'
    with 8 stored elements in Compressed Sparse Row format>
```

Just as in Recipe 6.8, the output is a spare matrix. However, if we want to view the output as a dense matrix, we can use .toarray:

```
# Show tf-idf feature matrix as dense matrix
feature_matrix.toarray()

array([[ 0.        , 0.        , 0.        , 0.89442719, 0.        ,
         0.        , 0.4472136 , 0.        ],
       [ 0.        , 0.57735027, 0.        , 0.        , 0.        ,
         0.57735027, 0.        , 0.57735027],
       [ 0.57735027, 0.        , 0.57735027, 0.        , 0.57735027,
         0.        , 0.        , 0.        ]])
```

vocabulary_ shows us the word of each feature:

```
# Show feature names
tfidf.vocabulary_

{'beats': 0,
 'best': 1,
 'both': 2,
 'brazil': 3,
 'germany': 4,
 'is': 5,
 'love': 6,
 'sweden': 7}
```

Discussion

The more a word appears in a document, the more likely it is important to that document. For example, if the word *economy* appears frequently, it is evidence that the document might be about economics. We call this *term frequency* (*tf*).

In contrast, if a word appears in many documents, it is likely less important to any individual document. For example, if every document in some text data contains the word *after* then it is probably an unimportant word. We call this document frequency (*df*).

By combining these two statistics, we can assign a score to every word representing how important that word is in a document. Specifically, we multiply *tf* to the inverse of document frequency (*idf*):

$$\text{tf-idf}(t, d) = tf(t, d) \times idf(t)$$

where *t* is a word and *d* is a document. There are a number of variations in how *tf* and *idf* are calculated. In scikit-learn, *tf* is simply the number of times a word appears in the document and *idf* is calculated as:

$$\text{idf}(t) = log\frac{1 + n_d}{1 + \text{df}(d, t)} + 1$$

where n_d is the number of documents and df(d,t) is term, t's document frequency (i.e., number of documents where the term appears).

By default, scikit-learn then normalizes the tf-idf vectors using the Euclidean norm (L2 norm). The higher the resulting value, the more important the word is to a document.

See Also

- scikit-learn documentation: tf–idf term weighting (*http://bit.ly/2HT2wmW*)

## CHAPTER 7

Handling Dates and Times

7.0 Introduction

Dates and times (datetimes) are frequently encountered during preprocessing for machine learning, whether the time of a particular sale or the year of some public health statistic. In this chapter, we will build a toolbox of strategies for handling time series data including tackling time zones and creating lagged time features. Specifically, we will focus on the time series tools in the pandas library, which centralizes the functionality of many other libraries.

7.1 Converting Strings to Dates

Problem

Given a vector of strings representing dates and times, you want to transform them into time series data.

Solution

Use pandas' to_datetime with the format of the date and/or time specified in the format parameter:

```
# Load libraries
import numpy as np
import pandas as pd

# Create strings
date_strings = np.array(['03-04-2005 11:35 PM',
                         '23-05-2010 12:01 AM',
                         '04-09-2009 09:09 PM'])
```

```
# Convert to datetimes
[pd.to_datetime(date, format='%d-%m-%Y %I:%M %p') for date in date_strings]

[Timestamp('2005-04-03 23:35:00'),
 Timestamp('2010-05-23 00:01:00'),
 Timestamp('2009-09-04 21:09:00')]
```

We might also want to add an argument to the `errors` parameter to handle problems:

```
# Convert to datetimes
[pd.to_datetime(date, format="%d-%m-%Y %I:%M %p", errors="coerce")
for date in date_strings]

[Timestamp('2005-04-03 23:35:00'),
 Timestamp('2010-05-23 00:01:00'),
 Timestamp('2009-09-04 21:09:00')]
```

If `errors="coerce"`, then any problem that occurs will not raise an error (the default behavior) but instead will set the value causing the error to NaT (i.e., a missing value).

Discussion

When dates and times come as strings, we need to convert them into a data type Python can understand. While there are a number of Python tools for converting strings to datetimes, following our use of pandas in other recipes we can use `to_date time` to conduct the transformation. One obstacle to strings representing dates and times is that the format of the strings can vary significantly between data sources. For example, one vector of dates might represent March 23rd, 2015 as "03-23-15" while another might use "3|23|2015". We can use the `format` parameter to specify the exact format of the string. Here are some common date and time formatting codes:

Code	Description	Example
%Y	Full year	2001
%m	Month w/ zero padding	04
%d	Day of the month w/ zero padding	09
%I	Hour (12hr clock) w/ zero padding	02
%p	AM or PM	AM
%M	Minute w/ zero padding	05
%S	Second w/ zero padding	09

See Also

- Complete List of Python String Time Codes (*http://strftime.org*)

7.2 Handling Time Zones

Problem

You have time series data and want to add or change time zone information.

Solution

If not specified, pandas objects have no time zone. However, we can add a time zone using `tz` during creation:

```
# Load library
import pandas as pd

# Create datetime
pd.Timestamp('2017-05-01 06:00:00', tz='Europe/London')

Timestamp('2017-05-01 06:00:00+0100', tz='Europe/London')
```

We can add a time zone to a previously created datetime using `tz_localize`:

```
# Create datetime
date = pd.Timestamp('2017-05-01 06:00:00')

# Set time zone
date_in_london = date.tz_localize('Europe/London')

# Show datetime
date_in_london

Timestamp('2017-05-01 06:00:00+0100', tz='Europe/London')
```

We can also convert to a different time zone:

```
# Change time zone
date_in_london.tz_convert('Africa/Abidjan')

Timestamp('2017-05-01 05:00:00+0000', tz='Africa/Abidjan')
```

Finally, pandas' Series objects can apply `tz_localize` and `tz_convert` to every element:

```
# Create three dates
dates = pd.Series(pd.date_range('2/2/2002', periods=3, freq='M'))

# Set time zone
dates.dt.tz_localize('Africa/Abidjan')

0   2002-02-28 00:00:00+00:00
1   2002-03-31 00:00:00+00:00
2   2002-04-30 00:00:00+00:00
dtype: datetime64[ns, Africa/Abidjan]
```

Discussion

pandas supports two sets of strings representing timezones; however, I suggest using pytz library's strings. We can see all the strings used to represent time zones by importing all_timezones:

```
# Load library
from pytz import all_timezones

# Show two time zones
all_timezones[0:2]

['Africa/Abidjan', 'Africa/Accra']
```

7.3 Selecting Dates and Times

Problem

You have a vector of dates and you want to select one or more.

Solution

Use two boolean conditions as the start and end dates:

```
# Load library
import pandas as pd

# Create data frame
dataframe = pd.DataFrame()

# Create datetimes
dataframe['date'] = pd.date_range('1/1/2001', periods=100000, freq='H')

# Select observations between two datetimes
dataframe[(dataframe['date'] > '2002-1-1 01:00:00') &
          (dataframe['date'] <= '2002-1-1 04:00:00')]
```

	date
8762	2002-01-01 02:00:00
8763	2002-01-01 03:00:00
8764	2002-01-01 04:00:00

Alternatively, we can set the date column as the DataFrame's index and then slice using loc:

```
# Set index
dataframe = dataframe.set_index(dataframe['date'])
```

```
# Select observations between two datetimes
dataframe.loc['2002-1-1 01:00:00':'2002-1-1 04:00:00']
```

	date
	date
2002-01-01 01:00:00	2002-01-01 01:00:00
2002-01-01 02:00:00	2002-01-01 02:00:00
2002-01-01 03:00:00	2002-01-01 03:00:00
2002-01-01 04:00:00	2002-01-01 04:00:00

Discussion

Whether we use boolean conditions or index slicing is situation dependent. If we wanted to do some complex time series manipulation, it might be worth the overhead of setting the date column as the index of the DataFrame, but if we wanted to do some simple data wrangling, the boolean conditions might be easier.

7.4 Breaking Up Date Data into Multiple Features

Problem

You have a column of dates and times and you want to create features for year, month, day, hour, and minute.

Solution

Use pandas Series.dt's time properties:

```
# Load library
import pandas as pd

# Create data frame
dataframe = pd.DataFrame()

# Create five dates
dataframe['date'] = pd.date_range('1/1/2001', periods=150, freq='W')

# Create features for year, month, day, hour, and minute
dataframe['year'] = dataframe['date'].dt.year
dataframe['month'] = dataframe['date'].dt.month
dataframe['day'] = dataframe['date'].dt.day
dataframe['hour'] = dataframe['date'].dt.hour
dataframe['minute'] = dataframe['date'].dt.minute

# Show three rows
dataframe.head(3)
```

	date	year	month	day	hour	minute
0	2001-01-07	2001	1	7	0	0
1	2001-01-14	2001	1	14	0	0
2	2001-01-21	2001	1	21	0	0

Discussion

Sometimes it can be useful to break up a column of dates into components. For example, we might want a feature that just includes the year of the observation or we might want only to consider the month of some observation so we can compare them regardless of year.

7.5 Calculating the Difference Between Dates

Problem

You have two datetime features and want to calculate the time between them for each observation.

Solution

Subtract the two date features using pandas:

```
# Load library
import pandas as pd

# Create data frame
dataframe = pd.DataFrame()

# Create two datetime features
dataframe['Arrived'] = [pd.Timestamp('01-01-2017'), pd.Timestamp('01-04-2017')]
dataframe['Left'] = [pd.Timestamp('01-01-2017'), pd.Timestamp('01-06-2017')]

# Calculate duration between features
dataframe['Left'] - dataframe['Arrived']

0    0 days
1    2 days
dtype: timedelta64[ns]
```

Often we will want to remove the days output and keep only the numerical value:

```
# Calculate duration between features
pd.Series(delta.days for delta in (dataframe['Left'] - dataframe['Arrived']))

0    0
1    2
dtype: int64
```

Discussion

There are times when the feature we want is the change (delta) between two points in time. For example, we might have the dates a customer checks in and checks out of a hotel, but the feature we want is the duration of his stay. pandas makes this calculation easy using the TimeDelta data type.

See Also

- Pandas documentation: Time Deltas (*http://bit.ly/2HOS3sJ*)

7.6 Encoding Days of the Week

Problem

You have a vector of dates and want to know the day of the week for each date.

Solution

Use pandas' Series.dt property weekday_name:

```
# Load library
import pandas as pd

# Create dates
dates = pd.Series(pd.date_range("2/2/2002", periods=3, freq="M"))

# Show days of the week
dates.dt.weekday_name

0     Thursday
1       Sunday
2      Tuesday
dtype: object
```

If we want the output to be a numerical value and therefore more usable as a machine learning feature, we can use weekday where the days of the week are represented as an integer (Monday is 0):

```
# Show days of the week
dates.dt.weekday

0    3
1    6
2    1
dtype: int64
```

Discussion

Knowing the weekday can be helpful if, for instance, we wanted to compare total sales on Sundays for the past three years. pandas makes creating a feature vector containing weekday information easy.

See Also

- pandas Series datetimelike properties (*http://bit.ly/2HShhq1*)

7.7 Creating a Lagged Feature

Problem

You want to create a feature that is lagged *n* time periods.

Solution

Use pandas' shift:

```
# Load library
import pandas as pd

# Create data frame
dataframe = pd.DataFrame()

# Create data
dataframe["dates"] = pd.date_range("1/1/2001", periods=5, freq="D")
dataframe["stock_price"] = [1.1,2.2,3.3,4.4,5.5]

# Lagged values by one row
dataframe["previous_days_stock_price"] = dataframe["stock_price"].shift(1)

# Show data frame
dataframe
```

	dates	stock_price	previous_days_stock_price
0	2001-01-01	1.1	NaN
1	2001-01-02	2.2	1.1
2	2001-01-03	3.3	2.2
3	2001-01-04	4.4	3.3
4	2001-01-05	5.5	4.4

Discussion

Very often data is based on regularly spaced time periods (e.g., every day, every hour, every three hours) and we are interested in using values in the past to make predictions (this is often called *lagging* a feature). For example, we might want to predict a stock's price using the price it was the day before. With pandas we can use `shift` to lag values by one row, creating a new feature containing past values.

In our solution, the first row for `previous_days_stock_price` is a missing value because there is no previous `stock_price` value.

7.8 Using Rolling Time Windows

Problem

Given time series data, you want to calculate some statistic for a rolling time.

Solution

```
# Load library
import pandas as pd

# Create datetimes
time_index = pd.date_range("01/01/2010", periods=5, freq="M")

# Create data frame, set index
dataframe = pd.DataFrame(index=time_index)

# Create feature
dataframe["Stock_Price"] = [1,2,3,4,5]

# Calculate rolling mean
dataframe.rolling(window=2).mean()
```

	Stock_Price
2010-01-31	NaN
2010-02-28	1.5
2010-03-31	2.5
2010-04-30	3.5
2010-05-31	4.5

Discussion

Rolling (also called moving) time windows are conceptually simple but can be difficult to understand at first. Imagine we have monthly observations for a stock's price. It is often useful to have a time window of a certain number of months and then move over the observations calculating a statistic for all observations in the time window.

For example, if we have a time window of three months and we want a rolling mean, we would calculate:

1. mean(January, February, March)
2. mean(February, March, April)
3. mean(March, April, May)
4. etc.

Another way to put it: our three-month time window "walks" over the observations, calculating the window's mean at each step.

pandas' rolling allows us to specify the size of the window using window and then quickly calculate some common statistics, including the max value (max()), mean value (mean()), count of values (count()), and rolling correlation (corr()).

Rolling means are often used to smooth out time series data because using the mean of the entire time window dampens the effect of short-term fluctuations.

See Also

- pandas documentation: Rolling Windows (*http://bit.ly/2HTIicA*)
- What are Moving Average or Smoothing Techniques? (*http://bit.ly/2HRRHBn*)

7.9 Handling Missing Data in Time Series

Problem

You have missing values in time series data.

Solution

In addition to the missing data strategies previously discussed, when we have time series data we can use interpolation to fill in gaps caused by missing values:

```
# Load libraries
import pandas as pd
import numpy as np

# Create date
time_index = pd.date_range("01/01/2010", periods=5, freq="M")

# Create data frame, set index
```

```
dataframe = pd.DataFrame(index=time_index)

# Create feature with a gap of missing values
dataframe["Sales"] = [1.0,2.0,np.nan,np.nan,5.0]

# Interpolate missing values
dataframe.interpolate()
```

	Sales
2010-01-31	1.0
2010-02-28	2.0
2010-03-31	3.0
2010-04-30	4.0
2010-05-31	5.0

Alternatively, we can replace missing values with the last known value (i.e., forward-filling):

```
# Forward-fill
dataframe.ffill()
```

	Sales
2010-01-31	1.0
2010-02-28	2.0
2010-03-31	2.0
2010-04-30	2.0
2010-05-31	5.0

We can also replace missing values with the latest known value (i.e., back-filling):

```
# Back-fill
dataframe.bfill()
```

	Sales
2010-01-31	1.0
2010-02-28	2.0
2010-03-31	5.0
2010-04-30	5.0
2010-05-31	5.0

Discussion

Interpolation is a technique for filling in gaps caused by missing values by, in effect, drawing a line or curve between the known values bordering the gap and using that line or curve to predict reasonable values. Interpolation can be particularly useful when the time intervals between are constant, the data is not prone to noisy fluctuations, and the gaps caused by missing values are small. For example, in our solution a gap of two missing values was bordered by 2.0 and 5.0. By fitting a line starting at 2.0 and ending at 5.0, we can make reasonable guesses for the two missing values in between of 3.0 and 4.0.

If we believe the line between the two known points is nonlinear, we can use `interpolate`'s `method` to specify the interpolation method:

```
# Interpolate missing values
dataframe.interpolate(method="quadratic")
```

	Sales
2010-01-31	1.000000
2010-02-28	2.000000
2010-03-31	3.059808
2010-04-30	4.038069
2010-05-31	5.000000

Finally, there might be cases when we have large gaps of missing values and do not want to interpolate values across the entire gap. In these cases we can use `limit` to restrict the number of interpolated values and `limit_direction` to set whether to interpolate values forward from at the last known value before the gap or vice versa:

```
# Interpolate missing values
dataframe.interpolate(limit=1, limit_direction="forward")
```

	Sales
2010-01-31	1.0
2010-02-28	2.0
2010-03-31	3.0
2010-04-30	NaN
2010-05-31	5.0

Back-filling and forward-filling can be thought of as a form of naive interpolation, where we draw a flat line from a known value and use it to fill in missing values. One (minor) advantage back- and forward-filling have over interpolation is the lack of the need for known values on *both* sides of missing value(s).

## CHAPTER 8

Handling Images

8.0 Introduction

Image classification is one of the most exciting areas of machine learning. The ability of computers to recognize patterns and objects from images is an incredibly powerful tool in our toolkit. However, before we can apply machine learning to images, we often first need to transform the raw images to features usable by our learning algorithms.

To work with images, we will use the Open Source Computer Vision Library (OpenCV). While there are a number of good libraries out there, OpenCV is the most popular and documented library for handling images. One of the biggest hurdles to using OpenCV is installing it. However, fortunately if we are using Python 3 (at the time of publication OpenCV does not work with Python 3.6+), we can use Anaconda's package manager tool conda to install OpenCV in a single line of code in our terminal:

```
conda install --channel https://conda.anaconda.org/menpo opencv3
```

Afterward, we can check the installation by opening a notebook, importing OpenCV, and checking the version number (3.1.0):

```
import cv2
```

```
cv2.__version__
```

If installing OpenCV using conda does not work, there are many guides online.

Finally, throughout this chapter we will use a set of images as examples, which are available to download on GitHub (*https://github.com/chrisalbon/simulated_datasets*).

8.1 Loading Images

Problem

You want to load an image for preprocessing.

Solution

Use OpenCV's `imread`:

```
# Load library
import cv2
import numpy as np
from matplotlib import pyplot as plt

# Load image as grayscale
image = cv2.imread("images/plane.jpg", cv2.IMREAD_GRAYSCALE)
```

If we want to view the image, we can use the Python plotting library Matplotlib:

```
# Show image
plt.imshow(image, cmap="gray"), plt.axis("off")
plt.show()
```

Discussion

Fundamentally, images are data and when we use `imread` we convert that data into a data type we are very familiar with—a NumPy array:

```
# Show data type
type(image)

numpy.ndarray
```

We have transformed the image into a matrix whose elements correspond to individual pixels. We can even take a look at the actual values of the matrix:

```
# Show image data
image

array([[140, 136, 146, ..., 132, 139, 134],
       [144, 136, 149, ..., 142, 124, 126],
       [152, 139, 144, ..., 121, 127, 134],
       ...,
       [156, 146, 144, ..., 157, 154, 151],
       [146, 150, 147, ..., 156, 158, 157],
       [143, 138, 147, ..., 156, 157, 157]], dtype=uint8)
```

The resolution of our image was 3600 × 2270, the exact dimensions of our matrix:

```
# Show dimensions
image.shape

(2270, 3600)
```

What does each element in the matrix actually represent? In grayscale images, the value of an individual element is the pixel intensity. Intensity values range from black (0) to white (255). For example, the intensity of the top-rightmost pixel in our image has a value of 140:

```
# Show first pixel
image[0,0]

140
```

In the matrix, each element contains three values corresponding to blue, green, red values (BGR):

```
# Load image in color
image_bgr = cv2.imread("images/plane.jpg", cv2.IMREAD_COLOR)

# Show pixel
image_bgr[0,0]

array([195, 144, 111], dtype=uint8)
```

One small caveat: by default OpenCV uses BGR, but many image applications—including Matplotlib—use red, green, blue (RGB), meaning the red and the blue values are swapped. To properly display OpenCV color images in Matplotlib, we need to first convert the color to RGB (apologies to hardcopy readers):

```
# Convert to RGB
image_rgb = cv2.cvtColor(image_bgr, cv2.COLOR_BGR2RGB)

# Show image
plt.imshow(image_rgb), plt.axis("off")
plt.show()
```

See Also

- Difference between RGB and BGR (*http://bit.ly/2Fws76E*)
- RGB color model (*http://bit.ly/2FxZjKZ*)

8.2 Saving Images

Problem

You want to save an image for preprocessing.

Solution

Use OpenCV's imwrite:

```
# Load libraries
import cv2
import numpy as np
from matplotlib import pyplot as plt

# Load image as grayscale
image = cv2.imread("images/plane.jpg", cv2.IMREAD_GRAYSCALE)

# Save image
cv2.imwrite("images/plane_new.jpg", image)

True
```

Discussion

OpenCV's `imwrite` saves images to the filepath specified. The format of the image is defined by the filename's extension (*.jpg*, *.png*, etc.). One behavior to be careful about: `imwrite` will overwrite existing files without outputting an error or asking for confirmation.

8.3 Resizing Images

Problem

You want to resize an image for further preprocessing.

Solution

Use `resize` to change the size of an image:

```
# Load image
import cv2
import numpy as np
from matplotlib import pyplot as plt

# Load image as grayscale
image = cv2.imread("images/plane_256x256.jpg", cv2.IMREAD_GRAYSCALE)

# Resize image to 50 pixels by 50 pixels
image_50x50 = cv2.resize(image, (50, 50))

# View image
plt.imshow(image_50x50, cmap="gray"), plt.axis("off")
plt.show()
```

Discussion

Resizing images is a common task in image preprocessing for two reasons. First, images come in all shapes and sizes, and to be usable as features, images must have the same dimensions. This standardization of image size does come with costs, however; images are matrices of information and when we reduce the size of the image we are reducing the size of that matrix and the information it contains. Second, machine learning can require thousands or hundreds of thousands of images. When those images are very large they can take up a lot of memory, and by resizing them we can dramatically reduce memory usage. Some common image sizes for machine learning are 32×32, 64×64, 96×96, and 256×256.

8.4 Cropping Images

Problem

You want to remove the outer portion of the image to change its dimensions.

Solution

The image is encoded as a two-dimensional NumPy array, so we can crop the image easily by slicing the array:

```
# Load image
import cv2
import numpy as np
from matplotlib import pyplot as plt

# Load image in grayscale
image = cv2.imread("images/plane_256x256.jpg", cv2.IMREAD_GRAYSCALE)

# Select first half of the columns and all rows
image_cropped = image[:,:128]

# Show image
plt.imshow(image_cropped, cmap="gray"), plt.axis("off")
plt.show()
```

Discussion

Since OpenCV represents images as a matrix of elements, by selecting the rows and columns we want to keep we are able to easily crop the image. Cropping can be particularly useful if we know that we only want to keep a certain part of every image.

For example, if our images come from a stationary security camera we can crop all the images so they only contain the area of interest.

See Also

- Slicing NumPy Arrays (*http://bit.ly/2FrVNBV*)

8.5 Blurring Images

Problem

You want to smooth out an image.

Solution

To blur an image, each pixel is transformed to be the average value of its neighbors. This neighbor and the operation performed are mathematically represented as a kernel (don't worry if you don't know what a kernel is). The size of this kernel determines the amount of blurring, with larger kernels producing smoother images. Here we blur an image by averaging the values of a 5×5 kernel around each pixel:

```
# Load libraries
import cv2
import numpy as np
from matplotlib import pyplot as plt

# Load image as grayscale
image = cv2.imread("images/plane_256x256.jpg", cv2.IMREAD_GRAYSCALE)

# Blur image
image_blurry = cv2.blur(image, (5,5))

# Show image
plt.imshow(image_blurry, cmap="gray"), plt.axis("off")
plt.show()
```

To highlight the effect of kernel size, here is the same blurring with a 100×100 kernel:

```
# Blur image
image_very_blurry = cv2.blur(image, (100,100))

# Show image
plt.imshow(image_very_blurry, cmap="gray"), plt.xticks([]), plt.yticks([])
plt.show()
```

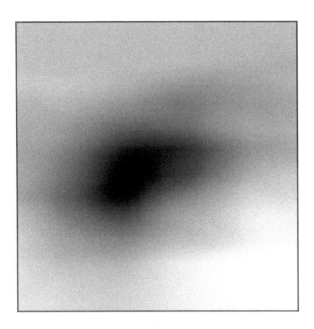

Discussion

Kernels are widely used in image processing to do everything from sharpening to edge detection, and will come up repeatedly in this chapter. The blurring kernel we used looks like this:

```
# Create kernel
kernel = np.ones((5,5)) / 25.0

# Show kernel
kernel
```

```
array([[ 0.04,  0.04,  0.04,  0.04,  0.04],
       [ 0.04,  0.04,  0.04,  0.04,  0.04],
       [ 0.04,  0.04,  0.04,  0.04,  0.04],
       [ 0.04,  0.04,  0.04,  0.04,  0.04],
       [ 0.04,  0.04,  0.04,  0.04,  0.04]])
```

The center element in the kernel is the pixel being examined, while the remaining elements are its neighbors. Since all elements have the same value (normalized to add up to 1), each has an equal say in the resulting value of the pixel of interest. We can manually apply a kernel to an image using filter2D to produce a similar blurring effect:

```
# Apply kernel
image_kernel = cv2.filter2D(image, -1, kernel)

# Show image
```

```
plt.imshow(image_kernel, cmap="gray"), plt.xticks([]), plt.yticks([])
plt.show()
```

See Also

- Image Kernels Explained Visually (*http://setosa.io/ev/image-kernels/*)
- Common Image Kernels (*http://bit.ly/2FxZCFD*)

8.6 Sharpening Images

Problem

You want to sharpen an image.

Solution

Create a kernel that highlights the target pixel. Then apply it to the image using `fil
ter2D`:

```
# Load libraries
import cv2
import numpy as np
from matplotlib import pyplot as plt
```

```
# Load image as grayscale
image = cv2.imread("images/plane_256x256.jpg", cv2.IMREAD_GRAYSCALE)

# Create kernel
kernel = np.array([[0, -1, 0],
                   [-1, 5,-1],
                   [0, -1, 0]])

# Sharpen image
image_sharp = cv2.filter2D(image, -1, kernel)

# Show image
plt.imshow(image_sharp, cmap="gray"), plt.axis("off")
plt.show()
```

Discussion

Sharpening works similarly to blurring, except instead of using a kernel to average the neighboring values, we constructed a kernel to highlight the pixel itself. The resulting effect makes contrasts in edges stand out more in the image.

8.7 Enhancing Contrast

Problem

We want to increase the contrast between pixels in an image.

Solution

Histogram equalization is a tool for image processing that can make objects and shapes stand out. When we have a grayscale image, we can apply OpenCV's equali zeHist directly on the image:

```
# Load libraries
import cv2
import numpy as np
from matplotlib import pyplot as plt

# Load image
image = cv2.imread("images/plane_256x256.jpg", cv2.IMREAD_GRAYSCALE)

# Enhance image
image_enhanced = cv2.equalizeHist(image)

# Show image
plt.imshow(image_enhanced, cmap="gray"), plt.axis("off")
plt.show()
```

However, when we have a color image, we first need to convert the image to the YUV color format. The Y is the luma, or brightness, and U and V denote the color. After the conversion, we can apply `equalizeHist` to the image and then convert it back to BGR or RGB:

```
# Load image
image_bgr = cv2.imread("images/plane.jpg")

# Convert to YUV
image_yuv = cv2.cvtColor(image_bgr, cv2.COLOR_BGR2YUV)

# Apply histogram equalization
image_yuv[:, :, 0] = cv2.equalizeHist(image_yuv[:, :, 0])

# Convert to RGB
image_rgb = cv2.cvtColor(image_yuv, cv2.COLOR_YUV2RGB)

# Show image
plt.imshow(image_rgb), plt.axis("off")
plt.show()
```

Discussion

While a detailed explanation of how histogram equalization works is beyond the scope of this book, the short explanation is that it transforms the image so that it uses a wider range of pixel intensities.

While the resulting image often does not look "realistic," we need to remember that the image is just a visual representation of the underlying data. If histogram equalization is able to make objects of interest more distinguishable from other objects or backgrounds (which is not always the case), then it can be a valuable addition to our image preprocessing pipeline.

8.8 Isolating Colors

Problem

You want to isolate a color in an image.

Solution

Define a range of colors and then apply a mask to the image:

```
# Load libraries
import cv2
import numpy as np
```

```
from matplotlib import pyplot as plt

# Load image
image_bgr = cv2.imread('images/plane_256x256.jpg')

# Convert BGR to HSV
image_hsv = cv2.cvtColor(image_bgr, cv2.COLOR_BGR2HSV)

# Define range of blue values in HSV
lower_blue = np.array([50,100,50])
upper_blue = np.array([130,255,255])

# Create mask
mask = cv2.inRange(image_hsv, lower_blue, upper_blue)

# Mask image
image_bgr_masked = cv2.bitwise_and(image_bgr, image_bgr, mask=mask)

# Convert BGR to RGB
image_rgb = cv2.cvtColor(image_bgr_masked, cv2.COLOR_BGR2RGB)

# Show image
plt.imshow(image_rgb), plt.axis("off")
plt.show()
```

Discussion

Isolating colors in OpenCV is straightforward. First we convert an image into HSV (hue, saturation, and value). Second, we define a range of values we want to isolate, which is probably the most difficult and time-consuming part. Third, we create a mask for the image (we will only keep the white areas):

```
# Show image
plt.imshow(mask, cmap='gray'), plt.axis("off")
plt.show()
```

Finally, we apply the mask to the image using `bitwise_and` and convert to our desired output format.

8.9 Binarizing Images

Problem

Given an image, you want to output a simplified version.

Solution

Thresholding is the process of setting pixels with intensity greater than some value to be white and less than the value to be black. A more advanced technique is *adaptive thresholding*, where the threshold value for a pixel is determined by the pixel intensities of its neighbors. This can be helpful when lighting conditions change over different regions in an image:

```
# Load libraries
import cv2
import numpy as np
from matplotlib import pyplot as plt

# Load image as grayscale
image_grey = cv2.imread("images/plane_256x256.jpg", cv2.IMREAD_GRAYSCALE)

# Apply adaptive thresholding
max_output_value = 255
neighborhood_size = 99
subtract_from_mean = 10
image_binarized = cv2.adaptiveThreshold(image_grey,
                                        max_output_value,
                                        cv2.ADAPTIVE_THRESH_GAUSSIAN_C,
                                        cv2.THRESH_BINARY,
                                        neighborhood_size,
                                        subtract_from_mean)

# Show image
plt.imshow(image_binarized, cmap="gray"), plt.axis("off")
plt.show()
```

Discussion

Our solution has four important arguments in `adaptiveThreshold`. `max_out put_value` simply determines the maximum intensity of the output pixel intensities. `cv2.ADAPTIVE_THRESH_GAUSSIAN_C` sets a pixel's threshold to be a weighted sum of the neighboring pixel intensities. The weights are determined by a Gaussian window. Alternatively we could set the threshold to simply the mean of the neighboring pixels with `cv2.ADAPTIVE_THRESH_MEAN_C`:

```
# Apply cv2.ADAPTIVE_THRESH_MEAN_C
image_mean_threshold = cv2.adaptiveThreshold(image_grey,
                                             max_output_value,
                                             cv2.ADAPTIVE_THRESH_MEAN_C,
                                             cv2.THRESH_BINARY,
                                             neighborhood_size,
                                             subtract_from_mean)

# Show image
plt.imshow(image_mean_threshold, cmap="gray"), plt.axis("off")
plt.show()
```

The last two parameters are the block size (the size of the neighborhood used to determine a pixel's threshold) and a constant subtracted from the calculated threshold (used to manually fine-tune the threshold).

A major benefit of thresholding is *denoising* an image—keeping only the most important elements. For example, thresholding is often applied to photos of printed text to isolate the letters from the page.

8.10 Removing Backgrounds

Problem

You want to isolate the foreground of an image.

Solution

Mark a rectangle around the desired foreground, then run the GrabCut algorithm:

```
# Load library
import cv2
import numpy as np
from matplotlib import pyplot as plt
```

```python
# Load image and convert to RGB
image_bgr = cv2.imread('images/plane_256x256.jpg')
image_rgb = cv2.cvtColor(image_bgr, cv2.COLOR_BGR2RGB)

# Rectangle values: start x, start y, width, height
rectangle = (0, 56, 256, 150)

# Create initial mask
mask = np.zeros(image_rgb.shape[:2], np.uint8)

# Create temporary arrays used by grabCut
bgdModel = np.zeros((1, 65), np.float64)
fgdModel = np.zeros((1, 65), np.float64)

# Run grabCut
cv2.grabCut(image_rgb, # Our image
            mask, # The Mask
            rectangle, # Our rectangle
            bgdModel, # Temporary array for background
            fgdModel, # Temporary array for background
            5, # Number of iterations
            cv2.GC_INIT_WITH_RECT) # Initiative using our rectangle

# Create mask where sure and likely backgrounds set to 0, otherwise 1
mask_2 = np.where((mask==2) | (mask==0), 0, 1).astype('uint8')

# Multiply image with new mask to subtract background
image_rgb_nobg = image_rgb * mask_2[:, :, np.newaxis]

# Show image
plt.imshow(image_rgb_nobg), plt.axis("off")
plt.show()
```

Discussion

The first thing we notice is that even though GrabCut did a pretty good job, there are still areas of background left in the image. We could go back and manually mark those areas as background, but in the real world we have thousands of images and manually fixing them individually is not feasible. Therefore, we would do well by simply accepting that the image data will still contain some background noise.

In our solution, we start out by marking a rectangle around the area that contains the foreground. GrabCut assumes everything outside this rectangle to be background and uses that information to figure out what is likely background inside the square (to learn how the algorithm does this, check out the external resources at the end of this solution). Then a mask is created that denotes the different definitely/likely background/foreground regions:

```
# Show mask
plt.imshow(mask, cmap='gray'), plt.axis("off")
plt.show()
```

The black region is the area outside our rectangle that is assumed to be definitely background. The gray area is what GrabCut considered likely background, while the white area is likely foreground.

This mask is then used to create a second mask that merges the black and gray regions:

```
# Show mask
plt.imshow(mask_2, cmap='gray'), plt.axis("off")
plt.show()
```

The second mask is then applied to the image so that only the foreground remains.

8.11 Detecting Edges

Problem

You want to find the edges in an image.

Solution

Use an edge detection technique like the Canny edge detector:

```
# Load library
import cv2
import numpy as np
from matplotlib import pyplot as plt

# Load image as grayscale
image_gray = cv2.imread("images/plane_256x256.jpg", cv2.IMREAD_GRAYSCALE)

# Calculate median intensity
median_intensity = np.median(image_gray)

# Set thresholds to be one standard deviation above and below median intensity
```

```
lower_threshold = int(max(0, (1.0 - 0.33) * median_intensity))
upper_threshold = int(min(255, (1.0 + 0.33) * median_intensity))

# Apply canny edge detector
image_canny = cv2.Canny(image_gray, lower_threshold, upper_threshold)

# Show image
plt.imshow(image_canny, cmap="gray"), plt.axis("off")
plt.show()
```

Discussion

Edge detection is a major topic of interest in computer vision. Edges are important because they are areas of high information. For example, in our image one patch of sky looks very much like another and is unlikely to contain unique or interesting information. However, patches where the background sky meets the airplane contain a lot of information (e.g., an object's shape). Edge detection allows us to remove low-information areas and isolate the areas of images containing the most information.

There are many edge detection techniques (Sobel filters, Laplacian edge detector, etc.). However, our solution uses the commonly used Canny edge detector. How the Canny detector works is too detailed for this book, but there is one point that we need to address. The Canny detector requires two parameters denoting low and high gradient threshold values. Potential edge pixels between the low and high thresholds are considered weak edge pixels, while those above the high threshold are considered strong edge pixels. OpenCV's Canny method includes the low and high thresholds as required parameters. In our solution, we set the lower and upper thresholds to be one standard deviation below and above the image's median pixel intensity. However, there are often cases when we might get better results if we used a good pair of low and high threshold values through manual trial and error using a few images before running Canny on our entire collection of images.

See Also

- Canny Edge Detector (*http://bit.ly/2FzDXNt*)
- Canny Edge Detection Auto Thresholding (*http://bit.ly/2nmQERq*)

8.12 Detecting Corners

Problem

You want to detect the corners in an image.

Solution

Use OpenCV's implementation of the Harris corner detector, `cornerHarris`:

```
# Load libraries
import cv2
import numpy as np
from matplotlib import pyplot as plt

# Load image as grayscale
image_bgr = cv2.imread("images/plane_256x256.jpg")
image_gray = cv2.cvtColor(image_bgr, cv2.COLOR_BGR2GRAY)
image_gray = np.float32(image_gray)

# Set corner detector parameters
block_size = 2
aperture = 29
free_parameter = 0.04

# Detect corners
detector_responses = cv2.cornerHarris(image_gray,
                                       block_size,
                                       aperture,
                                       free_parameter)

# Large corner markers
detector_responses = cv2.dilate(detector_responses, None)
```

```
# Only keep detector responses greater than threshold, mark as white
threshold = 0.02
image_bgr[detector_responses >
        threshold *
        detector_responses.max()] = [255,255,255]

# Convert to grayscale
image_gray = cv2.cvtColor(image_bgr, cv2.COLOR_BGR2GRAY)

# Show image
plt.imshow(image_gray, cmap="gray"), plt.axis("off")
plt.show()
```

Discussion

The Harris corner detector is a commonly used method of detecting the intersection
of two edges. Our interest in detecting corners is motivated by the same reason as for
deleting edges: corners are points of high information. A complete explanation of the
Harris corner detector is available in the external resources at the end of this recipe,
but a simplified explanation is that it looks for windows (also called *neighborhoods* or
patches) where small movements of the window (imagine shaking the window) creates big changes in the contents of the pixels inside the window. cornerHarris contains three important parameters that we can use to control the edges detected. First,
block_size is the size of the neighbor around each pixel used for corner detection.

Second, `aperture` is the size of the Sobel kernel used (don't worry if you don't know what that is), and finally there is a free parameter where larger values correspond to identifying softer corners.

The output is a grayscale image depicting potential corners:

```
# Show potential corners
plt.imshow(detector_responses, cmap='gray'), plt.axis("off")
plt.show()
```

We then apply thresholding to keep only the most likely corners. Alternatively, we can use a similar detector, the Shi-Tomasi corner detector, which works in a similar way to the Harris detector (goodFeaturesToTrack) to identify a fixed number of strong corners. goodFeaturesToTrack takes three major parameters—the number of corners to detect, the minimum quality of the corner (0 to 1), and the minimum Euclidean distance between corners:

```
# Load images
image_bgr = cv2.imread('images/plane_256x256.jpg')
image_gray = cv2.cvtColor(image_bgr, cv2.COLOR_BGR2GRAY)

# Number of corners to detect
corners_to_detect = 10
minimum_quality_score = 0.05
minimum_distance = 25
```

```
# Detect corners
corners = cv2.goodFeaturesToTrack(image_gray,
                                  corners_to_detect,
                                  minimum_quality_score,
                                  minimum_distance)
corners = np.float32(corners)

# Draw white circle at each corner
for corner in corners:
    x, y = corner[0]
    cv2.circle(image_bgr, (x,y), 10, (255,255,255), -1)

# Convert to grayscale
image_rgb = cv2.cvtColor(image_bgr, cv2.COLOR_BGR2GRAY)

# Show image
plt.imshow(image_rgb, cmap='gray'), plt.axis("off")
plt.show()
```

See Also

- OpenCV's cornerHarris (*http://bit.ly/2HQXwz6*)
- OpenCV's goodFeaturesToTrack (*http://bit.ly/2HRSVwF*)

8.13 Creating Features for Machine Learning

Problem

You want to convert an image into an observation for machine learning.

Solution

Use NumPy's `flatten` to convert the multidimensional array containing an image's data into a vector containing the observation's values:

```
# Load image
import cv2
import numpy as np
from matplotlib import pyplot as plt

# Load image as grayscale
image = cv2.imread("images/plane_256x256.jpg", cv2.IMREAD_GRAYSCALE)

# Resize image to 10 pixels by 10 pixels
image_10x10 = cv2.resize(image, (10, 10))

# Convert image data to one-dimensional vector
image_10x10.flatten()
```

```
array([133, 130, 130, 129, 130, 129, 129, 128, 128, 127, 135, 131, 131,
       131, 130, 130, 129, 128, 128, 128, 134, 132, 131, 131, 130, 129,
       129, 128, 130, 133, 132, 158, 130, 133, 130,  46,  97,  26, 132,
       143, 141,  36,  54,  91,   9,   9,  49, 144, 179,  41, 142,  95,
        32,  36,  29,  43, 113, 141, 179, 187, 141, 124,  26,  25, 132,
       135, 151, 175, 174, 184, 143, 151,  38, 133, 134, 139, 174, 177,
       169, 174, 155, 141, 135, 137, 137, 152, 169, 168, 168, 179, 152,
       139, 136, 135, 137, 143, 159, 166, 171, 175], dtype=uint8)
```

Discussion

Images are presented as a grid of pixels. If an image is in grayscale, each pixel is presented by one value (i.e., pixel intensity: 1 if white, 0 if black). For example, imagine we have a 10 × 10–pixel image:

```
plt.imshow(image_10x10, cmap="gray"), plt.axis("off")
plt.show()
```

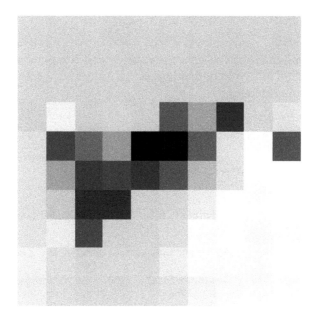

In this case the dimensions of the images data will be 10 × 10:

```
image_10x10.shape
```

```
(10, 10)
```

And if we flatten the array, we get a vector of length 100 (10 multiplied by 10):

```
image_10x10.flatten().shape
```

```
(100,)
```

This is the feature data for our image that can be joined with the vectors from other images to create the data we will feed to our machine learning algorithms.

If the image is in color, instead of each pixel being represented by one value, it is represented by multiple values (most often three) representing the channels (red, green, blue, etc.) that blend to make the final color of that pixel. For this reason, if our 10 × 10 image is in color, we will have 300 feature values for each observation:

```
# Load image in color
image_color = cv2.imread("images/plane_256x256.jpg", cv2.IMREAD_COLOR)

# Resize image to 10 pixels by 10 pixels
image_color_10x10 = cv2.resize(image_color, (10, 10))
```

```
# Convert image data to one-dimensional vector, show dimensions
image_color_10x10.flatten().shape
```

```
(300,)
```

One of the major challenges of image processing and computer vision is that since every pixel location in a collection of images is a feature, as the images get larger, the number of features explodes:

```
# Load image in grayscale
image_256x256_gray = cv2.imread("images/plane_256x256.jpg", cv2.IMREAD_GRAYSCALE)
```

```
# Convert image data to one-dimensional vector, show dimensions
image_256x256_gray.flatten().shape
```

```
(65536,)
```

And the number of features only intensifies when the image is in color:

```
# Load image in color
image_256x256_color = cv2.imread("images/plane_256x256.jpg", cv2.IMREAD_COLOR)
```

```
# Convert image data to one-dimensional vector, show dimensions
image_256x256_color.flatten().shape
```

```
(196608,)
```

As the output shows, even a small color image has almost 200,000 features, which can cause problems when we are training our models because the number of features might far exceed the number of observations.

This problem will motivate dimensionality strategies discussed in a later chapter, which attempt to reduce the number of features while not losing an excessive amount of information contained in the data.

8.14 Encoding Mean Color as a Feature

Problem

You want a feature based on the colors of an image.

Solution

Each pixel in an image is represented by the combination of multiple color channels (often three: red, green, and blue). Calculate the mean red, green, and blue channel values for an image to make three color features representing the average colors in that image:

```
# Load libraries
import cv2
import numpy as np
```

```
from matplotlib import pyplot as plt

# Load image as BGR
image_bgr = cv2.imread("images/plane_256x256.jpg", cv2.IMREAD_COLOR)

# Calculate the mean of each channel
channels = cv2.mean(image_bgr)

# Swap blue and red values (making it RGB, not BGR)
observation = np.array([(channels[2], channels[1], channels[0])])

# Show mean channel values
observation

array([[  90.53204346,  133.11735535,  169.03074646]])
```

We can view the mean channel values directly (apologies to printed book readers):

```
# Show image
plt.imshow(observation), plt.axis("off")
plt.show()
```

Discussion

The output is three feature values for an observation, one for each color channel in the image. These features can be used like any other features in learning algorithms to classify images according to their colors.

8.15 Encoding Color Histograms as Features

Problem

You want to create a set of features representing the colors appearing in an image.

Solution

Compute the histograms for each color channel:

```
# Load libraries
import cv2
import numpy as np
from matplotlib import pyplot as plt

# Load image
image_bgr = cv2.imread("images/plane_256x256.jpg", cv2.IMREAD_COLOR)

# Convert to RGB
image_rgb = cv2.cvtColor(image_bgr, cv2.COLOR_BGR2RGB)

# Create a list for feature values
features = []

# Calculate the histogram for each color channel
colors = ("r","g","b")

# For each channel: calculate histogram and add to feature value list
for i, channel in enumerate(colors):
    histogram = cv2.calcHist([image_rgb], # Image
                    [i], # Index of channel
                    None, # No mask
                    [256], # Histogram size
                    [0,256]) # Range
    features.extend(histogram)

# Create a vector for an observation's feature values
observation = np.array(features).flatten()

# Show the observation's value for the first five features
observation[0:5]

array([ 1008.,    217.,    184.,    165.,    116.], dtype=float32)
```

Discussion

In the RGB color model, each color is the combination of three color channels (i.e., red, green, blue). In turn, each channel can take on one of 256 values (represented by an integer between 0 and 255). For example, the top-leftmost pixel in our image has the following channel values:

```
# Show RGB channel values
image_rgb[0,0]

array([107, 163, 212], dtype=uint8)
```

A histogram is a representation of the distribution of values in data. Here is a simple example:

```
# Import pandas
import pandas as pd

# Create some data
data = pd.Series([1, 1, 2, 2, 3, 3, 3, 4, 5])

# Show the histogram
data.hist(grid=False)
plt.show()
```

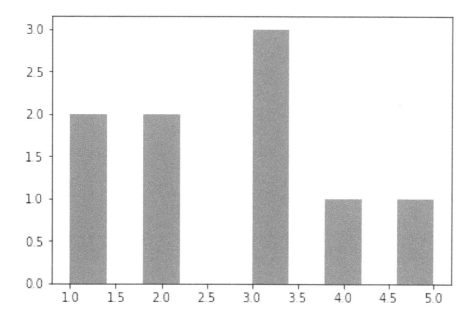

In this example, we have some data with two 1s, two 2s, three 3s, one 4, and one 5. In the histogram, each bar represents the number of times each value (1, 2, etc.) appears in our data.

We can apply this same technique to each of the color channels, but instead of five possible values, we have 256 (the range of possible values for a channel value). The x-axis represents the 256 possible channel values, and the y-axis represents the number of times a particular channel value appears across all pixels in an image:

```
# Calculate the histogram for each color channel
colors = ("r","g","b")

# For each channel: calculate histogram, make plot
for i, channel in enumerate(colors):
    histogram = cv2.calcHist([image_rgb], # Image
                    [i], # Index of channel
                    None, # No mask
```

```
                    [256], # Histogram size
                    [0,256]) # Range
        plt.plot(histogram, color = channel)
        plt.xlim([0,256])

    # Show plot
    plt.show()
```

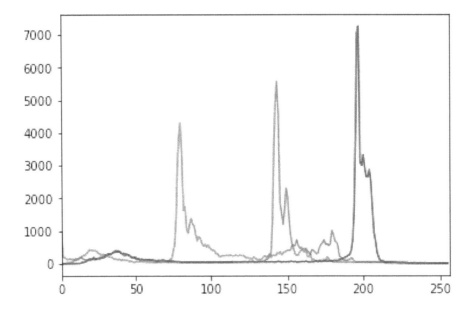

As we can see in the histogram, barely any pixels contain the blue channel values between 0 and ~180, while many pixels contain blue channel values between ~190 and ~210. This distribution of channel values is shown for all three channels. The histogram, however, is not simply a visualization; it is 256 features for each color channel, making for 768 total features representing the distribution of colors in an image.

See Also

- Histogram (*https://en.wikipedia.org/wiki/Histogram*)
- pandas Histogram documentation (*http://bit.ly/2HT4Fz0*)
- OpenCV Histogram tutorial (*http://bit.ly/2HSyoYH*)

## CHAPTER 9

Dimensionality Reduction Using Feature Extraction

9.0 Introduction

It is common to have access to thousands and even hundreds of thousands of features. For example, in Chapter 8 we transformed a 256 × 256–pixel color image into 196,608 features. Furthermore, because each of these pixels can take one of 256 possible values, there ends up being 256^{196608} different configurations our observation can take. This is problematic because we will practically never be able to collect enough observations to cover even a small fraction of those configurations and our learning algorithms do not have enough data to operate correctly.

Fortunately, not all features are created equal and the goal of feature extraction for dimensionality reduction is to transform our set of features, $p_{original}$, such that we end up with a new set, p_{new}, where $p_{original} > p_{new}$, while still keeping much of the underlying information. Put another way, we reduce the number of features with only a small loss in our data's ability to generate high-quality predictions. In this chapter, we will cover a number of feature extraction techniques to do just this.

One downside of the feature extraction techniques we discuss is that the new features we generate will not be interpretable by humans. They will contain as much or nearly as much ability to train our models, but will appear to the human eye as a collection of random numbers. If we wanted to maintain our ability to interpret our models, dimensionality reduction through feature selection is a better option.

9.1 Reducing Features Using Principal Components

Problem

Given a set of features, you want to reduce the number of features while retaining the variance in the data.

Solution

Use principal component analysis with scikit's PCA:

```
# Load libraries
from sklearn.preprocessing import StandardScaler
from sklearn.decomposition import PCA
from sklearn import datasets

# Load the data
digits = datasets.load_digits()

# Standardize the feature matrix
features = StandardScaler().fit_transform(digits.data)

# Create a PCA that will retain 99% of variance
pca = PCA(n_components=0.99, whiten=True)

# Conduct PCA
features_pca = pca.fit_transform(features)

# Show results
print("Original number of features:", features.shape[1])
print("Reduced number of features:", features_pca.shape[1])

Original number of features: 64
Reduced number of features: 54
```

Discussion

Principal component analysis (PCA) is a popular linear dimensionality reduction technique. PCA projects observations onto the (hopefully fewer) principal components of the feature matrix that retain the most variance. PCA is an unsupervised technique, meaning that it does not use the information from the target vector and instead only considers the feature matrix.

For a mathematical description of how PCA works, see the external resources listed at the end of this recipe. However, we can understand the intuition behind PCA using a simple example. In the following figure, our data contains two features, x_1 and x_2. Looking at the visualization, it should be clear that observations are spread out like a cigar, with a lot of length and very little height. More specifically, we can say that the variance of the "length" is significantly greater than the "height." Instead of length and height, we refer to the "directions" with the most variance as the first principal component and the "direction" with the second-most variance as the second principal component (and so on).

If we wanted to reduce our features, one strategy would be to project all observations in our 2D space onto the 1D principal component. We would lose the information captured in the second principal component, but in some situations that would be an acceptable trade-off. This is PCA.

PCA is implemented in scikit-learn using the `pca` method. `n_components` has two operations, depending on the argument provided. If the argument is greater than 1, `n_components` will return that many features. This leads to the question of how to select the number of features that is optimal. Fortunately for us, if the argument to `n_components` is between 0 and 1, `pca` returns the minimum amount of features that retain that much variance. It is common to use values of 0.95 and 0.99, meaning 95% and 99% of the variance of the original features has been retained, respectively. `whiten=True` transforms the values of each principal component so that they have zero mean and unit variance. Another parameter and argument is `svd_solver="randomized"`, which implements a stochastic algorithm to find the first principal components in often significantly less time.

The output of our solution shows that PCA let us reduce our dimensionality by 10 features while still retaining 99% of the information (variance) in the feature matrix.

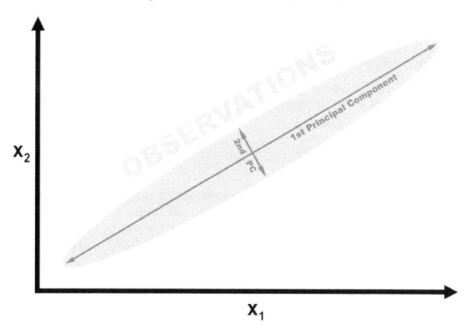

See Also

- scikit-learn documentation on PCA (*http://bit.ly/2FrSvyx*)
- Choosing the Number of Principal Components (*http://bit.ly/2FrSGtH*)
- Principal component analysis with linear algebra (*http://bit.ly/2FuzdIW*)

9.2 Reducing Features When Data Is Linearly Inseparable

Problem

You suspect you have linearly inseparable data and want to reduce the dimensions.

Solution

Use an extension of principal component analysis that uses kernels to allow for non-linear dimensionality reduction:

```
# Load libraries
from sklearn.decomposition import PCA, KernelPCA
from sklearn.datasets import make_circles

# Create linearly inseparable data
features, _ = make_circles(n_samples=1000, random_state=1, noise=0.1, factor=0.1)

# Apply kernal PCA with radius basis function (RBF) kernel
kpca = KernelPCA(kernel="rbf", gamma=15, n_components=1)
features_kpca = kpca.fit_transform(features)

print("Original number of features:", features.shape[1])
print("Reduced number of features:", features_kpca.shape[1])

Original number of features: 2
Reduced number of features: 1
```

Discussion

PCA is able to reduce the dimensionality of our feature matrix (e.g., the number of features). Standard PCA uses linear projection to reduce the features. If the data is linearly separable (i.e., you can draw a straight line or hyperplane between different classes) then PCA works well. However, if your data is not linearly separable (e.g., you can only separate classes using a curved decision boundary), the linear transformation will not work as well. In our solution we used scikit-learn's `make_circles` to generate a simulated dataset with a target vector of two classes and two features. `make_circles` makes linearly inseparable data; specifically, one class is surrounded on all sides by the other class.

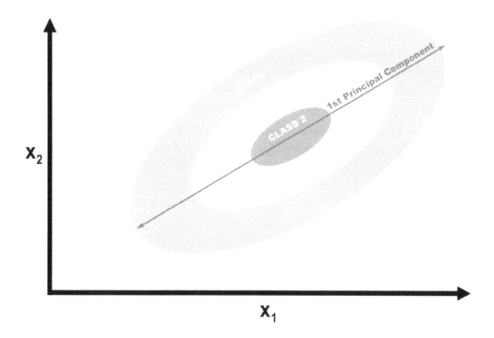

If we used linear PCA to reduce the dimensions of our data, the two classes would be linearly projected onto the first principal component such that they would become intertwined.

1st Principal Component

Ideally, we would want a transformation that would both reduce the dimensions and also make the data linearly separable. Kernel PCA can do both.

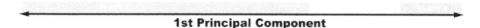

1st Principal Component

Kernels allow us to project the linearly inseparable data into a higher dimension where it is linearly separable; this is called the kernel trick. Don't worry if you don't understand the details of the kernel trick; just think of kernels as different ways of projecting the data. There are a number of kernels we can use in scikit-learn's `ker nelPCA`, specified using the `kernel` parameter. A common kernel to use is the Gaussian radial basis function kernel `rbf`, but other options are the polynomial kernel (`poly`) and sigmoid kernel (`sigmoid`). We can even specify a linear projection (`lin ear`), which will produce the same results as standard PCA.

One downside of kernel PCA is that there are a number of parameters we need to specify. For example, in Recipe 9.1 we set `n_components` to `0.99` to make PCA select the number of components to retain 99% of the variance. We don't have this option in kernel PCA. Instead we have to define the number of parameters (e.g., `n_compo` `nents=1`). Furthermore, kernels come with their own hyperparameters that we will have to set; for example, the radial basis function requires a `gamma` value.

So how do we know which values to use? Through trial and error. Specifically we can train our machine learning model multiple times, each time with a different kernel or different value of the parameter. Once we find the combination of values that produces the highest quality predicted values, we are done. We will learn about this strategy in depth in Chapter 12.

See Also

- scikit-learn documentation on Kernel PCA (*http://bit.ly/2HRkxC3*)
- Kernel tricks and nonlinear dimensionality reduction via RBF kernel PCA (*http://bit.ly/2HReP3f*)

9.3 Reducing Features by Maximizing Class Separability

Problem

You want to reduce the features to be used by a classifier.

Solution

Try linear discriminant analysis (LDA) to project the features onto component axes that maximize the separation of classes:

```
# Load libraries
from sklearn import datasets
from sklearn.discriminant_analysis import LinearDiscriminantAnalysis

# Load Iris flower dataset:
iris = datasets.load_iris()
features = iris.data
target = iris.target

# Create and run an LDA, then use it to transform the features
lda = LinearDiscriminantAnalysis(n_components=1)
features_lda = lda.fit(features, target).transform(features)

# Print the number of features
print("Original number of features:", features.shape[1])
print("Reduced number of features:", features_lda.shape[1])
```

```
Original number of features: 4
Reduced number of features: 1
```

We can use `explained_variance_ratio_` to view the amount of variance explained by each component. In our solution the single component explained over 99% of the variance:

```
lda.explained_variance_ratio_
```

```
array([ 0.99147248])
```

Discussion

LDA is a classification that is also a popular technique for dimensionality reduction. LDA works similarly to principal component analysis (PCA) in that it projects our feature space onto a lower-dimensional space. However, in PCA we were only interested in the component axes that maximize the variance in the data, while in LDA we have the additional goal of maximizing the differences between classes. In this pictured example, we have data comprising two target classes and two features. If we project the data onto the y-axis, the two classes are not easily separable (i.e., they overlap), while if we project the data onto the x-axis, we are left with a feature vector (i.e., we reduced our dimensionality by one) that still preserves class separability. In the real world, of course, the relationship between the classes will be more complex and the dimensionality will be higher, but the concept remains the same.

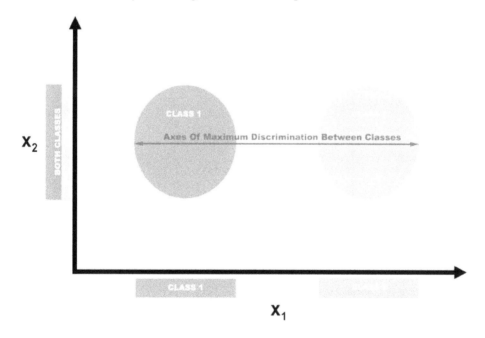

In scikit-learn, LDA is implemented using `LinearDiscriminantAnalysis`, which includes a parameter, `n_components`, indicating the number of features we want returned. To figure out what argument value to use with `n_components` (e.g., how many parameters to keep), we can take advantage of the fact that `explained_variance_ratio_` tells us the variance explained by each outputted feature and is a sorted array. For example:

```
lda.explained_variance_ratio_

array([ 0.99147248])
```

Specifically, we can run `LinearDiscriminantAnalysis` with `n_components` set to None to return the ratio of variance explained by every component feature, then calculate how many components are required to get above some threshold of variance explained (often 0.95 or 0.99):

```
# Create and run LDA
lda = LinearDiscriminantAnalysis(n_components=None)
features_lda = lda.fit(features, target)

# Create array of explained variance ratios
lda_var_ratios = lda.explained_variance_ratio_

# Create function
def select_n_components(var_ratio, goal_var: float) -> int:
    # Set initial variance explained so far
    total_variance = 0.0

    # Set initial number of features
    n_components = 0

    # For the explained variance of each feature:
    for explained_variance in var_ratio:

        # Add the explained variance to the total
        total_variance += explained_variance

        # Add one to the number of components
        n_components += 1

        # If we reach our goal level of explained variance
        if total_variance >= goal_var:
            # End the loop
            break

    # Return the number of components
    return n_components

# Run function
select_n_components(lda_var_ratios, 0.95)

1
```

See Also

- Comparison of LDA and PCA 2D projection of Iris dataset (*http://bit.ly/ 2Fs4cWe*)
- Linear Discriminant Analysis (*http://bit.ly/2FtiKEL*)

9.4 Reducing Features Using Matrix Factorization

Problem

You have a feature matrix of nonnegative values and want to reduce the dimensionality.

Solution

Use non-negative matrix factorization (NMF) to reduce the dimensionality of the feature matrix:

```
# Load libraries
from sklearn.decomposition import NMF
from sklearn import datasets

# Load the data
digits = datasets.load_digits()

# Load feature matrix
features = digits.data

# Create, fit, and apply NMF
nmf = NMF(n_components=10, random_state=1)
features_nmf = nmf.fit_transform(features)

# Show results
print("Original number of features:", features.shape[1])
print("Reduced number of features:", features_nmf.shape[1])

Original number of features: 64
Reduced number of features: 10
```

Discussion

NMF is an unsupervised technique for linear dimensionality reduction that factorizes (i.e., breaks up into multiple matrices whose product approximates the original matrix) the feature matrix into matrices representing the latent relationship between observations and their features. Intuitively, NMF can reduce dimensionality because in matrix multiplication, the two factors (matrices being multiplied) can have significantly fewer dimensions than the product matrix. Formally, given a desired number of returned features, r, NMF factorizes our feature matrix such that:

$$\mathbf{V} \approx \mathbf{WH}$$

where $\mathbf{V}$ is our $d \times \_n$ feature matrix (i.e., d features, n observations), $\mathbf{W}$ is a $d \times r$, and $\mathbf{H}$ is an $r \times n$ matrix. By adjusting the value of r we can set the amount of dimensionality reduction desired.

One major requirement of NMA is that, as the name implies, the feature matrix cannot contain negative values. Additionally, unlike PCA and other techniques we have examined, NMA does not provide us with the explained variance of the outputted features. Thus, the best way for us to find the optimum value of n_components is by trying a range of values to find the one that produces the best result in our end model (see Chapter 12).

See Also

- Non-Negative Matrix Factorization (NMF) (*http://bit.ly/2FvtWRj*)

9.5 Reducing Features on Sparse Data

Problem

You have a sparse feature matrix and want to reduce the dimensionality.

Solution

Use Truncated Singular Value Decomposition (TSVD):

```
# Load libraries
from sklearn.preprocessing import StandardScaler
from sklearn.decomposition import TruncatedSVD
from scipy.sparse import csr_matrix
from sklearn import datasets
import numpy as np

# Load the data
digits = datasets.load_digits()

# Standardize feature matrix
features = StandardScaler().fit_transform(digits.data)

# Make sparse matrix
features_sparse = csr_matrix(features)
```

```
# Create a TSVD
tsvd = TruncatedSVD(n_components=10)

# Conduct TSVD on sparse matrix
features_sparse_tsvd = tsvd.fit(features_sparse).transform(features_sparse)

# Show results
print("Original number of features:", features_sparse.shape[1])
print('"Reduced number of features:", features_sparse_tsvd.shape[1])

Original number of features: 64
Reduced number of features: 10
```

Discussion

TSVD is similar to PCA and in fact, PCA actually often uses non-truncated Singular Value Decomposition (SVD) in one of its steps. In regular SVD, given d features, SVD will create factor matrices that are $d \times d$, whereas TSVD will return factors that are $n \times n$, where n is previously specified by a parameter. The practical advantage of TSVD is that unlike PCA, it works on sparse feature matrices.

One issue with TSVD is that because of how it uses a random number generator, the signs of the output can flip between fittings. An easy workaround is to use fit only once per preprocessing pipeline, then use transform multiple times.

As with linear discriminant analysis, we have to specify the number of features (components) we want outputted. This is done with the n_components parameter. A natural question is then: what is the optimum number of components? One strategy is to include n_components as a hyperparameter to optimize during model selection (i.e., choose the value for n_components that produces the best trained model). Alternatively, because TSVD provides us with the ratio of the original feature matrix's variance explained by each component, we can select the number of components that explain a desired amount of variance (95% or 99% are common values). For example, in our solution the first three outputted components explain approximately 30% of the original data's variance:

```
# Sum of first three components' explained variance ratios
tsvd.explained_variance_ratio_[0:3].sum()

0.30039385386597783
```

We can automate the process by creating a function that runs TSVD with n_compo nents set to one less than the number of original features and then calculate the number of components that explain a desired amount of the original data's variance:

```
# Create and run an TSVD with one less than number of features
tsvd = TruncatedSVD(n_components=features_sparse.shape[1]-1)
features_tsvd = tsvd.fit(features)

# List of explained variances
```

```
tsvd_var_ratios = tsvd.explained_variance_ratio_

# Create a function
def select_n_components(var_ratio, goal_var):
    # Set initial variance explained so far
    total_variance = 0.0

    # Set initial number of features
    n_components = 0

    # For the explained variance of each feature:
    for explained_variance in var_ratio:

        # Add the explained variance to the total
        total_variance += explained_variance

        # Add one to the number of components
        n_components += 1

        # If we reach our goal level of explained variance
        if total_variance >= goal_var:
            # End the loop
            break

    # Return the number of components
    return n_components

# Run function
select_n_components(tsvd_var_ratios, 0.95)

40
```

See Also

- scikit-learn documentation TruncatedSVD (*http://bit.ly/2GTfxvh*)

## CHAPTER 10

Dimensionality Reduction Using Feature Selection

10.0 Introduction

In Chapter 9, we discussed how to reduce the dimensionality of our feature matrix by creating new features with (ideally) similar ability to train quality models but with significantly fewer dimensions. This is called feature extraction. In this chapter we will cover an alternative approach: selecting high-quality, informative features and dropping less useful features. This is called feature selection.

There are three types of feature selection methods: filter, wrapper, and embedded. Filter methods select the best features by examining their statistical properties. Wrapper methods use trial and error to find the subset of features that produce models with the highest quality predictions. Finally, embedded methods select the best feature subset as part or as an extension of a learning algorithm's training process.

Ideally, we'd describe all three methods in this chapter. However, since embedded methods are closely intertwined with specific learning algorithms, they are difficult to explain prior to a deeper dive into the algorithms themselves. Therefore, in this chapter we cover only filter and wrapper feature selection methods, leaving the discussion of particular embedded methods until the chapters where those learning algorithms are discussed in depth.

10.1 Thresholding Numerical Feature Variance

Problem

You have a set of numerical features and want to remove those with low variance (i.e., likely containing little information).

Solution

Select a subset of features with variances above a given threshold:

```
# Load libraries
from sklearn import datasets
from sklearn.feature_selection import VarianceThreshold

# import some data to play with
iris = datasets.load_iris()

# Create features and target
features = iris.data
target = iris.target

# Create thresholder
thresholder = VarianceThreshold(threshold=.5)

# Create high variance feature matrix
features_high_variance = thresholder.fit_transform(features)

# View high variance feature matrix
features_high_variance[0:3]
array([[ 5.1,   1.4,   0.2],
       [ 4.9,   1.4,   0.2],
       [ 4.7,   1.3,   0.2]])
```

Discussion

Variance thresholding (VT) is one of the most basic approaches to feature selection. It is motivated by the idea that features with low variance are likely less interesting (and useful) than features with high variance. VT first calculates the variance of each feature:

$$\operatorname{Var}(x) = \frac{1}{n} \sum_{i=1}^{n} \left(x_i - \mu\right)^2$$

where x is the feature vector, x_i is an individual feature value, and μ is that feature's mean value. Next, it drops all features whose variance does not meet that threshold.

There are two things to keep in mind when employing VT. First, the variance is not centered; that is, it is in the squared unit of the feature itself. Therefore, the VT will not work when feature sets contain different units (e.g., one feature is in years while a different feature is in dollars). Second, the variance threshold is selected manually, so we have to use our own judgment for a good value to select (or use a model selection technique described in Chapter 12). We can see the variance for each feature using variances_:

```
# View variances
thresholder.fit(features).variances_

array([ 0.68112222,  0.18675067,  3.09242489,  0.57853156])
```

Finally, if the features have been standardized (to mean zero and unit variance), then for obvious reasons variance thresholding will not work correctly:

```
# Load library
from sklearn.preprocessing import StandardScaler

# Standardize feature matrix
scaler = StandardScaler()
features_std = scaler.fit_transform(features)

# Caculate variance of each feature
selector = VarianceThreshold()
selector.fit(features_std).variances_

array([ 1.,  1.,  1.,  1.])
```

10.2 Thresholding Binary Feature Variance

Problem

You have a set of binary categorical features and want to remove those with low variance (i.e., likely containing little information).

Solution

Select a subset of features with a Bernoulli random variable variance above a given threshold:

```
# Load library
from sklearn.feature_selection import VarianceThreshold

# Create feature matrix with:
# Feature 0: 80% class 0
# Feature 1: 80% class 1
# Feature 2: 60% class 0, 40% class 1
features = [[0, 1, 0],
            [0, 1, 1],
```

```
                        [0, 1, 0],
                        [0, 1, 1],
                        [1, 0, 0]]

# Run threshold by variance
thresholder = VarianceThreshold(threshold=(.75 * (1 - .75)))
thresholder.fit_transform(features)

array([[0],
       [1],
       [0],
       [1],
       [0]])
```

Discussion

Just like with numerical features, one strategy for selecting highly informative categorical features is to examine their variances. In binary features (i.e., Bernoulli random variables), variance is calculated as:

$$\text{Var}(x) = p(1 - p)$$

where p is the proportion of observations of class 1. Therefore, by setting p, we can remove features where the vast majority of observations are one class.

10.3 Handling Highly Correlated Features

Problem

You have a feature matrix and suspect some features are highly correlated.

Solution

Use a correlation matrix to check for highly correlated features. If highly correlated features exist, consider dropping one of the correlated features:

```
# Load libraries
import pandas as pd
import numpy as np

# Create feature matrix with two highly correlated features
features = np.array([[1, 1, 1],
                     [2, 2, 0],
                     [3, 3, 1],
                     [4, 4, 0],
                     [5, 5, 1],
                     [6, 6, 0],
                     [7, 7, 1],
                     [8, 7, 0],
```

```
                [9, 7, 1]])

# Convert feature matrix into DataFrame
dataframe = pd.DataFrame(features)

# Create correlation matrix
corr_matrix = dataframe.corr().abs()

# Select upper triangle of correlation matrix
upper = corr_matrix.where(np.triu(np.ones(corr_matrix.shape),
                          k=1).astype(np.bool))

# Find index of feature columns with correlation greater than 0.95
to_drop = [column for column in upper.columns if any(upper[column] > 0.95)]

# Drop features
dataframe.drop(dataframe.columns[to_drop], axis=1).head(3)
```

	0	2
0	1	1
1	2	0
2	3	1

Discussion

One problem we often run into in machine learning is highly correlated features. If two features are highly correlated, then the information they contain is very similar, and it is likely redundant to include both features. The solution to highly correlated features is simple: remove one of them from the feature set.

In our solution, first we create a correlation matrix of all features:

```
# Correlation matrix
dataframe.corr()
```

	0	1	2
0	1.000000	0.976103	0.000000
1	0.976103	1.000000	-0.034503
2	0.000000	-0.034503	1.000000

Second, we look at the upper triangle of the correlation matrix to identify pairs of highly correlated features:

```
# Upper triangle of correlation matrix
upper
```

	0	1	2
0	NaN	0.976103	0.000000
1	NaN	NaN	0.034503
2	NaN	NaN	NaN

Third, we remove one feature from each of those pairs from the feature set.

10.4 Removing Irrelevant Features for Classification

Problem

You have a categorical target vector and want to remove uninformative features.

Solution

If the features are categorical, calculate a chi-square (χ^2) statistic between each feature and the target vector:

```
# Load libraries
from sklearn.datasets import load_iris
from sklearn.feature_selection import SelectKBest
from sklearn.feature_selection import chi2, f_classif

# Load data
iris = load_iris()
features = iris.data
target = iris.target

# Convert to categorical data by converting data to integers
features = features.astype(int)

# Select two features with highest chi-squared statistics
chi2_selector = SelectKBest(chi2, k=2)
features_kbest = chi2_selector.fit_transform(features, target)

# Show results
print("Original number of features:", features.shape[1])
print("Reduced number of features:", features_kbest.shape[1])

Original number of features: 4
Reduced number of features: 2
```

If the features are quantitative, compute the ANOVA F-value between each feature and the target vector:

```
# Select two features with highest F-values
fvalue_selector = SelectKBest(f_classif, k=2)
features_kbest = fvalue_selector.fit_transform(features, target)
```

```
# Show results
print("Original number of features:", features.shape[1])
print("Reduced number of features:", features_kbest.shape[1])

Original number of features: 4
Reduced number of features: 2
```

Instead of selecting a specific number of features, we can also use `SelectPercentile` to select the top *n* percent of features:

```
# Load library
from sklearn.feature_selection import SelectPercentile

# Select top 75% of features with highest F-values
fvalue_selector = SelectPercentile(f_classif, percentile=75)
features_kbest = fvalue_selector.fit_transform(features, target)

# Show results
print("Original number of features:", features.shape[1])
print("Reduced number of features:", features_kbest.shape[1])

Original number of features: 4
Reduced number of features: 3
```

Discussion

Chi-square statistics examines the independence of two categorical vectors. That is, the statistic is the difference between the observed number of observations in each class of a categorical feature and what we would expect if that feature was independent (i.e., no relationship) with the target vector:

$$\chi^2 = \sum_{i=1}^{n} \frac{(O_i - E_i)^2}{E_i}$$

where O_i is the number of observations in class i and E_i is the number of observations in class i we would expect if there is no relationship between the feature and target vector.

A chi-squared statistic is a single number that tells you how much difference exists between your observed counts and the counts you would expect if there were no relationship at all in the population. By calculating the chi-squared statistic between a feature and the target vector, we obtain a measurement of the independence between the two. If the target is independent of the feature variable, then it is irrelevant for our purposes because it contains no information we can use for classification. On the other hand, if the two features are highly dependent, they likely are very informative for training our model.

To use chi-squared in feature selection, we calculate the chi-squared statistic between each feature and the target vector, then select the features with the best chi-square statistics. In scikit-learn, we can use `SelectKBest` to select the features with the best statistics. The parameter k determines the number of features we want to keep.

It is important to note that chi-square statistics can only be calculated between two categorical vectors. For this reason, chi-squared for feature selection requires that both the target vector and the features are categorical. However, if we have a numerical feature we can use the chi-squared technique by first transforming the quantitative feature into a categorical feature. Finally, to use our chi-squared approach, all values need to be non-negative.

Alternatively, if we have a numerical feature we can use `f_classif` to calculate the ANOVA F-value statistic with each feature and the target vector. F-value scores examine if, when we group the numerical feature by the target vector, the means for each group are significantly different. For example, if we had a binary target vector, gender, and a quantitative feature, test scores, the F-value score would tell us if the mean test score for men is different than the mean test score for women. If it is not, then test score doesn't help us predict gender and therefore the feature is irrelevant.

10.5 Recursively Eliminating Features

Problem

You want to automatically select the best features to keep.

Solution

Use scikit-learn's `RFECV` to conduct recursive feature elimination (RFE) using cross-validation (CV). That is, repeatedly train a model, each time removing a feature until model performance (e.g., accuracy) becomes worse. The remaining features are the best:

```
# Load libraries
import warnings
from sklearn.datasets import make_regression
from sklearn.feature_selection import RFECV
from sklearn import datasets, linear_model

# Suppress an annoying but harmless warning
warnings.filterwarnings(action="ignore", module="scipy",
                        message="^internal gelsd")

# Generate features matrix, target vector, and the true coefficients
features, target = make_regression(n_samples = 10000,
                                   n_features = 100,
                                   n_informative = 2,
```

```
                              random_state = 1)

    # Create a linear regression
    ols = linear_model.LinearRegression()

    # Recursively eliminate features
    rfecv = RFECV(estimator=ols, step=1, scoring="neg_mean_squared_error")
    rfecv.fit(features, target)
    rfecv.transform(features)

    array([[ 0.00850799,  0.7031277 , -1.2416911 , -0.25651883, -0.10738769],
           [-1.07500204,  2.56148527,  0.5540926 , -0.72602474, -0.91773159],
           [ 1.37940721, -1.77039484, -0.59609275,  0.51485979, -1.17442094],
           ...,
           [-0.80331656, -1.60648007,  0.37195763,  0.78006511, -0.20756972],
           [ 0.39508844, -1.34564911, -0.9639982 ,  1.7983361 , -0.61308782],
           [-0.55383035,  0.82880112,  0.24597833, -1.71411248,  0.3816852 ]])
```

Once we have conducted RFE, we can see the number of features we should keep:

```
    # Number of best features
    rfecv.n_features_

    5
```

We can also see which of those features we should keep:

```
    # Which categories are best
    rfecv.support_

    array([False, False, False, False, False,  True, False, False, False,
           False, False, False, False, False, False, False, False, False,
           False, False, False, False, False, False, False, False, False,
           False, False, False, False, False, False, False, False, False,
           False, False, False,  True, False, False, False,  True, False,
           False, False, False, False, False, False, False, False, False,
           False, False, False, False, False, False,  True, False, False,
           False, False, False, False, False,  True, False, False, False,
           False, False, False, False, False, False, False, False, False,
           False, False, False, False, False, False, False, False, False,
           False, False, False, False, False, False, False, False, False,
           False], dtype=bool)
```

We can even view the rankings of the features:

```
    # Rank features best (1) to worst
    rfecv.ranking_

    array([11, 92, 96, 87, 46,  1, 48, 23, 16,  2, 66, 83, 33, 27, 70, 75, 29,
           84, 54, 88, 37, 42, 85, 62, 74, 50, 80, 10, 38, 59, 79, 57, 44,  8,
           82, 45, 89, 69, 94,  1, 35, 47, 39,  1, 34, 72, 19,  4, 17, 91, 90,
           24, 32, 13, 49, 26, 12, 71, 68, 40,  1, 43, 63, 28, 73, 58, 21, 67,
            1, 95, 77, 93, 22, 52, 30, 60, 81, 14, 86, 18, 15, 41,  7, 53, 65,
           51, 64,  6,  9, 20,  5, 55, 56, 25, 36, 61, 78, 31,  3, 76])
```

Discussion

This is likely the most advanced recipe in this book up to this point, combining a number of topics we have yet to address in detail. However, the intuition is straight-forward enough that we can address it here rather than holding off until a later chapter. The idea behind RFE is to train a model that contains some parameters (also called *weights* or *coefficients*) like linear regression or support vector machines repeatedly. The first time we train the model, we include all the features. Then, we find the feature with the smallest parameter (notice that this assumes the features are either rescaled or standardized), meaning it is less important, and remove the feature from the feature set.

The obvious question then is: how many features should we keep? We can (hypothetically) repeat this loop until we only have one feature left. A better approach requires that we include a new concept called cross-validation (CV). We will discuss cross-validation in detail in the next chapter, but here is the general idea.

Given data containing 1) a target we want to predict and 2) a feature matrix, first we split the data into two groups: a training set and a test set. Second, we train our model using the training set. Third, we pretend that we do not know the target of the test set, and apply our model to the test set's features in order to predict the values of the test set. Finally, we compare our predicted target values with the true target values to evaluate our model.

We can use CV to find the optimum number of features to keep during RFE. Specifically, in RFE with CV after every iteration, we use cross-validation to evaluate our model. If CV shows that our model improved after we eliminated a feature, then we continue on to the next loop. However, if CV shows that our model got worse after we eliminated a feature, we put that feature back into the feature set and select those features as the best.

In scikit-learn, RFE with CV is implemented using `RFECV` and contains a number of important parameters. The `estimator` parameter determines the type of model we want to train (e.g., linear regression). The `step` regression sets the number or proportion of features to drop during each loop. The `scoring` parameter sets the metric of quality we use to evaluate our model during cross-validation.

See Also

- Recursive feature elimination with cross-validation (*http://bit.ly/2Ftuffz*)

## CHAPTER 11

Model Evaluation

11.0 Introduction

In this chapter we will examine strategies for evaluating the quality of models created through our learning algorithms. It might appear strange to discuss model evaluation before discussing how to create them, but there is a method to our madness. Models are only as useful as the quality of their predictions, and thus fundamentally our goal is not to create models (which is easy) but to create high-quality models (which is hard). Therefore, before we explore the myriad learning algorithms, we first set up how we can evaluate the models they produce.

11.1 Cross-Validating Models

Problem

You want to evaluate how well your model will work in the real world.

Solution

Create a pipeline that preprocesses the data, trains the model, and then evaluates it using cross-validation:

```
# Load libraries
from sklearn import datasets
from sklearn import metrics
from sklearn.model_selection import KFold, cross_val_score
from sklearn.pipeline import make_pipeline
from sklearn.linear_model import LogisticRegression
from sklearn.preprocessing import StandardScaler

# Load digits dataset
```

```
digits = datasets.load_digits()

# Create features matrix
features = digits.data

# Create target vector
target = digits.target

# Create standardizer
standardizer = StandardScaler()

# Create logistic regression object
logit = LogisticRegression()

# Create a pipeline that standardizes, then runs logistic regression
pipeline = make_pipeline(standardizer, logit)

# Create k-Fold cross-validation
kf = KFold(n_splits=10, shuffle=True, random_state=1)

# Conduct k-fold cross-validation
cv_results = cross_val_score(pipeline, # Pipeline
                             features, # Feature matrix
                             target, # Target vector
                             cv=kf, # Cross-validation technique
                             scoring="accuracy", # Loss function
                             n_jobs=-1) # Use all CPU scores

# Calculate mean
cv_results.mean()
```

```
0.96493171942892597
```

Discussion

At first consideration, evaluating supervised-learning models might appear straight-forward: train a model and then calculate how well it did using some performance metric (accuracy, squared errors, etc.). However, this approach is fundamentally flawed. If we train a model using our data, and then evaluate how well it did on that data, we are not achieving our desired goal. Our goal is not to evaluate how well the model does on our training data, but how well it does on data it has never seen before (e.g., a new customer, a new crime, a new image). For this reason, our method of evaluation should help us understand how well models are able to make predictions from data they have never seen before.

One strategy might be to hold off a slice of data for testing. This is called *validation* (or *hold-out*). In validation our observations (features and targets) are split into two sets, traditionally called the *training set* and the *test set*. We take the test set and put it off to the side, pretending that we have never seen it before. Next we train our model using our training set, using the features and target vector to teach the model how to make the best prediction. Finally, we simulate having never before seen external data by evaluating how our model trained on our training set performs on our test set. However, the validation approach has two major weaknesses. First, the performance of the model can be highly dependent on which few observations were selected for the test set. Second, the model is not being trained using all the available data, and not being evaluated on all the available data.

A better strategy, which overcomes these weaknesses, is called *k-fold cross-validation* (KFCV). In KFCV, we split the data into *k* parts called "folds." The model is then trained using *k* - *1* folds—combined into one training set—and then the last fold is used as a test set. We repeat this *k* times, each time using a different fold as the test set. The performance on the model for each of the *k* iterations is then averaged to produce an overall measurement.

In our solution, we conducted k-fold cross-validation using 10 folds and outputted the evaluation scores to cv_results:

```
# View score for all 10 folds
cv_results

array([ 0.97222222,  0.97777778,  0.95555556,  0.95      ,  0.95555556,
        0.98333333,  0.97777778,  0.96648045,  0.96089385,  0.94972067])
```

There are three important points to consider when we are using KFCV. First, KFCV assumes that each observation was created independent from the other (i.e., the data is independent identically distributed [IID]). If the data is IID, it is a good idea to shuffle observations when assigning to folds. In scikit-learn we can set shuffle=True to perform shuffling.

Second, when we are using KFCV to evaluate a classifier, it is often beneficial to have folds containing roughly the same percentage of observations from each of the different target classes (called *stratified k-fold*). For example, if our target vector contained gender and 80% of the observations were male, then each fold would contain 80% male and 20% female observations. In scikit-learn, we can conduct stratified k-fold cross-validation by replacing the KFold class with StratifiedKFold.

Finally, when we are using validation sets or cross-validation, it is important to pre-process data based on the training set and then apply those transformations to both the training and test set. For example, when we fit our standardization object, stand ardizer, we calculate the mean and variance of only the training set. Then we apply that transformation (using transform) to both the training and test sets:

```
# Import library
from sklearn.model_selection import train_test_split

# Create training and test sets
features_train, features_test, target_train, target_test = train_test_split(
    features, target, test_size=0.1, random_state=1)
```

```
# Fit standardizer to training set
standardizer.fit(features_train)

# Apply to both training and test sets
features_train_std = standardizer.transform(features_train)
features_test_std = standardizer.transform(features_test)
```

The reason for this is because we are pretending that the test set is unknown data. If we fit both our preprocessors using observations from both training and test sets, some of the information from the test set leaks into our training set. This rule applies for any preprocessing step such as feature selection.

scikit-learn's pipeline package makes this easy to do while using cross-validation techniques. We first create a pipeline that preprocesses the data (e.g., `standardizer`) and then trains a model (logistic regression, `logit`):

```
# Create a pipeline
pipeline = make_pipeline(standardizer, logit)
```

Then we run KFCV using that pipeline and scikit does all the work for us:

```
# Do k-fold cross-validation
cv_results = cross_val_score(pipeline, # Pipeline
                             features, # Feature matrix
                             target, # Target vector
                             cv=kf, # Cross-validation technique
                             scoring="accuracy", # Loss function
                             n_jobs=-1) # Use all CPU scores
```

`cross_val_score` comes with three parameters that we have not discussed that are worth noting. `cv` determines our cross-validation technique. K-fold is the most common by far, but there are others, like leave-one-out-cross-validation where the number of folds k equals the number of observations. The `scoring` parameter defines our metric for success, a number of which are discussed in other recipes in this chapter. Finally, `n_jobs=-1` tells scikit-learn to use every core available. For example, if your computer has four cores (a common number for laptops), then scikit-learn will use all four cores at once to speed up the operation.

See Also

- Why every statistician should know about cross-validation (*http://bit.ly/2Fzhz6X*)
- Cross-Validation Gone Wrong (*http://bit.ly/2Fzfliw*)

11.2 Creating a Baseline Regression Model

Problem

You want a simple baseline regression model to compare against your model.

Solution

Use scikit-learn's `DummyRegressor` to create a simple model to use as a baseline:

```python
# Load libraries
from sklearn.datasets import load_boston
from sklearn.dummy import DummyRegressor
from sklearn.model_selection import train_test_split

# Load data
boston = load_boston()

# Create features
features, target = boston.data, boston.target

# Make test and training split
features_train, features_test, target_train, target_test = train_test_split(
    features, target, random_state=0)

# Create a dummy regressor
dummy = DummyRegressor(strategy='mean')

# "Train" dummy regressor
dummy.fit(features_train, target_train)

# Get R-squared score
dummy.score(features_test, target_test)
```

```
-0.0011193592039553391
```

To compare, we train our model and evaluate the performance score:

```python
# Load library
from sklearn.linear_model import LinearRegression

# Train simple linear regression model
ols = LinearRegression()
ols.fit(features_train, target_train)

# Get R-squared score
ols.score(features_test, target_test)
```

```
0.63536207866746675
```

Discussion

DummyRegressor allows us to create a very simple model that we can use as a baseline to compare against our actual model. This can often be useful to simulate a "naive" existing prediction process in a product or system. For example, a product might have been originally hardcoded to assume that all new users will spend $100 in the first month, regardless of their features. If we encode that assumption into a baseline model, we are able to concretely state the benefits of using a machine learning approach.

DummyRegressor uses the strategy parameter to set the method of making predictions, including the mean or median value in the training set. Furthermore, if we set strategy to constant and use the constant parameter, we can set the dummy regressor to predict some constant value for every observation:

```
# Create dummy regressor that predicts 20's for everything
clf = DummyRegressor(strategy='constant', constant=20)
clf.fit(features_train, target_train)

# Evaluate score
clf.score(features_test, target_test)
```

```
-0.065105020293257265
```

One small note regarding score. By default, score returns the coefficient of determination (R-squared, R^2) score:

$$R^2 = 1 - \frac{\Sigma_i(y_i - \hat{y}_i)^2}{\Sigma_i(y_i - \bar{y})^2}$$

where y_i is the true value of the target observation, $\hat{y}_i$ is the predicted value, and $\bar{y}$ is the mean value for the target vector.

The closer R^2 is to 1, the more of the variance in the target vector that is explained by the features.

11.3 Creating a Baseline Classification Model

Problem

You want a simple baseline classifier to compare against your model.

Solution

Use scikit-learn's DummyClassifier:

```
# Load libraries
from sklearn.datasets import load_iris
from sklearn.dummy import DummyClassifier
from sklearn.model_selection import train_test_split

# Load data
iris = load_iris()

# Create target vector and feature matrix
features, target = iris.data, iris.target

# Split into training and test set
features_train, features_test, target_train, target_test = train_test_split(
features, target, random_state=0)

# Create dummy classifier
dummy = DummyClassifier(strategy='uniform', random_state=1)

# "Train" model
dummy.fit(features_train, target_train)

# Get accuracy score
dummy.score(features_test, target_test)

0.42105263157894735
```

By comparing the baseline classifier to our trained classifier, we can see the improvement:

```
# Load library
from sklearn.ensemble import RandomForestClassifier

# Create classifier
classifier = RandomForestClassifier()

# Train model
classifier.fit(features_train, target_train)

# Get accuracy score
classifier.score(features_test, target_test)

0.94736842105263153
```

Discussion

A common measure of a classifier's performance is how much better it is than random guessing. scikit-learn's DummyClassifier makes this comparison easy. The strat egy parameter gives us a number of options for generating values. There are two particularly useful strategies. First, stratified makes predictions that are proportional to the training set's target vector's class proportions (i.e., if 20% of the observations in the training data are women, then DummyClassifier will predict women 20% of the time). Second, `uniform` will generate predictions uniformly at random between the different classes. For example, if 20% of observations are women and 80% are men, `uniform` will produce predictions that are 50% women and 50% men.

See Also

- scikit-learn documentation: DummyClassifier (*http://bit.ly/2Fr178G*)

11.4 Evaluating Binary Classifier Predictions

Problem

Given a trained classification model, you want to evaluate its quality.

Solution

Use scikit-learn's `cross_val_score` to conduct cross-validation while using the `scor ing` parameter to define one of a number of performance metrics, including accuracy, precision, recall, and F_1.

Accuracy is a common performance metric. It is simply the proportion of observations predicted correctly:

$$Accuracy = \frac{TP + TN}{TP + TN + FP + FN}$$

where:

- *TP* is the number of true positives. Observations that are part of the *positive* class (has the disease, purchased the product, etc.) and that we predicted correctly.

- *TN* is the number of true negatives. Observations that are part of the *negative* class (does not have the disease, did not purchase the product, etc.) and that we predicted correctly.

- *FP* is the number of false positives. Also called a Type I error. Observations predicted to be part of the *positive* class that are actually part of the *negative* class.

- *FN* is the number of false negatives. Also called a Type II error. Observations predicted to be part of the *negative* class that are actually part of the *positive* class.

We can measure accuracy in three-fold (the default number of folds) cross-validation by setting `scoring="accuracy"`:

```
# Load libraries
from sklearn.model_selection import cross_val_score
from sklearn.linear_model import LogisticRegression
from sklearn.datasets import make_classification

# Generate features matrix and target vector
X, y = make_classification(n_samples = 10000,
                           n_features = 3,
                           n_informative = 3,
                           n_redundant = 0,
                           n_classes = 2,
                           random_state = 1)

# Create logistic regression
logit = LogisticRegression()

# Cross-validate model using accuracy
cross_val_score(logit, X, y, scoring="accuracy")
```

```
array([ 0.95170966,  0.9580084 ,  0.95558223])
```

The appeal of accuracy is that it has an intuitive and plain English explanation: proportion of observations predicted correctly. However, in the real world, often our data has imbalanced classes (e.g., the 99.9% of observations are of class 1 and only 0.1% are class 2). When in the presence of imbalanced classes, accuracy suffers from a paradox where a model is highly accurate but lacks predictive power. For example, imagine we are trying to predict the presence of a very rare cancer that occurs in 0.1% of the population. After training our model, we find the accuracy is at 95%. However, 99.9% of people do not have the cancer: if we simply created a model that "predicted" that nobody had that form of cancer, our naive model would be 4.9% more accurate, but clearly is not able to *predict* anything. For this reason, we are often motivated to use other metrics like precision, recall, and the F_1 score.

Precision is the proportion of every observation predicted to be positive that is actually positive. We can think about it as a measurement noise in our predictions— that is, when we predict something is positive, how likely we are to be right. Models with high precision are pessimistic in that they only predict an observation is of the positive class when they are very certain about it. Formally, precision is:

$$\text{Precision} = \frac{TP}{TP + FP}$$

```
# Cross-validate model using precision
cross_val_score(logit, X, y, scoring="precision")
```

```
array([ 0.95252404,  0.96583282,  0.95558223])
```

Recall is the proportion of every positive observation that is truly positive. Recall measures the model's ability to identify an observation of the positive class. Models with high recall are optimistic in that they have a low bar for predicting that an observation is in the positive class:

$$\text{Recall} = \frac{TP}{TP + FN}$$

```
# Cross-validate model using recall
cross_val_score(logit, X, y, scoring="recall")
```

```
array([ 0.95080984,  0.94961008,  0.95558223])
```

If this is the first time you have encountered precision and recall, it is understandable if it takes you a little while to fully understand them. This is one of the downsides to accuracy; precision and recall are less intuitive. Almost always we want some kind of balance between precision and recall, and this role is filled by the F_1 score. The F_1 score is the harmonic mean (a kind of average used for ratios):

$$F_1 = 2 \times \frac{\text{Precision} \times \text{Recall}}{\text{Precision} + \text{Recall}}$$

It is a measure of correctness achieved in positive prediction—that is, of observations labeled as positive, how many are actually positive:

```
# Cross-validate model using f1
cross_val_score(logit, X, y, scoring="f1")
```

```
array([ 0.95166617,  0.95765275,  0.95558223])
```

Discussion

As an evaluation metric, accuracy has some valuable properties, especially its simple intuition. However, better metrics often involve using some balance of precision and recall—that is, a trade-off between the optimism and pessimism of our model. F_1 represents a balance between the recall and precision, where the relative contributions of both are equal.

Alternatively to using `cross_val_score`, if we already have the true y values and the predicted y values, we can calculate metrics like accuracy and recall directly:

```
# Load library
from sklearn.model_selection import train_test_split
from sklearn.metrics import accuracy_score

# Create training and test split
X_train, X_test, y_train, y_test = train_test_split(X,
                                                     y,
                                                     test_size=0.1,
                                                     random_state=1)
```

```
# Predict values for training target vector
y_hat = logit.fit(X_train, y_train).predict(X_test)

# Calculate accuracy
accuracy_score(y_test, y_hat)

0.94699999999999995
```

See Also

- Accuracy paradox (*http://bit.ly/2FxTpK0*)

11.5 Evaluating Binary Classifier Thresholds

Problem

You want to evaluate a binary classifier and various probability thresholds.

Solution

The Receiving Operating Characteristic (ROC) curve is a common method for evaluating the quality of a binary classifier. ROC compares the presence of true positives and false positives at every probability threshold (i.e., the probability at which an observation is predicted to be a class). By plotting the ROC curve, we can see how the model performs. A classifier that predicts every observation correctly would look like the solid light gray line in the following chart, going straight up to the top immediately. A classifier that predicts at random will appear as the diagonal line. The better the model, the closer it is to the solid line. In scikit-learn, we can use roc_curve to calculate the true and false positives at each threshold, then plot them:

```
# Load libraries
import matplotlib.pyplot as plt
from sklearn.datasets import make_classification
from sklearn.linear_model import LogisticRegression
from sklearn.metrics import roc_curve, roc_auc_score
from sklearn.model_selection import train_test_split

# Create feature matrix and target vector
features, target = make_classification(n_samples=10000,
                                       n_features=10,
                                       n_classes=2,
                                       n_informative=3,
                                       random_state=3)

# Split into training and test sets
features_train, features_test, target_train, target_test = train_test_split(
    features, target, test_size=0.1, random_state=1)
```

```
# Create classifier
logit = LogisticRegression()

# Train model
logit.fit(features_train, target_train)

# Get predicted probabilities
target_probabilities = logit.predict_proba(features_test)[:,1]

# Create true and false positive rates
false_positive_rate, true_positive_rate, threshold = roc_curve(target_test,
                                                        target_probabilities)

# Plot ROC curve
plt.title("Receiver Operating Characteristic")
plt.plot(false_positive_rate, true_positive_rate)
plt.plot([0, 1], ls="--")
plt.plot([0, 0], [1, 0] , c=".7"), plt.plot([1, 1] , c=".7")
plt.ylabel("True Positive Rate")
plt.xlabel("False Positive Rate")
plt.show()
```

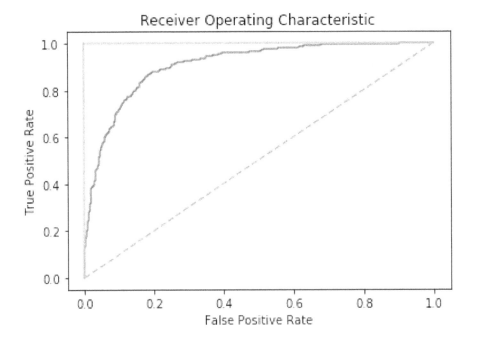

Discussion

Up until now we have only examined models based on the values they predict. However, in many learning algorithms those predicted values are based off of probability estimates. That is, each observation is given an explicit probability of belonging in each class. In our solution, we can use `predict_proba` to see the predicted probabilities for the first observation:

```
# Get predicted probabilities
logit.predict_proba(features_test)[0:1]

array([[ 0.8688938,  0.1311062]])
```

We can see the classes using `classes_`:

```
logit.classes_

array([0, 1])
```

In this example, the first observation has an ~87% chance of being in the negative class (0) and a 13% chance of being in the positive class (1). By default, scikit-learn predicts an observation is part of the positive class if the probability is greater than 0.5 (called the *threshold*). However, instead of a middle ground, we will often want to explicitly bias our model to use a different threshold for substantive reasons. For example, if a false positive is very costly to our company, we might prefer a model that has a high probability threshold. We fail to predict some positives, but when an observation is predicted to be positive, we can be very confident that the prediction is correct. This trade-off is represented in the true positive rate (TPR) and the false positive rate (FPR). The true positive rate is the number of observations correctly predicted true divided by all true positive observations:

$$TPR = \frac{\text{True Positives}}{\text{True Positives+False Negatives}}$$

The false positive rate is the number of incorrectly predicted positives divided by all true negative observations:

$$FPR = \frac{\text{False Positives}}{\text{False Positives+True Negatives}}$$

The ROC curve represents the respective TPR and FPR for every probability threshold. For example, in our solution a threshold of roughly 0.50 has a TPR of \0.81 and an FPR of \0.15:

```
print("Threshold:", threshold[116])
print("True Positive Rate:", true_positive_rate[116])
print("False Positive Rate:", false_positive_rate[116])
```

```
Threshold: 0.528224777887
True Positive Rate: 0.810204081633
False Positive Rate: 0.154901960784
```

However, if we increase the threshold to ~80% (i.e., increase how certain the model has to be before it predicts an observation as positive) the TPR drops significantly but so does the FPR:

```
print("Threshold:", threshold[45])
print("True Positive Rate:", true_positive_rate[45])
print("False Positive Rate:", false_positive_rate[45])

Threshold: 0.808019566563
True Positive Rate: 0.563265306122
False Positive Rate: 0.0470588235294
```

This is because our higher requirement for being predicted to be in the positive class has made the model not identify a number of positive observations (the lower TPR), but also reduce the noise from negative observations being predicted as positive (the lower FPR).

In addition to being able to visualize the trade-off between TPR and FPR, the ROC curve can also be used as a general metric for a model. The better a model is, the higher the curve and thus the greater the area under the curve. For this reason, it is common to calculate the area under the ROC curve (AUCROC) to judge the overall equality of a model at all possible thresholds. The closer the AUCROC is to 1, the better the model. In scikit-learn we can calculate the AUCROC using `roc_auc_score`:

```
# Calculate area under curve
roc_auc_score(target_test, target_probabilities)

0.90733893557422962
```

See Also

- ROC Curves in Python and R (*http://bit.ly/2FuqoyV*)
- The Area Under an ROC Curve (*http://bit.ly/2FxTrl6*)

11.6 Evaluating Multiclass Classifier Predictions

Problem

You have a model that predicts three or more classes and want to evaluate its performance.

Solution

Use cross-validation with an evaluation metric capable of handling more than two classes:

```
# Load libraries
from sklearn.model_selection import cross_val_score
from sklearn.linear_model import LogisticRegression
from sklearn.datasets import make_classification

# Generate features matrix and target vector
features, target = make_classification(n_samples = 10000,
                                       n_features = 3,
                                       n_informative = 3,
                                       n_redundant = 0,
                                       n_classes = 3,
                                       random_state = 1)

# Create logistic regression
logit = LogisticRegression()

# Cross-validate model using accuracy
cross_val_score(logit, features, target, scoring='accuracy')
```

```
array([ 0.83653269,  0.8259826 ,  0.81308131])
```

Discussion

When we have balanced classes (e.g., a roughly equal number of observations in each class of the target vector), accuracy is—just like in the binary class setting—a simple and interpretable choice for an evaluation metric. Accuracy is the number of correct predictions divided by the number of observations and works just as well in the multiclass as binary setting. However, when we have imbalanced classes (a common scenario), we should be inclined to use other evaluation metrics.

Many of scikit-learn's built-in metrics are for evaluating binary classifiers. However, many of these metrics can be extended for use when we have more than two classes. Precision, recall, and F1 scores are useful metrics that we have already covered in detail in previous recipes. While all of them were originally designed for binary classifiers, we can apply them to multiclass settings by treating our data as a set of binary classes. Doing so enables us to apply the metrics to each class as if it were the only class in the data, and then aggregate the evaluation scores for all the classes by averaging them:

```
# Cross-validate model using macro averaged F1 score
cross_val_score(logit, features, target, scoring='f1_macro')
```

```
array([ 0.83613125,  0.82562258,  0.81293539])
```

In this code, _macro refers to the method used to average the evaluation scores from the classes:

macro
> Calculate mean of metric scores for each class, weighting each class equally.

weighted
> Calculate mean of metric scores for each class, weighting each class proportional to its size in the data.

micro
> Calculate mean of metric scores for each observation-class combination.

11.7 Visualizing a Classifier's Performance

Problem

Given predicted classes and true classes of the test data, you want to visually compare the model's quality.

Solution

Use a confusion matrix, which compares predicted classes and true classes:

```
# Load libraries
import matplotlib.pyplot as plt
import seaborn as sns
from sklearn import datasets
from sklearn.linear_model import LogisticRegression
from sklearn.model_selection import train_test_split
from sklearn.metrics import confusion_matrix
import pandas as pd

# Load data
iris = datasets.load_iris()

# Create feature matrix
features = iris.data

# Create target vector
target = iris.target

# Create list of target class names
class_names = iris.target_names

# Create training and test set
features_train, features_test, target_train, target_test = train_test_split(
    features, target, random_state=1)
```

```
# Create logistic regression
classifier = LogisticRegression()

# Train model and make predictions
target_predicted = classifier.fit(features_train,
    target_train).predict(features_test)

# Create confusion matrix
matrix = confusion_matrix(target_test, target_predicted)

# Create pandas dataframe
dataframe = pd.DataFrame(matrix, index=class_names, columns=class_names)

# Create heatmap
sns.heatmap(dataframe, annot=True, cbar=None, cmap="Blues")
plt.title("Confusion Matrix"), plt.tight_layout()
plt.ylabel("True Class"), plt.xlabel("Predicted Class")
plt.show()
```

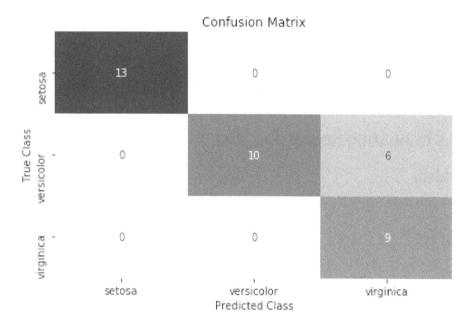

Discussion

Confusion matrices are an easy, effective visualization of a classifier's performance. One of the major benefits of confusion matrices is their interpretability. Each column of the matrix (often visualized as a heatmap) represents predicted classes, while every row shows true classes. The end result is that every cell is one possible combination of predict and true classes. This is probably best explained using an example. In the solution, the top-left cell is the number of observations predicted to be *Iris setosa* (indicated by the column) that are actually *Iris setosa* (indicated by the row). This means the models accurately predicted all *Iris setosa* flowers. However, the model does not do as well at predicting *Iris virginica*. The bottom-right cell indicates that the model successfully predicted nine observations were *Iris virginica*, but (looking one cell up) predicted six flowers to be *viriginica* that were actually *Iris versicolor*.

There are three things worth noting about confusion matrices. First, a perfect model will have values along the diagonal and zeros everywhere else. A bad model will look like the observation counts will be spread evenly around cells. Second, a confusion matrix lets us see not only where the model was wrong, but also how it was wrong. That is, we can look at patterns of misclassification. For example, our model had an easy time differentiating *Iris virginica* and *Iris setosa*, but a much more difficult time classifying *Iris virginica* and *Iris versicolor*. Finally, confusion matrices work with any number of classes (although if we had one million classes in our target vector, the confusion matrix visualization might be difficult to read).

See Also

- Confusion Matrix (*http://bit.ly/2FuGKaP*)
- scikit-learn documentation: Confusion Matrix (*http://bit.ly/2DmnICk*)

11.8 Evaluating Regression Models

Problem

You want to evaluate the performance of a regression model.

Solution

Use mean squared error (MSE):

```
# Load libraries
from sklearn.datasets import make_regression
from sklearn.model_selection import cross_val_score
from sklearn.linear_model import LinearRegression

# Generate features matrix, target vector
features, target = make_regression(n_samples = 100,
                                   n_features = 3,
                                   n_informative = 3,
                                   n_targets = 1,
                                   noise = 50,
                                   coef = False,
                                   random_state = 1)
```

```
# Create a linear regression object
ols = LinearRegression()

# Cross-validate the linear regression using (negative) MSE
cross_val_score(ols, features, target, scoring='neg_mean_squared_error')

    array([-1718.22817783, -3103.4124284 , -1377.17858823])
```

Another common regression metric is the coefficient of determination, R^2:

```
# Cross-validate the linear regression using R-squared
cross_val_score(ols, features, target, scoring='r2')

    array([ 0.87804558,  0.76395862,  0.89154377])
```

Discussion

MSE is one of the most common evaluation metrics for regression models. Formally, MSE is:

$$\text{MSE} = \frac{1}{n} \sum_{i=1}^{n} (\widehat{y}_i - y_i)^2$$

where n is the number of observations, y_i is the true value of the target we are trying to predict for observation i, and $\widehat{y}_i$ is the model's predicted value for y_i. MSE is a measurement of the squared sum of all distances between predicted and true values. The higher the value of MSE, the greater the total squared error and thus the worse the model. There are a number of mathematical benefits to squaring the error term, including that it forces all error values to be positive, but one often unrealized implication is that squaring penalizes a few large errors more than many small errors, even if the absolute value of the errors is the same. For example, imagine two models, A and B, each with two observations:

- Model A has errors of 0 and 10 and thus its MSE is $0^2 + 10^2 = 100$.
- Model B has two errors of 5 each, and thus its MSE is $5^2 + 5^2 = 50$.

Both models have the same total error, 10; however, MSE would consider Model A (MSE = 100) worse than Model B (MSE = 50). In practice this implication is rarely an issue (and indeed can be theoretically beneficial) and MSE works perfectly fine as an evaluation metric.

One important note: by default in scikit-learn arguments of the `scoring` parameter assume that higher values are better than lower values. However, this is not the case for MSE, where higher values mean a worse model. For this reason, scikit-learn looks at the *negative* MSE using the `neg_mean_squared_error` argument.

A common alternative regression evaluation metric is R^2, which measures the amount of variance in the target vector that is explained by the model:

$$R^2 = 1 - \frac{\sum_{i=1}^{n}\left(y_i - \hat{y}_i\right)^2}{\sum_{i=1}^{n}\left(y_i - \bar{y}\right)^2}$$

where y_i is the true target value of the ith observation, $\hat{y}_i$ is the predicted value for the ith observation, and $\bar{y}$ is the mean value of the target vector. The closer to 1.0, the better the model.

See Also

- Mean squared error (*http://bit.ly/2HgALnc*)
- Coefficient of determination (*http://bit.ly/2HjW7Qn*)

11.9 Evaluating Clustering Models

Problem

You have used an unsupervised learning algorithm to cluster your data. Now you want to know how well it did.

Solution

The short answer is that you probably can't, at least not in the way you want.

That said, one option is to evaluate clustering using silhouette coefficients, which measure the quality of the clusters:

```python
import numpy as np
from sklearn.metrics import silhouette_score
from sklearn import datasets
from sklearn.cluster import KMeans
from sklearn.datasets import make_blobs

# Generate feature matrix
features, _ = make_blobs(n_samples = 1000,
                         n_features = 10,
                         centers = 2,
                         cluster_std = 0.5,
                         shuffle = True,
                         random_state = 1)

# Cluster data using k-means to predict classes
```

```
model = KMeans(n_clusters=2, random_state=1).fit(features)

# Get predicted classes
target_predicted = model.labels_

# Evaluate model
silhouette_score(features, target_predicted)
```

```
0.89162655640721422
```

Discussion

Supervised model evaluation compares predictions (e.g., classes or quantitative values) with the corresponding true values in the target vector. However, the most common motivation for using clustering methods is that your data doesn't have a target vector. There are a number of clustering evaluation metrics that require a target vector, but again, using unsupervised learning approaches like clustering when you have a target vector available to you is probably handicapping yourself unnecessarily.

While we cannot evaluate predictions versus true values if we don't have a target vector, we can evaluate the nature of the clusters themselves. Intuitively, we can imagine "good" clusters having very small distances between observations in the same cluster (i.e., dense clusters) and large distances between the different clusters (i.e., well-separated clusters). Silhouette coefficients provide a single value measuring both traits. Formally, the ith observation's silhouette coefficient is:

$$s_i = \frac{b_i - a_i}{\max(a_i, b_i)}$$

where s_i is the silhouette coefficient for observation i, a_i is the mean distance between i and all observations of the same class, and b_i is the mean distance between i and all observations from the closest cluster of a different class. The value returned by `silhouette_score` is the mean silhouette coefficient for all observations. Silhouette coefficients range between –1 and 1, with 1 indicating dense, well-separated clusters.

See Also

- scikit-learn documentation: silhouette_score (*http://bit.ly/2BEVQV5*)

11.10 Creating a Custom Evaluation Metric

Problem

You want to evaluate a model using a metric you created.

Solution

Create the metric as a function and convert it into a scorer function using scikit-learn's make_scorer:

```
# Load libraries
from sklearn.metrics import make_scorer, r2_score
from sklearn.model_selection import train_test_split
from sklearn.linear_model import Ridge
from sklearn.datasets import make_regression

# Generate features matrix and target vector
features, target = make_regression(n_samples = 100,
                                   n_features = 3,
                                   random_state = 1)

# Create training set and test set
features_train, features_test, target_train, target_test = train_test_split(
    features, target, test_size=0.10, random_state=1)

# Create custom metric
def custom_metric(target_test, target_predicted):
    # Calculate r-squared score
    r2 = r2_score(target_test, target_predicted)
    # Return r-squared score
    return r2

# Make scorer and define that higher scores are better
score = make_scorer(custom_metric, greater_is_better=True)

# Create ridge regression object
classifier = Ridge()

# Train ridge regression model
model = classifier.fit(features_train, target_train)

# Apply custom scorer
score(model, features_test, target_test)
```

```
0.99979061028820582
```

Discussion

While scikit-learn has a number of built-in metrics for evaluating model performance, it is often useful to define our own metrics. scikit-learn makes this easy using make_scorer. First, we define a function that takes in two arguments—the ground truth target vector and our predicted values—and outputs some score. Second, we use make_scorer to create a scorer object, making sure to specify whether higher or lower scores are desirable (using the greater_is_better parameter).

The custom metric in the solution (`custom_metric`) is a toy example since it simply wraps a built-in metric for calculating the R^2 score. In a real-world situation, we would replace the `custom_metric` function with whatever custom metric we wanted. However, we can see that the custom metric that calculates R^2 does work by comparing the results to scikit-learn's `r2_score` built-in method:

```
# Predict values
target_predicted = model.predict(features_test)

# Calculate r-squared score
r2_score(target_test, target_predicted)
```

```
0.99979061028820582
```

See Also

- scikit-learn documentation: make_scorer (*http://bit.ly/2FwMm4m*)

11.11 Visualizing the Effect of Training Set Size

Problem

You want to evaluate the effect of the number of observations in your training set on some metric (accuracy, F1, etc.).

Solution

Plot the learning curve:

```
# Load libraries
import numpy as np
import matplotlib.pyplot as plt
from sklearn.ensemble import RandomForestClassifier
from sklearn.datasets import load_digits
from sklearn.model_selection import learning_curve

# Load data
digits = load_digits()

# Create feature matrix and target vector
features, target = digits.data, digits.target

# Create CV training and test scores for various training set sizes
train_sizes, train_scores, test_scores = learning_curve(# Classifier
                                                        RandomForestClassifier(),
                                                        # Feature matrix
                                                        features,
                                                        # Target vector
```

```
                                                        target,
                                                        # Number of folds
                                                        cv=10,
                                                        # Performance metric
                                                        scoring='accuracy',
                                                        # Use all computer cores
                                                        n_jobs=-1,
                                                        # Sizes of 50
                                                        # training set
                                                        train_sizes=np.linspace(
                                                        0.01,
                                                        1.0,
                                                        50))

# Create means and standard deviations of training set scores
train_mean = np.mean(train_scores, axis=1)
train_std = np.std(train_scores, axis=1)

# Create means and standard deviations of test set scores
test_mean = np.mean(test_scores, axis=1)
test_std = np.std(test_scores, axis=1)

# Draw lines
plt.plot(train_sizes, train_mean, '--', color="#111111",  label="Training score")
plt.plot(train_sizes, test_mean, color="#111111", label="Cross-validation score")

# Draw bands
plt.fill_between(train_sizes, train_mean - train_std,
                 train_mean + train_std, color="#DDDDDD")
plt.fill_between(train_sizes, test_mean - test_std,
                 test_mean + test_std, color="#DDDDDD")

# Create plot
plt.title("Learning Curve")
plt.xlabel("Training Set Size"), plt.ylabel("Accuracy Score"),
plt.legend(loc="best")
plt.tight_layout()
plt.show()
```

Discussion

Learning curves visualize the performance (e.g., accuracy, recall) of a model on the training set and during cross-validation as the number of observations in the training set increases. They are commonly used to determine if our learning algorithms would benefit from gathering additional training data.

In our solution, we plot the accuracy of a random forest classifier at 50 different training set sizes ranging from 1% of observations to 100%. The increasing accuracy score of the cross-validated models tell us that we would likely benefit from additional observations (although in practice this might not be feasible).

See Also

- scikit-learn documentation: Learning Curve (*http://bit.ly/2FwjBVe*)

11.12 Creating a Text Report of Evaluation Metrics

Problem

You want a quick description of a classifier's performance.

Solution

Use scikit-learn's `classification_report`:

```
# Load libraries
from sklearn import datasets
from sklearn.linear_model import LogisticRegression
from sklearn.model_selection import train_test_split
from sklearn.metrics import classification_report

# Load data
iris = datasets.load_iris()

# Create feature matrix
features = iris.data

# Create target vector
target = iris.target

# Create list of target class names
class_names = iris.target_names

# Create training and test set
features_train, features_test, target_train, target_test = train_test_split(
    features, target, random_state=1)

# Create logistic regression
classifier = LogisticRegression()

# Train model and make predictions
model = classifier.fit(features_train, target_train)
target_predicted = model.predict(features_test)

# Create a classification report
print(classification_report(target_test,
                            target_predicted,
                            target_names=class_names))
```

	precision	recall	f1-score	support
setosa	1.00	1.00	1.00	13
versicolor	1.00	0.62	0.77	16
virginica	0.60	1.00	0.75	9
avg / total	0.91	0.84	0.84	38

Discussion

`classification_report` provides a quick means for us to see some common evaluation metrics, including precision, recall, and F1-score (described earlier in this chapter). Support refers to the number of observations in each class.

See Also

- Precision and recall (*https://en.wikipedia.org/wiki/Precision_and_recall*)

11.13 Visualizing the Effect of Hyperparameter Values

Problem

You want to understand how the performance of a model changes as the value of some hyperparameter changes.

Solution

Plot the validation curve:

```
# Load libraries
import matplotlib.pyplot as plt
import numpy as np
from sklearn.datasets import load_digits
from sklearn.ensemble import RandomForestClassifier
from sklearn.model_selection import validation_curve

# Load data
digits = load_digits()

# Create feature matrix and target vector
features, target = digits.data, digits.target

# Create range of values for parameter
param_range = np.arange(1, 250, 2)

# Calculate accuracy on training and test set using range of parameter values
train_scores, test_scores = validation_curve(
    # Classifier
    RandomForestClassifier(),
    # Feature matrix
    features,
    # Target vector
    target,
    # Hyperparameter to examine
    param_name="n_estimators",
    # Range of hyperparameter's values
    param_range=param_range,
    # Number of folds
    cv=3,
    # Performance metric
    scoring="accuracy",
    # Use all computer cores
    n_jobs=-1)
```

```
# Calculate mean and standard deviation for training set scores
train_mean = np.mean(train_scores, axis=1)
train_std = np.std(train_scores, axis=1)

# Calculate mean and standard deviation for test set scores
test_mean = np.mean(test_scores, axis=1)
test_std = np.std(test_scores, axis=1)

# Plot mean accuracy scores for training and test sets
plt.plot(param_range, train_mean, label="Training score", color="black")
plt.plot(param_range, test_mean, label="Cross-validation score", color="dimgrey")

# Plot accurancy bands for training and test sets
plt.fill_between(param_range, train_mean - train_std,
                 train_mean + train_std, color="gray")
plt.fill_between(param_range, test_mean - test_std,
                 test_mean + test_std, color="gainsboro")

# Create plot
plt.title("Validation Curve With Random Forest")
plt.xlabel("Number Of Trees")
plt.ylabel("Accuracy Score")
plt.tight_layout()
plt.legend(loc="best")
plt.show()
```

Discussion

Most training algorithms (including many covered in this book) contain hyperparameters that must be chosen before the training process begins. For example, a random forest classifier creates a "forest" of decision trees, each of which votes on the predicted class of an observation. One hyperparameter in random forest classifiers is the number of trees in the forest. Most often hyperparameter values are selected during model selection (see Chapter 12). However, it is occasionally useful to visualize how model performance changes as the hyperparameter value changes. In our solution, we plot the changes in accuracy for a random forest classifier for the training set and during cross-validation as the number of trees increases. When we have a small number of trees, both the training and cross-validation score are low, suggesting the model is underfitted. As the number of trees increases to 250, the accuracy of both levels off, suggesting there is probably not much value in the computational cost of training a massive forest.

In scikit-learn, we can calculate the validation curve using `validation_curve`, which contains three important parameters:

- `param_name` is the name of the hyperparameter to vary.
- `param_range` is the value of the hyperparameter to use.
- `scoring` is the evaluation metric used to judge to model.

See Also

- scikit-learn documentation: Validation Curve (*http://bit.ly/2FuwYFG*)

## CHAPTER 12

Model Selection

12.0 Introduction

In machine learning, we use training algorithms to learn the parameters of a model by minimizing some loss function. However, in addition many learning algorithms (e.g., support vector classifier and random forests) also have hyperparameters that must be defined outside of the learning process. For example, random forests are collections of decision trees (hence the word *forest*); however, the number of decision trees in the forest is not learned by the algorithm and must be set prior to fitting. This is often referred to as *hyperparameter tuning*, *hyperparameter optimization*, or *model selection*. Additionally, often we might want to try multiple learning algorithms (for example, trying both support vector classifier and random forests to see which learning method produces the best model).

While there is widespread variation in the use of terminology in this area, in this book we refer to both selecting the best learning algorithm and its best hyperparameters as model selection. The reason is straightforward: imagine we have data and want to train a support vector classifier with 10 candidate hyperparameter values and a random forest classifier with 10 candidate hyperparameter values. The result is that we are trying to select the best model from a set of 20 candidate models. In this chapter, we will cover techniques to efficiently select the best model from the set of candidates.

Throughout this chapter we will refer to specific hyperparameters, such as C (the inverse of regularization strength). Do not worry if you don't know what the hyperparameters are. We will cover them in later chapters. Instead, just treat hyperparameters like the settings for the learning algorithm that we must choose before starting training.

12.1 Selecting Best Models Using Exhaustive Search

Problem

You want to select the best model by searching over a range of hyperparameters.

Solution

Use scikit-learn's `GridSearchCV`:

```
# Load libraries
import numpy as np
from sklearn import linear_model, datasets
from sklearn.model_selection import GridSearchCV

# Load data
iris = datasets.load_iris()
features = iris.data
target = iris.target

# Create logistic regression
logistic = linear_model.LogisticRegression()

# Create range of candidate penalty hyperparameter values
penalty = ['l1', 'l2']

# Create range of candidate regularization hyperparameter values
C = np.logspace(0, 4, 10)

# Create dictionary hyperparameter candidates
hyperparameters = dict(C=C, penalty=penalty)

# Create grid search
gridsearch = GridSearchCV(logistic, hyperparameters, cv=5, verbose=0)

# Fit grid search
best_model = gridsearch.fit(features, target)
```

Discussion

`GridSearchCV` is a brute-force approach to model selection using cross-validation. Specifically, a user defines sets of possible values for one or multiple hyperparameters, and then `GridSearchCV` trains a model using every value and/or combination of values. The model with the best performance score is selected as the best model. For example, in our solution we used logistic regression as our learning algorithm, containing two hyperparameters: C and the regularization penalty. Don't worry if you don't know what C and regularization mean; we cover them in the next few chapters. Just realize that C and the regularization penalty can take a range of values, which have to be specified prior to training. For C, we define 10 possible values:

```
np.logspace(0, 4, 10)

array([ 1.00000000e+00,   2.78255940e+00,   7.74263683e+00,
        2.15443469e+01,   5.99484250e+01,   1.66810054e+02,
        4.64158883e+02,   1.29154967e+03,   3.59381366e+03,
        1.00000000e+04])
```

And similarly we define two possible values for the regularization penalty: `['l1'`, `'l2']`. For each combination of C and regularization penalty values, we train the model and evaluate it using k-fold cross-validation. In our solution, we had 10 possible values of C, 2 possible values of regularization penalty, and 5 folds. They created $10 \times 2 \times 5 = 100$ candidate models from which the best was selected.

Once `GridSearchCV` is complete, we can see the hyperparameters of the best model:

```
# View best hyperparameters
print('Best Penalty:', best_model.best_estimator_.get_params()['penalty'])
print('Best C:', best_model.best_estimator_.get_params()['C'])

Best Penalty: l1
Best C: 7.74263682681
```

By default, after identifying the best hyperparameters, `GridSearchCV` will retrain a model using the best hyperparameters on the entire dataset (rather than leaving a fold out for cross-validation). We can use this model to predict values like any other scikit-learn model:

```
# Predict target vector
best_model.predict(features)

array([0, 0, 0, 0, 0, 0, 0, 0, 0, 0, 0, 0, 0, 0, 0, 0, 0, 0, 0, 0, 0, 0,
       0, 0, 0, 0, 0, 0, 0, 0, 0, 0, 0, 0, 0, 0, 0, 0, 0, 0, 0, 0, 0, 0,
       0, 0, 0, 0, 1, 1, 1, 1, 1, 1, 1, 1, 1, 1, 1, 1, 1, 1, 1, 1, 1, 1,
       1, 2, 1, 1, 1, 1, 1, 1, 1, 1, 1, 1, 1, 1, 2, 1, 1, 1, 1, 1, 1, 1,
       1, 1, 1, 1, 1, 1, 1, 1, 2, 2, 2, 2, 2, 2, 2, 2, 2, 2, 2, 2, 2, 2,
       2, 2, 2, 2, 2, 2, 2, 2, 2, 2, 2, 2, 2, 2, 1, 2, 2, 2, 2,
       2, 2, 2, 2, 2, 2, 2, 2, 2, 2, 2, 2])
```

One `GridSearchCV` parameter is worth noting: `verbose`. While mostly unnecessary, it can be reassuring during long searching processes to receive an indication that the search is progressing. The `verbose` parameter determines the amount of messages outputted during the search, with 0 showing no output, and 1 to 3 outputting messages with increasing detail.

See Also

- scikit-learn documentation: GridSearchCV (*http://bit.ly/2Fuctc4*)

12.2 Selecting Best Models Using Randomized Search

Problem

You want a computationally cheaper method than exhaustive search to select the best model.

Solution

Use scikit-learn's `RandomizedSearchCV`:

```
# Load libraries
from scipy.stats import uniform
from sklearn import linear_model, datasets
from sklearn.model_selection import RandomizedSearchCV

# Load data
iris = datasets.load_iris()
features = iris.data
target = iris.target

# Create logistic regression
logistic = linear_model.LogisticRegression()

# Create range of candidate regularization penalty hyperparameter values
penalty = ['l1', 'l2']

# Create distribution of candidate regularization hyperparameter values
C = uniform(loc=0, scale=4)

# Create hyperparameter options
hyperparameters = dict(C=C, penalty=penalty)

# Create randomized search
randomizedsearch = RandomizedSearchCV(
    logistic, hyperparameters, random_state=1, n_iter=100, cv=5, verbose=0,
    n_jobs=-1)

# Fit randomized search
best_model = randomizedsearch.fit(features, target)
```

Discussion

In Recipe 12.1, we used `GridSearchCV` on a user-defined set of hyperparameter values to search for the best model according to a score function. A more efficient method than `GridSearchCV`'s brute-force search is to search over a specific number of random combinations of hyperparameter values from user-supplied distributions (e.g., normal, uniform). scikit-learn implements this randomized search technique with `RandomizedSearchCV`.

With `RandomizedSearchCV`, if we specify a distribution, scikit-learn will randomly sample without replacement hyperparameter values from that distribution. As an example of the general concept, here we randomly sample 10 values from a uniform distribution ranging from 0 to 4:

```
# Define a uniform distribution between 0 and 4, sample 10 values
uniform(loc=0, scale=4).rvs(10)

array([ 1.97118721,  1.34786898,  3.79867719,  1.15999967,  3.33485021,
        1.20394179,  0.88117832,  0.47855329,  0.48521699,  1.5479854 ])
```

Alternatively, if we specify a list of values such as two regularization penalty hyperparameter values, `['l1', 'l2']`, `RandomizedSearchCV` will randomly sample with replacement from the list.

Just like with `GridSearchCV`, we can see the hyperparameter values of the best model:

```
# View best hyperparameters
print('Best Penalty:', best_model.best_estimator_.get_params()['penalty'])
print('Best C:', best_model.best_estimator_.get_params()['C'])

Best Penalty: l1
Best C: 1.66808801881
```

And just like with `GridSearchCV`, after the search is complete `RandomizedSearchCV` fits a new model using the best hyperparameters on the entire dataset. We can use this model like any other in scikit-learn; for example, to make predictions:

```
# Predict target vector
best_model.predict(features)

array([0, 0, 0, 0, 0, 0, 0, 0, 0, 0, 0, 0, 0, 0, 0, 0, 0, 0, 0, 0, 0, 0,
       0, 0, 0, 0, 0, 0, 0, 0, 0, 0, 0, 0, 0, 0, 0, 0, 0, 0, 0, 0, 0, 0,
       0, 0, 0, 0, 1, 1, 1, 1, 1, 1, 1, 1, 1, 1, 1, 1, 1, 1, 1, 1, 1, 1,
       1, 2, 1, 1, 1, 1, 1, 1, 1, 1, 1, 1, 1, 1, 2, 2, 1, 1, 1, 1, 1, 1,
       1, 1, 1, 1, 1, 1, 1, 1, 2, 2, 2, 2, 2, 2, 2, 2, 2, 2, 2, 2, 2, 2,
       2, 2, 2, 2, 2, 2, 2, 2, 2, 2, 1, 2, 2, 2, 1, 2, 2, 2, 2,
       2, 2, 2, 2, 2, 2, 2, 2, 2, 2, 2, 2])
```

The number of sampled combinations of hyperparameters (i.e., the number of candidate models trained) is specified with the `n_iter` (number of iterations) setting.

See Also

- scikit-learn documentation: RandomizedSearchCV (*http://bit.ly/2B7p1zT*)
- Random Search for Hyper-Parameter Optimization (*http://bit.ly/2FrUinf*)

12.3 Selecting Best Models from Multiple Learning Algorithms

Problem

You want to select the best model by searching over a range of learning algorithms and their respective hyperparameters.

Solution

Create a dictionary of candidate learning algorithms and their hyperparameters:

```
# Load libraries
import numpy as np
from sklearn import datasets
from sklearn.linear_model import LogisticRegression
from sklearn.ensemble import RandomForestClassifier
from sklearn.model_selection import GridSearchCV
from sklearn.pipeline import Pipeline

# Set random seed
np.random.seed(0)

# Load data
iris = datasets.load_iris()
features = iris.data
target = iris.target

# Create a pipeline
pipe = Pipeline([("classifier", RandomForestClassifier())])

# Create dictionary with candidate learning algorithms and their hyperparameters
search_space = [{"classifier": [LogisticRegression()],
                 "classifier__penalty": ['l1', 'l2'],
                 "classifier__C": np.logspace(0, 4, 10)},
                {"classifier": [RandomForestClassifier()],
                 "classifier__n_estimators": [10, 100, 1000],
                 "classifier__max_features": [1, 2, 3]}]

# Create grid search
gridsearch = GridSearchCV(pipe, search_space, cv=5, verbose=0)

# Fit grid search
best_model = gridsearch.fit(features, target)
```

Discussion

In the previous two recipes we found the best model by searching over possible hyperparameter values of a learning algorithm. However, what if we are not certain which learning algorithm to use? Recent versions of scikit-learn allow us to include learning algorithms as part of the search space. In our solution we define a search space that includes two learning algorithms: logistic regression and random forest classifier. Each learning algorithm has its own hyperparameters, and we define their candidate values using the format classifier__[*hyperparameter name*]. For example, for our logistic regression, to define the set of possible values for regularization hyperparameter space, C, and potential types of regularization penalties, penalty, we create a dictionary:

```
{'classifier': [LogisticRegression()],
 'classifier__penalty': ['l1', 'l2'],
 'classifier__C': np.logspace(0, 4, 10)}
```

We can also create a similar dictionary for the random forest hyperparameters:

```
{'classifier': [RandomForestClassifier()],
 'classifier__n_estimators': [10, 100, 1000],
 'classifier__max_features': [1, 2, 3]}
```

After the search is complete, we can use best_estimator_ to view the best model's learning algorithm and hyperparameters:

```
# View best model
best_model.best_estimator_.get_params()["classifier"]
```

```
LogisticRegression(C=7.7426368268112693, class_weight=None, dual=False,
        fit_intercept=True, intercept_scaling=1, max_iter=100,
        multi_class='ovr', n_jobs=1, penalty='l1', random_state=None,
        solver='liblinear', tol=0.0001, verbose=0, warm_start=False)
```

Just like with the last two recipes, once we have fit the model selection search, we can use this best model just like any other scikit-learn model:

```
# Predict target vector
best_model.predict(features)
```

```
array([0, 0, 0, 0, 0, 0, 0, 0, 0, 0, 0, 0, 0, 0, 0, 0, 0, 0, 0, 0, 0, 0,
       0, 0, 0, 0, 0, 0, 0, 0, 0, 0, 0, 0, 0, 0, 0, 0, 0, 0, 0, 0, 0, 0,
       0, 0, 0, 0, 1, 1, 1, 1, 1, 1, 1, 1, 1, 1, 1, 1, 1, 1, 1, 1, 1, 1,
       1, 2, 1, 1, 1, 1, 1, 1, 1, 1, 1, 1, 1, 1, 2, 1, 1, 1, 1, 1, 1, 1,
       1, 1, 1, 1, 1, 1, 1, 1, 2, 2, 2, 2, 2, 2, 2, 2, 2, 2, 2, 2, 2, 2,
       2, 2, 2, 2, 2, 2, 2, 2, 2, 2, 2, 2, 2, 2, 1, 2, 2, 2, 2,
       2, 2, 2, 2, 2, 2, 2, 2, 2, 2, 2, 2])
```

12.4 Selecting Best Models When Preprocessing

Problem

You want to include a preprocessing step during model selection.

Solution

Create a pipeline that includes the preprocessing step and any of its parameters:

```
# Load libraries
import numpy as np
from sklearn import datasets
from sklearn.linear_model import LogisticRegression
from sklearn.model_selection import GridSearchCV
from sklearn.pipeline import Pipeline, FeatureUnion
from sklearn.decomposition import PCA
from sklearn.preprocessing import StandardScaler

# Set random seed
np.random.seed(0)

# Load data
iris = datasets.load_iris()
features = iris.data
target = iris.target

# Create a preprocessing object that includes StandardScaler features and PCA
preprocess = FeatureUnion([("std", StandardScaler()), ("pca", PCA())])

# Create a pipeline
pipe = Pipeline([("preprocess", preprocess),
                 ("classifier", LogisticRegression())])

# Create space of candidate values
search_space = [{"preprocess__pca__n_components": [1, 2, 3],
                 "classifier__penalty": ["l1", "l2"],
                 "classifier__C": np.logspace(0, 4, 10)}]

# Create grid search
clf = GridSearchCV(pipe, search_space, cv=5, verbose=0, n_jobs=-1)

# Fit grid search
best_model = clf.fit(features, target)
```

Discussion

Very often we will need to preprocess our data before using it to train a model. We have to be careful to properly handle preprocessing when conducting model selection. First, GridSearchCV uses cross-validation to determine which model has the highest performance. However, in cross-validation we are in effect pretending that the fold held out, as the test set is not seen, and thus not part of fitting any preprocessing steps (e.g., scaling or standardization). For this reason, we cannot preprocess the data and then run GridSearchCV. Rather, the preprocessing steps must be a part of the set of actions taken by GridSearchCV. While this might appear complex, the reality is that scikit-learn makes it simple. FeatureUnion allows us to combine multiple preprocessing actions properly. In our solution we use `FeatureUnion` to combine two preprocessing steps: standardize the feature values (`StandardScaler`) and Principal Component Analysis (`PCA`). This object is called `preprocess` and contains both of our preprocessing steps. We then include `preprocess` into a pipeline with our learning algorithm. The end result is that this allows us to outsource the proper (and confusing) handling of fitting, transforming, and training the models with combinations of hyperparameters to scikit-learn.

Second, some preprocessing methods have their own parameters, which often have to be supplied by the user. For example, dimensionality reduction using PCA requires the user to define the number of principal components to use to produce the transformed feature set. Ideally, we would choose the number of components that produces a model with the greatest performance for some evaluation test metric. Luckily, scikit-learn makes this easy. When we include candidate component values in the search space, they are treated like any other hyperparameter to be searched over. In our solution, we defined `features__pca__n_components': [1, 2, 3]` in the search space to indicate that we wanted to discover if one, two, or three principal components produced the best model.

After model selection is complete, we can view the preprocessing values that produced the best model. For example, we can see the best number of principal components:

```
# View best model
best_model.best_estimator_.get_params()['preprocess__pca__n_components']

1
```

12.5 Speeding Up Model Selection with Parallelization

Problem

You need to speed up model selection.

Solution

Use all the cores in your machine by setting `n_jobs=-1`:

```
# Load libraries
import numpy as np
from sklearn import linear_model, datasets
from sklearn.model_selection import GridSearchCV

# Load data
iris = datasets.load_iris()
features = iris.data
target = iris.target
```

```
# Create logistic regression
logistic = linear_model.LogisticRegression()

# Create range of candidate regularization penalty hyperparameter values
penalty = ["l1", "l2"]

# Create range of candidate values for C
C = np.logspace(0, 4, 1000)

# Create hyperparameter options
hyperparameters = dict(C=C, penalty=penalty)

# Create grid search
gridsearch = GridSearchCV(logistic, hyperparameters, cv=5, n_jobs=-1, verbose=1)

# Fit grid search
best_model = gridsearch.fit(features, target)

Fitting 5 folds for each of 2000 candidates, totalling 10000 fits


[Parallel(n_jobs=-1)]: Done 1352 tasks      | elapsed:    7.2s
[Parallel(n_jobs=-1)]: Done 5120 tasks      | elapsed:   30.3s
[Parallel(n_jobs=-1)]: Done 10000 out of 10000 | elapsed:  1.1min finished
```

Discussion

In the recipes of this chapter, we have kept the number of candidate models small to make the code complete quickly. However, in the real world we will often have many thousands or tens of thousands of models to train. The end result is that it can take many hours to find the best model. To speed up the process, scikit-learn lets us train multiple models simultaneously. Without going into too much technical detail, scikit-learn can simultaneously train models up to the number of cores on the machine. Most modern laptops have four cores, so (assuming you are currently on a laptop) we can potentially train four models at the same time. This will dramatically increase the speed of our model selection process. The parameter n_jobs defines the number of models to train in parallel.

In our solution, we set n_jobs to -1, which tells scikit-learn to use *all* cores. However, by default n_jobs is set to 1, meaning it only uses one core. To demonstrate this, if we run the same GridSearch as in the solution, but with n_jobs=1, we can see it takes significantly longer to find the best model (note that exact time will depend on your computer):

```
# Create grid search using one core
clf = GridSearchCV(logistic, hyperparameters, cv=5, n_jobs=1, verbose=1)

# Fit grid search
best_model = clf.fit(features, target)
```

```
Fitting 5 folds for each of 2000 candidates, totalling 10000 fits


[Parallel(n_jobs=1)]: Done 10000 out of 10000 | elapsed:  2.8min finished
```

12.6 Speeding Up Model Selection Using Algorithm-Specific Methods

Problem

You need to speed up model selection.

Solution

If you are using a select number of learning algorithms, use scikit-learn's model-specific cross-validation hyperparameter tuning. For example, `LogisticRegressionCV`:

```
# Load libraries
from sklearn import linear_model, datasets

# Load data
iris = datasets.load_iris()
features = iris.data
target = iris.target

# Create cross-validated logistic regression
logit = linear_model.LogisticRegressionCV(Cs=100)

# Train model
logit.fit(features, target)

LogisticRegressionCV(Cs=100, class_weight=None, cv=None, dual=False,
          fit_intercept=True, intercept_scaling=1.0, max_iter=100,
          multi_class='ovr', n_jobs=1, penalty='l2', random_state=None,
          refit=True, scoring=None, solver='lbfgs', tol=0.0001, verbose=0)
```

Discussion

Sometimes the characteristics of a learning algorithm allow us to search for the best hyperparameters significantly faster than either brute force or randomized model search methods. In scikit-learn, many learning algorithms (e.g., ridge, lasso, and elastic net regression) have an algorithm-specific cross-validation method to take advantage of this. For example, `LogisticRegression` is used to conduct a standard logistic regression classifier, while `LogisticRegressionCV` implements an efficient cross-validated logistic regression classifier that has the ability to identify the optimum value of the hyperparameter C.

scikit-learn's `LogisticRegressionCV` method includes a parameter `Cs`. If supplied a list, `Cs` is the candidate hyperparameter values to select from. If supplied an integer, the parameter `Cs` generates a list of that many candidate values. The candidate values are drawn logarithmically from a range between 0.0001 and 1,0000 (a range of reasonable values for C).

However, a major downside to `LogisticRegressionCV` is that it can only search a range of values for C. In Recipe 12.1 our possible hyperparameter space included both C and another hyperparameter (the regularization penalty norm). This limitation is common to many of scikit-learn's model-specific cross-validated approaches.

See Also

- scikit-learn documentation: LogisticRegressionCV (*http://bit.ly/2GPJvjY*)
- scikit-learn documentation: Model specific cross-validation (*http://bit.ly/2F0TQsL*)

12.7 Evaluating Performance After Model Selection

Problem

You want to evaluate the performance of a model found through model selection.

Solution

Use nested cross-validation to avoid biased evaluation:

```
# Load libraries
import numpy as np
from sklearn import linear_model, datasets
from sklearn.model_selection import GridSearchCV, cross_val_score

# Load data
iris = datasets.load_iris()
features = iris.data
target = iris.target

# Create logistic regression
logistic = linear_model.LogisticRegression()

# Create range of 20 candidate values for C
C = np.logspace(0, 4, 20)

# Create hyperparameter options
hyperparameters = dict(C=C)
```

```
# Create grid search
gridsearch = GridSearchCV(logistic, hyperparameters, cv=5, n_jobs=-1, verbose=0)

# Conduct nested cross-validation and outut the average score
cross_val_score(gridsearch, features, target).mean()
```

```
0.95343137254901966
```

Discussion

Nested cross-validation during model selection is a difficult concept for many people to grasp the first time. Remember that in k-fold cross-validation, we train our model on *k-1* folds of the data, use this model to make predictions on the remaining fold, and then evaluate our model best on how well our model's predictions compare to the true values. We then repeat this process *k* times.

In the model selection searches described in this chapter (i.e., GridSearchCV and Ran domizedSearchCV), we used cross-validation to evaluate which hyperparameter values produced the best models. However, a nuanced and generally underappreciated problem arises: since we used the data to select the best hyperparameter values, we cannot use that same data to evaluate the model's performance. The solution? Wrap the cross-validation used for model search in another cross-validation! In nested cross-validation, the "inner" cross-validation selects the best model, while the "outer" cross-validation provides us with an unbiased evaluation of the model's performance. In our solution, the inner cross-validation is our GridSearchCV object, which we then wrap in an outer cross-validation using cross_val_score.

If you are confused, try a simple experiment. First, set verbose=1 so we can see what is happening:

```
gridsearch = GridSearchCV(logistic, hyperparameters, cv=5, verbose=1)
```

Next, run gridsearch.fit(features, target), which is our inner cross-validation used to find the best model:

```
best_model = gridsearch.fit(features, target)
```

```
Fitting 5 folds for each of 20 candidates, totalling 100 fits
```

```
[Parallel(n_jobs=1)]: Done 100 out of 100 | elapsed:    0.4s finished
```

From the output you can see the inner cross-validation trained 20 candidate models five times, totaling 100 models. Next, nest clf inside a new cross-validation, which defaults to three folds:

```
scores = cross_val_score(gridsearch, features, target)
```

```
Fitting 5 folds for each of 20 candidates, totalling 100 fits
```

```
[Parallel(n_jobs=1)]: Done 100 out of 100 | elapsed:    0.5s finished

Fitting 5 folds for each of 20 candidates, totalling 100 fits

[Parallel(n_jobs=1)]: Done 100 out of 100 | elapsed:    0.7s finished

Fitting 5 folds for each of 20 candidates, totalling 100 fits

[Parallel(n_jobs=1)]: Done 100 out of 100 | elapsed:    0.5s finished
```

The output shows that the inner cross-validation trained 20 models five times to find the best model, and this model was evaluated using an outer three-fold cross-validation, creating a total of 300 models trained.

## CHAPTER 13

Linear Regression

13.0 Introduction

Linear regression is one of the simplest supervised learning algorithms in our toolkit. If you have ever taken an introductory statistics course in college, likely the final topic you covered was linear regression. In fact, it is so simple that it is sometimes not considered machine learning at all! Whatever you believe, the fact is that linear regression—and its extensions—continues to be a common and useful method of making predictions when the target vector is a quantitative value (e.g., home price, age). In this chapter we will cover a variety of linear regression methods (and some extensions) for creating well-performing prediction models.

13.1 Fitting a Line

Problem

You want to train a model that represents a linear relationship between the feature and target vector.

Solution

Use a linear regression (in scikit-learn, `LinearRegression`):

```
# Load libraries
from sklearn.linear_model import LinearRegression
from sklearn.datasets import load_boston

# Load data with only two features
boston = load_boston()
features = boston.data[:,0:2]
target = boston.target
```

```
# Create linear regression
regression = LinearRegression()

# Fit the linear regression
model = regression.fit(features, target)
```

Discussion

Linear regression assumes that the relationship between the features and the target vector is approximately linear. That is, the *effect* (also called *coefficient, weight,* or *parameter*) of the features on the target vector is constant. In our solution, for the sake of explanation we have trained our model using only two features. This means our linear model will be:

$$\hat{y} = \hat{\beta}_0 + \hat{\beta}_1 x_1 + \hat{\beta}_2 x_2 + \epsilon$$

where $\hat{y}$ is our target, x_i is the data for a single feature, $\hat{\beta}_1$ and $\hat{\beta}_2$ are the coefficients identified by fitting the model, and ϵ is the error. After we have fit our model, we can view the value of each parameter. For example, $\hat{\beta}_0$, also called the *bias* or *intercept*, can be viewed using intercept_:

```
# View the intercept
model.intercept_
```

```
22.46681692105723
```

And $\hat{\beta}_1$ and $\hat{\beta}_2$ are shown using coef_:

```
# View the feature coefficients
model.coef_
```

```
array([-0.34977589,  0.11642402])
```

In our dataset, the target value is the median value of a Boston home (in the 1970s) in thousands of dollars. Therefore the price of the first home in the dataset is:

```
# First value in the target vector multiplied by 1000
target[0]*1000
```

```
24000.0
```

Using the predict method, we can predict a value for that house:

```
# Predict the target value of the first observation, multiplied by 1000
model.predict(features)[0]*1000
```

```
24560.23872370844
```

Not bad! Our model was only off by $560.24!

The major advantage of linear regression is its interpretability, in large part because the coefficients of the model are the effect of a one-unit change on the target vector. For example, the first feature in our solution is the number of crimes per resident. Our model's coefficient of this feature was ~–0.35, meaning that if we multiply this coefficient by 1,000 (since the target vector is the house price in thousands of dollars), we have the change in house price for each additional one crime per capita:

```
# First coefficient multiplied by 1000
model.coef_[0]*1000
```

```
-349.77588707748947
```

This says that every single crime per capita will decrease the price of the house by approximately $350!

13.2 Handling Interactive Effects

Problem

You have a feature whose effect on the target variable depends on another feature.

Solution

Create an interaction term to capture that dependence using scikit-learn's PolynomialFeatures:

```
# Load libraries
from sklearn.linear_model import LinearRegression
from sklearn.datasets import load_boston
from sklearn.preprocessing import PolynomialFeatures

# Load data with only two features
boston = load_boston()
features = boston.data[:,0:2]
target = boston.target

# Create interaction term
interaction = PolynomialFeatures(
    degree=3, include_bias=False, interaction_only=True)
features_interaction = interaction.fit_transform(features)

# Create linear regression
regression = LinearRegression()

# Fit the linear regression
model = regression.fit(features_interaction, target)
```

Discussion

Sometimes a feature's effect on our target variable is at least partially dependent on another feature. For example, imagine a simple coffee-based example where we have two binary features—the presence of sugar (`sugar`) and whether or not we have stirred (`stirred`)—and we want to predict if the coffee tastes sweet. Just putting sugar in the coffee (`sugar=1, stirred=0`) won't make the coffee taste sweet (all the sugar is at the bottom!) and just stirring the coffee without adding sugar (`sugar=0, stirred=1`) won't make it sweet either. Instead it is the interaction of putting sugar in the coffee *and* stirring the coffee (`sugar=1, stirred=1`) that will make a coffee taste sweet. The effects of `sugar` and `stir` on sweetness are dependent on each other. In this case we say there is an interaction effect between the features `sugar` and `stirred`.

We can account for interaction effects by including a new feature comprising the product of corresponding values from the interacting features:

$$\hat{y} = \hat{\beta}_0 + \hat{\beta}_1 x_1 + \hat{\beta}_2 x_2 + \hat{\beta}_3 x_1 x_2 + \epsilon$$

where x_1 and x_2 are the values of the `sugar` and `stirred`, respectively, and $x_1 x_2$ represents the interaction between the two.

In our solution, we used a dataset containing only two features. Here is the first observation's values for each of those features:

```
# View the feature values for first observation
features[0]

array([  6.32000000e-03,   1.80000000e+01])
```

To create an interaction term, we simply multiply those two values together for every observation:

```
# Import library
import numpy as np

# For each observation, multiply the values of the first and second feature
interaction_term = np.multiply(features[:, 0], features[:, 1])
```

We can then view the interaction term for the first observation:

```
# View interaction term for first observation
interaction_term[0]

0.11376
```

However, while often we will have a substantive reason for believing there is an interaction between two features, sometimes we will not. In those cases it can be useful to use scikit-learn's `PolynomialFeatures` to create interaction terms for all combinations of features. We can then use model selection strategies to identify the combination of features and interaction terms that produce the best model.

To create interaction terms using `PolynomialFeatures`, there are three important parameters we must set. Most important, `interaction_only=True` tells `Polynomial Features` to only return interaction terms (and not polynomial features, which we will discuss in Recipe 13.3). By default, `PolynomialFeatures` will add a feature containing ones called a bias. We can prevent that with `include_bias=False`. Finally, the `degree` parameter determines the maximum number of features to create interaction terms from (in case we wanted to create an interaction term that is the combination of three features). We can see the output of `PolynomialFeatures` from our solution by checking to see if the first observation's feature values and interaction term value match our manually calculated version:

```
# View the values of the first observation
features_interaction[0]

array([  6.32000000e-03,   1.80000000e+01,   1.13760000e-01])
```

13.3 Fitting a Nonlinear Relationship

Problem

You want to model a nonlinear relationship.

Solution

Create a polynomial regression by including polynomial features in a linear regression model:

```
# Load library
from sklearn.linear_model import LinearRegression
from sklearn.datasets import load_boston
from sklearn.preprocessing import PolynomialFeatures

# Load data with one feature
boston = load_boston()
features = boston.data[:,0:1]
target = boston.target

# Create polynomial features x^2 and x^3
polynomial = PolynomialFeatures(degree=3, include_bias=False)
features_polynomial = polynomial.fit_transform(features)

# Create linear regression
regression = LinearRegression()

# Fit the linear regression
model = regression.fit(features_polynomial, target)
```

Discussion

So far we have only discussed modeling linear relationships. An example of a linear relationship would be the number of stories a building has and the building's height. In linear regression, we assume the effect of number of stories and building height is approximately constant, meaning a 20-story building will be roughly twice as high as a 10-story building, which will be roughly twice as high as a 5-story building. Many relationships of interest, however, are not strictly linear.

Often we want to model a non-linear relationship—for example, the relationship between the number of hours a student studies and the score she gets on the test. Intuitively, we can imagine there is a big difference in test scores between students who study for one hour compared to students who did not study at all. However, there is a much smaller difference in test scores between a student who studied for 99 hours and a student who studied for 100 hours. The effect one hour of studying has on a student's test score decreases as the number of hours increases.

Polynomial regression is an extension of linear regression to allow us to model non-linear relationships. To create a polynomial regression, convert the linear function we used in Recipe 13.1:

$$\hat{y} = \hat{\beta}_0 + \hat{\beta}_1 x_1 + \epsilon$$

into a polynomial function by adding polynomial features:

$$\hat{y} = \hat{\beta}_0 + \hat{\beta}_1 x_1 + \hat{\beta}_2 x_1^2 + \ldots + \hat{\beta}_d x_i^d + \epsilon$$

where d is the degree of the polynomial. How are we able to use a linear regression for a nonlinear function? The answer is that we do not change how the linear regression fits the model, but rather only add polynomial features. That is, the linear regression does not "know" that the x^2 is a quadratic transformation of x. It just considers it one more variable.

A more practical description might be in order. To model nonlinear relationships, we can create new features that raise an existing feature, x, up to some power: x^2, x^3, and so on. The more of these new features we add, the more flexible the "line" created by our model. To make this more explicit, imagine we want to create a polynomial to the third degree. For the sake of simplicity, we will focus on only one observation (the first observation in the dataset), x_0:

```
# View first observation
features[0]

array([ 0.00632])
```

To create a polynomial feature, we would raise the first observation's value to the second degree, x_1^2:

```
# View first observation raised to the second power, x^2
features[0]**2

array([  3.99424000e-05])
```

This would be our new feature. We would then also raise the first observation's value to the third degree, x_1^3:

```
# View first observation raised to the third power, x^3
features[0]**3

array([  2.52435968e-07])
```

By including all three features (x, x^2, and x^3) in our feature matrix and then running a linear regression, we have conducted a polynomial regression:

```
# View the first observation's values for x, x^2, and x^3
features_polynomial[0]

array([  6.32000000e-03,   3.99424000e-05,   2.52435968e-07])
```

PolynomialFeatures has two important parameters. First, degree determines the maximum number of degrees for the polynomial features. For example, degree=3 will generate x^2 and x^3. Finally, by default PolynomialFeatures includes a feature containing only ones (called a bias). We can remove that by setting include_bias=False.

13.4 Reducing Variance with Regularization

Problem

You want to reduce the variance of your linear regression model.

Solution

Use a learning algorithm that includes a *shrinkage penalty* (also called *regularization*) like ridge regression and lasso regression:

```
# Load libraries
from sklearn.linear_model import Ridge
from sklearn.datasets import load_boston
from sklearn.preprocessing import StandardScaler

# Load data
boston = load_boston()
features = boston.data
target = boston.target

# Standardize features
scaler = StandardScaler()
```

```
features_standardized = scaler.fit_transform(features)

# Create ridge regression with an alpha value
regression = Ridge(alpha=0.5)

# Fit the linear regression
model = regression.fit(features_standardized, target)
```

Discussion

In standard linear regression the model trains to minimize the sum of squared error between the true (y_i) and prediction, ($\hat{y}_i$) target values, or residual sum of squares (RSS):

$$RSS = \sum_{i=1}^{n} (y_i - \hat{y}_i)^2$$

Regularized regression learners are similar, except they attempt to minimize RSS *and* some penalty for the total size of the coefficient values, called a shrinkage penalty because it attempts to "shrink" the model. There are two common types of regularized learners for linear regression: ridge regression and the lasso. The only formal difference is the type of shrinkage penalty used. In ridge regression, the shrinkage penalty is a tuning hyperparameter multiplied by the squared sum of all coefficients:

$$RSS + \alpha \sum_{j=1}^{p} \hat{\beta}_j^2$$

where $\hat{\beta}_j$ is the coefficient of the jth of p features and α is a hyperparameter (discussed next). The lasso is similar, except the shrinkage penalty is a tuning hyperparameter multiplied by the sum of the absolute value of all coefficients:

$$\frac{1}{2n}RSS + \alpha \sum_{j=1}^{p} |\hat{\beta}_j|$$

where n is the number of observations. So which one should we use? As a very general rule of thumb, ridge regression often produces slightly better predictions than lasso, but lasso (for reasons we will discuss in Recipe 13.5) produces more interpretable models. If we want a balance between ridge and lasso's penalty functions we can use elastic net, which is simply a regression model with both penalties included. Regardless of which one we use, both ridge and lasso regressions can penalize large or complex models by including coefficient values in the loss function we are trying to minimize.

The hyperparameter, α, lets us control how much we penalize the coefficients, with higher values of α creating simpler models. The ideal value of α should be tuned like any other hyperparameter. In scikit-learn, α is set using the alpha parameter.

scikit-learn includes a RidgeCV method that allows us to select the ideal value for α:

```
# Load library
from sklearn.linear_model import RidgeCV

# Create ridge regression with three alpha values
regr_cv = RidgeCV(alphas=[0.1, 1.0, 10.0])

# Fit the linear regression
model_cv = regr_cv.fit(features_standardized, target)

# View coefficients
model_cv.coef_

array([-0.91215884,  1.0658758 ,  0.11942614,  0.68558782, -2.03231631,
        2.67922108,  0.01477326, -3.0777265 ,  2.58814315, -2.00973173,
       -2.05390717,  0.85614763, -3.73565106])
```

We can then easily view the best model's α value:

```
# View alpha
model_cv.alpha_

1.0
```

One final note: because in linear regression the value of the coefficients is partially determined by the scale of the feature, and in regularized models all coefficients are summed together, we must make sure to standardize the feature prior to training.

13.5 Reducing Features with Lasso Regression

Problem

You want to simplify your linear regression model by reducing the number of features.

Solution

Use a lasso regression:

```
# Load library
from sklearn.linear_model import Lasso
from sklearn.datasets import load_boston
from sklearn.preprocessing import StandardScaler

# Load data
boston = load_boston()
```

```
features = boston.data
target = boston.target

# Standardize features
scaler = StandardScaler()
features_standardized = scaler.fit_transform(features)

# Create lasso regression with alpha value
regression = Lasso(alpha=0.5)

# Fit the linear regression
model = regression.fit(features_standardized, target)
```

Discussion

One interesting characteristic of lasso regression's penalty is that it can shrink the coefficients of a model to zero, effectively reducing the number of features in the model. For example, in our solution we set `alpha` to `0.5` and we can see that many of the coefficients are 0, meaning their corresponding features are not used in the model:

```
# View coefficients
model.coef_

array([-0.10697735,  0.        , -0.        ,  0.39739898, -0.        ,
        2.97332316, -0.        , -0.16937793, -0.        , -0.        ,
       -1.59957374,  0.54571511, -3.66888402])
```

However, if we increase α to a much higher value, we see that literally none of the features are being used:

```
# Create lasso regression with a high alpha
regression_a10 = Lasso(alpha=10)
model_a10 = regression_a10.fit(features_standardized, target)
model_a10.coef_

array([-0.,  0., -0.,  0., -0.,  0., -0.,  0., -0., -0., -0.,  0., -0.])
```

The practical benefit of this effect is that it means that we could include 100 features in our feature matrix and then, through adjusting lasso's α hyperparameter, produce a model that uses only 10 (for instance) of the most important features. This lets us reduce variance while improving the interpretability of our model (since fewer features is easier to explain).

## CHAPTER 14

Trees and Forests

14.0 Introduction

Tree-based learning algorithms are a broad and popular family of related non-parametric, supervised methods for both classification and regression. The basis of tree-based learners is the decision tree wherein a series of decision rules (e.g., "If their gender is male...") are chained. The result looks vaguely like an upside-down tree, with the first decision rule at the top and subsequent decision rules spreading out below. In a decision tree, every decision rule occurs at a decision node, with the rule creating branches leading to new nodes. A branch without a decision rule at the end is called a *leaf*.

One reason for the popularity of tree-based models is their interpretability. In fact, decision trees can literally be drawn out in their complete form (see Recipe 14.3) to create a highly intuitive model. From this basic tree system comes a wide variety of extensions from random forests to stacking. In this chapter we will cover how to train, handle, adjust, visualize, and evaluate a number of tree-based models.

14.1 Training a Decision Tree Classifier

Problem

You need to train a classifier using a decision tree.

Solution

Use scikit-learn's `DecisionTreeClassifier`:

```
# Load libraries
from sklearn.tree import DecisionTreeClassifier
```

```
from sklearn import datasets

# Load data
iris = datasets.load_iris()
features = iris.data
target = iris.target

# Create decision tree classifier object
decisiontree = DecisionTreeClassifier(random_state=0)

# Train model
model = decisiontree.fit(features, target)
```

Discussion

Decision tree learners attempt to find a decision rule that produces the greatest decrease in impurity at a node. While there are a number of measurements of impurity, by default `DecisionTreeClassifier` uses Gini impurity:

$$G(t) = 1 - \sum_{i=1}^{c} p_i^2$$

where $G(t)$ is the Gini impurity at node t and p_i is the proportion of observations of class c at node t. This process of finding the decision rules that create splits to increase impurity is repeated recursively until all leaf nodes are pure (i.e., contain only one class) or some arbitrary cut-off is reached.

In scikit-learn, `DecisionTreeClassifier` operates like other learning methods; after the model is trained using `fit` we can use the model to predict the class of an observation:

```
# Make new observation
observation = [[ 5,   4,   3,   2]]

# Predict observation's class
model.predict(observation)

array([1])
```

We can also see the predicted class probabilities of the observation:

```
# View predicted class probabilities for the three classes
model.predict_proba(observation)

array([[ 0.,   1.,   0.]])
```

Finally, if we want to use a different impurity measurement we can use the `criterion` parameter:

```
# Create decision tree classifier object using entropy
decisiontree_entropy = DecisionTreeClassifier(
```

```
          criterion='entropy', random_state=0)

# Train model
model_entropy = decisiontree_entropy.fit(features, target)
```

See Also

- Decision Tree Learning, Princeton (*http://bit.ly/2FqJxlj*)

14.2 Training a Decision Tree Regressor

Problem

You need to train a regression model using a decision tree.

Solution

Use scikit-learn's `DecisionTreeRegressor`:

```
# Load libraries
from sklearn.tree import DecisionTreeRegressor
from sklearn import datasets

# Load data with only two features
boston = datasets.load_boston()
features = boston.data[:,0:2]
target = boston.target

# Create decision tree classifier object
decisiontree = DecisionTreeRegressor(random_state=0)

# Train model
model = decisiontree.fit(features, target)
```

Discussion

Decision tree regression works similarly to decision tree classification; however, instead of reducing Gini impurity or entropy, potential splits are by default measured on how much they reduce mean squared error (MSE):

$$\text{MSE} = \frac{1}{n} \sum_{i=1}^{n} \left(y_i - \hat{y}_i \right)^2$$

where y_i is the true value of the target and $\hat{y}_i$ is the predicted value. In scikit-learn, decision tree regression can be conducted using `DecisionTreeRegressor`. Once we have trained a decision tree, we can use it to predict the target value for an observation:

```
# Make new observation
observation = [[0.02, 16]]

# Predict observation's value
model.predict(observation)

array([ 33.])
```

Just like with `DecisionTreeClassifier` we can use the `criterion` parameter to select the desired measurement of split quality. For example, we can construct a tree whose splits reduce mean absolute error (MAE):

```
# Create decision tree classifier object using entropy
decisiontree_mae = DecisionTreeRegressor(criterion="mae", random_state=0)

# Train model
model_mae = decisiontree_mae.fit(features, target)
```

See Also

- Decision Tree Regression, scikit-learn (*http://bit.ly/2GR63AZ*)

14.3 Visualizing a Decision Tree Model

Problem

You need to visualize a model created by a decision tree learning algorithm.

Solution

Export the decision tree model into DOT format, then visualize:

```
# Load libraries
import pydotplus
from sklearn.tree import DecisionTreeClassifier
from sklearn import datasets
from IPython.display import Image
from sklearn import tree

# Load data
iris = datasets.load_iris()
features = iris.data
target = iris.target

# Create decision tree classifier object
decisiontree = DecisionTreeClassifier(random_state=0)
```

```
# Train model
model = decisiontree.fit(features, target)

# Create DOT data
dot_data = tree.export_graphviz(decisiontree,
                                out_file=None,
                                feature_names=iris.feature_names,
                                class_names=iris.target_names)

# Draw graph
graph = pydotplus.graph_from_dot_data(dot_data)

# Show graph
Image(graph.create_png())
```

Discussion

One of the advantages of decision tree classifiers is that we can visualize the entire trained model—making decision trees one of the most interpretable models in machine learning. In our solution, we exported our trained model in DOT format (a graph description language) and then used that to draw the graph.

If we look at the root node, we can see the decision rule is that if petal widths are less than or equal to 0.8, then go to the left branch; if not, go to the right branch. We can also see the Gini impurity index (0.667), the number of observations (150), the number of observations in each class ([50,50,50]), and the class the observations would be predicted to be if we stopped at that node (setosa). We can also see that at that node the learner found that a single decision rule (petal width (cm) <= 0.8) was able to perfectly identify all of the setosa class observations. Furthermore, with one more decision rule with the same feature (petal width (cm) <= 1.75) the decision tree is able to correctly classify 144 of 150 observations. This makes petal width a very important feature!

If we want to use the decision tree in other applications or reports, we can easily export the visualization into PDF or a PNG image:

```
# Create PDF
graph.write_pdf("iris.pdf")

True

# Create PNG
graph.write_png("iris.png")

True
```

While this solution visualized a decision tree classifier, it can just as easily be used to visualize a decision tree regressor.

Note: macOS users might have to install GraphViz's executable to run the preceding code. This can be done using Homebrew: brew install graphviz. For Homebrew installation instructions, visit Homebrew's website.

See Also

- Homebrew (*https://brew.sh*)

14.4 Training a Random Forest Classifier

Problem

You want to train a classification model using a "forest" of randomized decision trees.

Solution

Train a random forest classification model using scikit-learn's RandomForestClassifier:

```
# Load libraries
from sklearn.ensemble import RandomForestClassifier
from sklearn import datasets

# Load data
iris = datasets.load_iris()
features = iris.data
target = iris.target

# Create random forest classifier object
randomforest = RandomForestClassifier(random_state=0, n_jobs=-1)

# Train model
model = randomforest.fit(features, target)
```

Discussion

A common problem with decision trees is that they tend to fit the training data too closely (i.e., overfitting). This has motivated the widespread use of an ensemble learning method called *random forest*. In a random forest, many decision trees are trained, but each tree only receives a bootstrapped sample of observations (i.e., a random sample of observations with replacement that matches the original number of observations) and each node only considers a subset of features when determining the best split. This forest of randomized decision trees (hence the name) votes to determine the predicted class.

As we can see by comparing this solution to Recipe 14.1, scikit-learn's RandomForest Classifier works similarly to DecisionTreeClassifier:

```
# Make new observation
observation = [[ 5,  4,  3,  2]]

# Predict observation's class
model.predict(observation)

array([1])
```

RandomForestClassifier also uses many of the same parameters as DecisionTree Classifier. For example, we can change the measure of split quality used:

```
# Create random forest classifier object using entropy
randomforest_entropy = RandomForestClassifier(
    criterion="entropy", random_state=0)

# Train model
model_entropy = randomforest_entropy.fit(features, target)
```

However, being a forest rather than an individual decision tree, RandomForestClassi fier has certain parameters that are either unique to random forests or particularly important. First, the max_features parameter determines the maximum number of features to be considered at each node and takes a number of arguments including integers (number of features), floats (percentage of features), and `sqrt` (square root of the number of features). By default, `max_features` is set to `auto`, which acts the same as `sqrt`. Second, the `bootstrap` parameter allows us to set whether the subset of observations considered for a tree is created using sampling with replacement (the default setting) or without replacement. Third, `n_estimators` sets the number of decision trees to include in the forest. In Recipe 10.4 we treated `n_estimators` as a hyperparameter and visualized the effect of increasing the number of trees on an evaluation metric. Finally, while not specific to random forest classifiers, because we are effectively training many decision tree models, it is often useful to use all available cores by setting `n_jobs=-1`.

See Also

- Random Forests, Berkeley Statistics (*http://bit.ly/2Fxm0Ps*)

14.5 Training a Random Forest Regressor

Problem

You want to train a regression model using a "forest" of randomized decision trees.

Solution

Train a random forest regression model using scikit-learn's `RandomForestRegressor`:

```
# Load libraries
from sklearn.ensemble import RandomForestRegressor
from sklearn import datasets

# Load data with only two features
boston = datasets.load_boston()
features = boston.data[:,0:2]
target = boston.target

# Create random forest classifier object
randomforest = RandomForestRegressor(random_state=0, n_jobs=-1)

# Train model
model = randomforest.fit(features, target)
```

Discussion

Just like how we can make a forest of decision tree classifiers, we can make a forest of decision tree regressors where each tree uses a bootstrapped subset of observations and at each node the decision rule considers only a subset of features. As with Random ForestClassifier we have certain important parameters:

- max_features sets the maximum number of features to consider at each node. Defaults to $\sqrt{p}$ features, where p is the total number of features.
- bootstrap sets whether or not to sample with replacement. Defaults to True.
- n_estimators sets the number of decision trees to construct. Defaults to 10.

See Also

- RandomForestRegressor, scikit-learn (*http://bit.ly/2GQZ3nx*)

14.6 Identifying Important Features in Random Forests

Problem

You need to know which features are most important in a random forest model.

Solution

Calculate and visualize the importance of each feature:

```
# Load libraries
import numpy as np
import matplotlib.pyplot as plt
from sklearn.ensemble import RandomForestClassifier
from sklearn import datasets

# Load data
iris = datasets.load_iris()
features = iris.data
target = iris.target

# Create random forest classifier object
randomforest = RandomForestClassifier(random_state=0, n_jobs=-1)

# Train model
model = randomforest.fit(features, target)

# Calculate feature importances
importances = model.feature_importances_

# Sort feature importances in descending order
indices = np.argsort(importances)[::-1]

# Rearrange feature names so they match the sorted feature importances
```

```
names = [iris.feature_names[i] for i in indices]

# Create plot
plt.figure()

# Create plot title
plt.title("Feature Importance")

# Add bars
plt.bar(range(features.shape[1]), importances[indices])

# Add feature names as x-axis labels
plt.xticks(range(features.shape[1]), names, rotation=90)

# Show plot
plt.show()
```

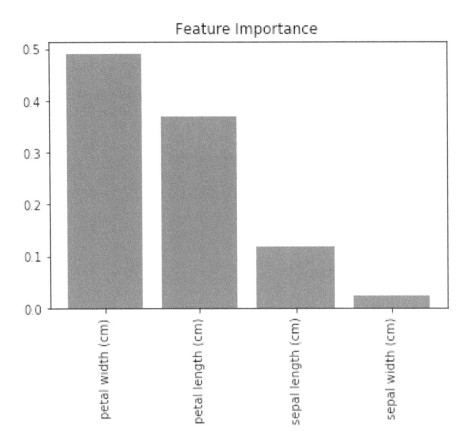

Discussion

One of the major benefits of decision trees is interpretability. Specifically, we can visualize the entire model (see Recipe 13.3). However, a random forest model is comprised of tens, hundreds, even thousands of decision trees. This makes a simple, intuitive visualization of a random forest model impractical. That said, there is another option: we can compare (and visualize) the relative importance of each feature.

In Recipe 13.3, we visualized a decision tree classifier model and saw that decision rules based only on petal width were able to classify many observations correctly. Intuitively, we can say that this means that petal width is an important feature in our classifier. More formally, features with splits that have the greater mean decrease in impurity (e.g., Gini impurity or entropy in classifiers and variance in regressors) are considered more important.

However, there are two things to keep in mind regarding feature importance. First, scikit-learn requires that we break up nominal categorical features into multiple binary features. This has the effect of spreading the importance of that feature across all of the binary features and can often make each feature appear to be unimportant even when the original nominal categorical feature is highly important. Second, if two features are highly correlated, one feature will claim much of the importance, making the other feature appear to be far less important—which has implications for interpretation if not considered.

In scikit-learn, classification and regression decision trees and random forests can report the relative importance of each feature using the `feature_importances_` method:

```
# View feature importances
model.feature_importances_

array([ 0.11896532,  0.0231668 ,  0.36804744,  0.48982043])
```

The higher the number, the more important the feature (all importance scores sum to 1). By plotting these values we can add interpretability to our random forest models.

14.7 Selecting Important Features in Random Forests

Problem

You need to conduct feature selection on a random forest.

Solution

Identify the importance features and retrain the model using only the most important features:

```
# Load libraries
from sklearn.ensemble import RandomForestClassifier
from sklearn import datasets
from sklearn.feature_selection import SelectFromModel

# Load data
iris = datasets.load_iris()
features = iris.data
target = iris.target

# Create random forest classifier
randomforest = RandomForestClassifier(random_state=0, n_jobs=-1)

# Create object that selects features with importance greater
# than or equal to a threshold
selector = SelectFromModel(randomforest, threshold=0.3)

# Feature new feature matrix using selector
features_important = selector.fit_transform(features, target)

# Train random forest using most important featres
model = randomforest.fit(features_important, target)
```

Discussion

There are situations where we might want to reduce the number of features in our model. For example, we might want to reduce the model's variance or we might want to improve interpretability by including only the most important features.

In scikit-learn we can use a simple two-stage workflow to create a model with reduced features. First, we train a random forest model using all features. Then, we use this model to identify the most important features. Next, we create a new feature matrix that includes only these features. In our solution, we used the `SelectFromMo del` method to create a feature matrix containing only features with an importance greater than or equal to some `threshold` value. Finally, we created a new model using only those features.

It must be noted that there are two caveats to this approach. First, nominal categorical features that have been one-hot encoded will see the feature importance diluted across the binary features. Second, the feature importance of highly correlated features will be effectively assigned to one feature and not evenly distributed across both features.

See Also

- Variable selection using Random Forests, Robin Genuer, Jean-Michel Poggi, Christine Tuleau-Malot (*http://bit.ly/2FvG70D*)

14.8 Handling Imbalanced Classes

Problem

You have a target vector with highly imbalanced classes and want to train a random forest model.

Solution

Train a decision tree or random forest model with `class_weight="balanced"`:

```
# Load libraries
import numpy as np
from sklearn.ensemble import RandomForestClassifier
from sklearn import datasets

# Load data
iris = datasets.load_iris()
features = iris.data
target = iris.target

# Make class highly imbalanced by removing first 40 observations
features = features[40:,:]
target = target[40:]

# Create target vector indicating if class 0, otherwise 1
target = np.where((target == 0), 0, 1)

# Create random forest classifier object
randomforest = RandomForestClassifier(
    random_state=0, n_jobs=-1, class_weight="balanced")

# Train model
model = randomforest.fit(features, target)
```

Discussion

Imbalanced classes are a common problem when we are doing machine learning in the real world. Left unaddressed, the presence of imbalanced classes can reduce the performance of our model. We already talked about a few strategies for handling imbalanced classes during preprocessing in Recipe 17.5. However, many learning algorithms in scikit-learn come with built-in methods for correcting for imbalanced classes. We can set `RandomForestClassifier` to correct for imbalanced classes using the `class_weight` parameter. If supplied with a dictionary in the form of class names and respective desired weights (e.g., `{"male": 0.2, "female": 0.8}`), `RandomForestClassifier` will weight the classes accordingly. However, often a more useful argument is `balanced`, wherein classes are automatically weighted inversely proportional to how frequently they appear in the data:

$$w_j = \frac{n}{kn_j}$$

where w_j is the weight to class j, n is the number of observations, n_j is the number of observations in class j, and k is the total number of classes. For example, in our solution we have 2 classes (k), 110 observations (n), and 10 and 100 observations in each class, respectively (n_j). If we weight the classes using class_weight="balanced", then the smaller class is weighted more:

```
# Calculate weight for small class
110/(2*10)

5.5
```

while the larger class is weighted less:

```
# Calculate weight for large class
110/(2*100)

0.55
```

14.9 Controlling Tree Size

Problem

You want to manually determine the structure and size of a decision tree.

Solution

Use the tree structure parameters in scikit-learn tree-based learning algorithms:

```
# Load libraries
from sklearn.tree import DecisionTreeClassifier
from sklearn import datasets

# Load data
iris = datasets.load_iris()
features = iris.data
target = iris.target

# Create decision tree classifier object
decisiontree = DecisionTreeClassifier(random_state=0,
                                      max_depth=None,
                                      min_samples_split=2,
                                      min_samples_leaf=1,
                                      min_weight_fraction_leaf=0,
                                      max_leaf_nodes=None,
                                      min_impurity_decrease=0)
```

```
# Train model
model = decisiontree.fit(features, target)
```

Discussion

scikit-learn's tree-based learning algorithms have a variety of techniques for control-ling the size of the decision tree(s). These are accessed through parameters:

max_depth
> Maximum depth of the tree. If None, the tree is grown until all leaves are pure. If an integer, the tree is effectively "pruned" to that depth.

min_samples_split
> Minimum number of observations at a node before that node is split. If an inte-ger is supplied as an argument it determines the raw minimum, while if a float is supplied the minimum is the percent of total observations.

min_samples_leaf
> Minimum number of observations required to be at a leaf. Uses the same argu-ments as min_samples_split.

max_leaf_nodes
> Maximum number of leaves.

min_impurity_split
> Minimum impurity decrease required before a split is performed.

While it is useful to know these parameters exist, most likely we will only be using max_depth and min_impurity_split because shallower trees (sometimes called *stumps*) are simpler models and thus have lower variance.

14.10 Improving Performance Through Boosting

Problem

You need a model with better performance than decision trees or random forests.

Solution

Train a boosted model using AdaBoostClassifier or AdaBoostRegressor:

```
# Load libraries
from sklearn.ensemble import AdaBoostClassifier
from sklearn import datasets

# Load data
iris = datasets.load_iris()
features = iris.data
```

```
target = iris.target

# Create adaboost tree classifier object
adaboost = AdaBoostClassifier(random_state=0)

# Train model
model = adaboost.fit(features, target)
```

Discussion

In random forest, an ensemble (group) of randomized decision trees predicts the target vector. An alternative, and often more powerful, approach is called *boosting*. In one form of boosting called AdaBoost, we iteratively train a series of weak models (most often a shallow decision tree, sometimes called a stump), each iteration giving higher priority to observations the previous model predicted incorrectly. More specifically, in AdaBoost:

1. Assign every observation, x_i, an initial weight value, $w_i = \frac{1}{n}$, where n is the total number of observations in the data.

2. Train a "weak" model on the data.

3. For each observation:

    a. If weak model predicts x_i correctly, w_i is increased.

    b. If weak model predicts x_i incorrectly, w_i is decreased.

4. Train a new weak model where observations with greater w_i are given greater priority.

5. Repeat steps 4 and 5 until the data is perfectly predicted or a preset number of weak models has been trained.

The end result is an aggregated model where individual weak models focus on more difficult (from a prediction perspective) observations. In scikit-learn, we can implement AdaBoost using `AdaBoostClassifier` or `AdaBoostRegressor`. The most important parameters are `base_estimator`, `n_estimators`, and `learning_rate`:

- `base_estimator` is the learning algorithm to use to train the weak models. This will almost always not need to be changed because by far the most common learner to use with AdaBoost is a decision tree—the parameter's default argument.

- `n_estimators` is the number of models to iteratively train.

- `learning_rate` is the contribution of each model to the weights and defaults to 1. Reducing the learning rate will mean the weights will be increased or decreased to a small degree, forcing the model to train slower (but sometimes resulting in better performance scores).

- loss is exclusive to `AdaBoostRegressor` and sets the loss function to use when updating weights. This defaults to a linear loss function, but can be changed to `square` or `exponential`.

See Also

- Explaining AdaBoost, Robert E. Schapire (*http://bit.ly/2FCS30E*)

14.11 Evaluating Random Forests with Out-of-Bag Errors

Problem

You need to evaluate a random forest model without using cross-validation.

Solution

Calculate the model's out-of-bag score:

```
# Load libraries
from sklearn.ensemble import RandomForestClassifier
from sklearn import datasets

# Load data
iris = datasets.load_iris()
features = iris.data
target = iris.target

# Create random tree classifier object
randomforest = RandomForestClassifier(
    random_state=0, n_estimators=1000, oob_score=True, n_jobs=-1)

# Train model
model = randomforest.fit(features, target)

# View out-of-bag-error
randomforest.oob_score_

0.95333333333333337
```

Discussion

In random forests, each decision tree is trained using a bootstrapped subset of observations. This means that for every tree there is a separate subset of observations not being used to train that tree. These are called out-of-bag (OOB) observations. We can use OOB observations as a test set to evaluate the performance of our random forest.

For every observation, the learning algorithm compares the observation's true value with the prediction from a subset of trees not trained using that observation. The overall score is calculated and provides a single measure of a random forest's performance. OOB score estimation is an alternative to cross-validation.

In scikit-learn, we can OOB scores of a random forest by setting oob_score=True in the random forest object (i.e., RandomForestClassifier). The score can be retrieved using oob_score_.

## CHAPTER 15

K-Nearest Neighbors

15.0 Introduction

The K-Nearest Neighbors classifier (KNN) is one of the simplest yet most commonly used classifiers in supervised machine learning. KNN is often considered a lazy learner; it doesn't technically train a model to make predictions. Instead an observation is predicted to be the class of that of the largest proportion of the k nearest observations. For example, if an observation with an unknown class is surrounded by an observation of class 1, then the observation is classified as class 1. In this chapter we will explore how to use scikit-learn to create and use a KNN classifier.

15.1 Finding an Observation's Nearest Neighbors

Problem

You need to find an observation's k nearest observations (neighbors).

Solution

Use scikit-learn's NearestNeighbors:

```
# Load libraries
from sklearn import datasets
from sklearn.neighbors import NearestNeighbors
from sklearn.preprocessing import StandardScaler

# Load data
iris = datasets.load_iris()
features = iris.data

# Create standardizer
```

```
standardizer = StandardScaler()

# Standardize features
features_standardized = standardizer.fit_transform(features)

# Two nearest neighbors
nearest_neighbors = NearestNeighbors(n_neighbors=2).fit(features_standardized)

# Create an observation
new_observation = [ 1,  1,  1,  1]

# Find distances and indices of the observation's nearest neighbors
distances, indices = nearest_neighbors.kneighbors([new_observation])

# View the nearest neighbors
features_standardized[indices]
array([[[ 1.03800476,  0.56925129,  1.10395287,  1.1850097 ],
        [ 0.79566902,  0.33784833,  0.76275864,  1.05353673]]])
```

Discussion

In our solution we used the dataset of Iris flowers. We created an observation, new_observation, with some values and then found the two observations that are closest to our observation. indices contains the locations of the observations in our dataset that are closest, so X[indices] displays the values of those observations. Intuitively, distance can be thought of as a measure of similarity, so the two closest observations are the two flowers most similar to the flower we created.

How do we measure distance? scikit-learn offers a wide variety of distance metrics, d, including Euclidean:

$$d_{euclidean} = \sqrt{\sum_{i=1}^{n}(x_i - y_i)^2}$$

and Manhattan distance:

$$d_{manhattan} = \sum_{i=1}^{n}|x_i - y_i|$$

By default, NearestNeighbors uses Minkowski distance:

$$d_{minkowski} = \left(\sum_{i=1}^{n}|x_i - y_i|^p\right)^{1/p}$$

where x_i and y_i are the two observations we are calculating the distance between. Minkowski includes a hyperparameter, p, where $p = 1$ is Manhattan distance and $p = 2$ is Euclidean distance, and so on. By default in scikit-learn $p = 2$.

We can set the distance metric using the metric parameter:

```
# Find two nearest neighbors based on euclidean distance
nearestneighbors_euclidean = NearestNeighbors(
n_neighbors=2, metric='euclidean').fit(features_standardized)
```

The distance variable we created contains the actual distance measurement to each of the two nearest neighbors:

```
# View distances
distances
```

```
array([[ 0.48168828,  0.73440155]])
```

In addition, we can use kneighbors_graph to create a matrix indicating each observation's nearest neighbors:

```
# Find each observation's three nearest neighbors
# based on euclidean distance (including itself)
nearestneighbors_euclidean = NearestNeighbors(
n_neighbors=3, metric="euclidean").fit(features_standardized)

# List of lists indicating each observation's 3 nearest neighbors
# (including itself)
nearest_neighbors_with_self = nearestneighbors_euclidean.kneighbors_graph(
    features_standardized).toarray()

# Remove 1's marking an observation is a nearest neighbor to itself
for i, x in enumerate(nearest_neighbors_with_self):
    x[i] = 0

# View first observation's two nearest neighbors
nearest_neighbors_with_self[0]
```

```
array([ 0.,  0.,  0.,  0.,  0.,  0.,  0.,  0.,  0.,  0.,  0.,  0.,  0.,
        0.,  0.,  0.,  0.,  1.,  0.,  0.,  0.,  0.,  0.,  0.,  0.,  0.,
        0.,  1.,  0.,  0.,  0.,  0.,  0.,  0.,  0.,  0.,  0.,  0.,  0.,
        0.,  0.,  0.,  0.,  0.,  0.,  0.,  0.,  0.,  0.,  0.,  0.,  0.,
        0.,  0.,  0.,  0.,  0.,  0.,  0.,  0.,  0.,  0.,  0.,  0.,  0.,
        0.,  0.,  0.,  0.,  0.,  0.,  0.,  0.,  0.,  0.,  0.,  0.,  0.,
        0.,  0.,  0.,  0.,  0.,  0.,  0.,  0.,  0.,  0.,  0.,  0.,  0.,
        0.,  0.,  0.,  0.,  0.,  0.,  0.,  0.,  0.,  0.,  0.,  0.,  0.,
        0.,  0.,  0.,  0.,  0.,  0.,  0.,  0.,  0.,  0.,  0.,  0.,  0.,
        0.,  0.,  0.,  0.,  0.,  0.,  0.,  0.,  0.,  0.,  0.,  0.,  0.,
        0.,  0.,  0.,  0.,  0.,  0.,  0.,  0.,  0.,  0.,  0.,  0.,  0.,
        0.,  0.,  0.,  0.,  0.,  0.,  0.])
```

When we are finding nearest neighbors or using any learning algorithm based on distance, it is important to transform features so that they are on the same scale. The reason is because the distance metrics treat all features as if they were on the same scale, but if one feature is in millions of dollars and a second feature is in percentages, the distance calculated will be biased toward the former. In our solution we addressed this potential issue by standardizing the features using `StandardScaler`.

15.2 Creating a K-Nearest Neighbor Classifier

Problem

Given an observation of unknown class, you need to predict its class based on the class of its neighbors.

Solution

If the dataset is not very large, use `KNeighborsClassifier`:

```
# Load libraries
from sklearn.neighbors import KNeighborsClassifier
from sklearn.preprocessing import StandardScaler
from sklearn import datasets

# Load data
iris = datasets.load_iris()
X = iris.data
y = iris.target

# Create standardizer
standardizer = StandardScaler()

# Standardize features
X_std = standardizer.fit_transform(X)

# Train a KNN classifier with 5 neighbors
knn = KNeighborsClassifier(n_neighbors=5, n_jobs=-1).fit(X_std, y)

# Create two observations
new_observations = [[ 0.75,  0.75,  0.75,  0.75],
                    [ 1,  1,  1,  1]]

# Predict the class of two observations
knn.predict(new_observations)

array([1, 2])
```

Discussion

In KNN, given an observation, x_u, with an unknown target class, the algorithm first identifies the k closest observations (sometimes called x_u's neighborhood) based on some distance metric (e.g., Euclidean distance), then these k observations "vote" based on their class, and the class that wins the vote is x_u's predicted class. More formally, the probability x_u is some class j is:

$$\frac{1}{k} \sum_{i \in v} I(y_i = j)$$

where v is the k observation in x_u's neighborhood, y_i is the class of the ith observation, and I is an indicator function (i.e., 1 is true, 0 otherwise). In scikit-learn we can see these probabilities using `predict_proba`:

```
# View probability each observation is one of three classes
knn.predict_proba(new_observations)

array([[ 0. ,  0.6,  0.4],
       [ 0. ,  0. ,  1. ]])
```

The class with the highest probability becomes the predicted class. For example, in the preceding output, the first observation should be class 1 ($Pr = 0.6$) while the second observation should be class 2 ($Pr = 1$), and this is just what we see:

```
knn.predict(new_observations)

array([1, 2])
```

`KNeighborsClassifier` contains a number of important parameters to consider. First, `metric` sets the distance metric used (discussed more in Recipe 14.1). Second, `n_jobs` determines how many of the computer's cores to use. Because making a prediction requires calculating the distance from a point to every single point in the data, using multiple cores is highly recommended. Third, `algorithm` sets the method used to calculate the nearest neighbors. While there are real differences in the algorithms, by default `KNeighborsClassifier` attempts to auto-select the best algorithm so you often don't need to worry about this parameter. Fourth, by default `KNeighborsClassifier` works how we described previously, with each observation in the neighborhood getting one vote; however, if we set the `weights` parameter to `distance`, the closer observations' votes are weighted more than observations farther away. Intuitively this make sense, since more similar neighbors might tell us more about an observation's class than others.

Finally, as discussed in Recipe 14.1, because distance calculations treat all features as if they are on the same scale, it is important to standardize the features prior to using a KNN classifier.

15.3 Identifying the Best Neighborhood Size

Problem

You want to select the best value for k in a k-nearest neighbors classifier.

Solution

Use model selection techniques like `GridSearchCV`:

```
# Load libraries
from sklearn.neighbors import KNeighborsClassifier
from sklearn import datasets
from sklearn.preprocessing import StandardScaler
from sklearn.pipeline import Pipeline, FeatureUnion
from sklearn.model_selection import GridSearchCV

# Load data
iris = datasets.load_iris()
features = iris.data
target = iris.target

# Create standardizer
standardizer = StandardScaler()

# Standardize features
features_standardized = standardizer.fit_transform(features)

# Create a KNN classifier
knn = KNeighborsClassifier(n_neighbors=5, n_jobs=-1)

# Create a pipeline
pipe = Pipeline([("standardizer", standardizer), ("knn", knn)])

# Create space of candidate values
search_space = [{"knn__n_neighbors": [1, 2, 3, 4, 5, 6, 7, 8, 9, 10]}]

# Create grid search
classifier = GridSearchCV(
    pipe, search_space, cv=5, verbose=0).fit(features_standardized, target)
```

Discussion

The size of k has real implications in KNN classifiers. In machine learning we are try-ing to find a balance between bias and variance, and in few places is that as explicit as the value of k. If $k = n$ where n is the number of observations, then we have high bias but low variance. If $k = 1$, we will have low bias but high variance. The best model will come from finding the value of k that balances this bias-variance trade-off. In our sol-ution, we used `GridSearchCV` to conduct five-fold cross-validation on KNN classifiers with different values of *k*. When that is completed, we can see the *k* that produces the best model:

```
# Best neighborhood size (k)
classifier.best_estimator_.get_params()["knn__n_neighbors"]
```

```
6
```

15.4 Creating a Radius-Based Nearest Neighbor Classifier

Problem

Given an observation of unknown class, you need to predict its class based on the class of all observations within a certain distance.

Solution

Use RadiusNeighborsClassifier:

```
# Load libraries
from sklearn.neighbors import RadiusNeighborsClassifier
from sklearn.preprocessing import StandardScaler
from sklearn import datasets

# Load data
iris = datasets.load_iris()
features = iris.data
target = iris.target

# Create standardizer
standardizer = StandardScaler()

# Standardize features
features_standardized = standardizer.fit_transform(features)

# Train a radius neighbors classifier
rnn = RadiusNeighborsClassifier(
    radius=.5, n_jobs=-1).fit(features_standardized, target)

# Create two observations
new_observations = [[ 1,  1,  1,  1]]

# Predict the class of two observations
rnn.predict(new_observations)
```

```
array([2])
```

Discussion

In KNN classification, an observation's class is predicted from the classes of its *k* neighbors. A less common technique is classification in a radius-based (RNN) classifier, where an observation's class is predicted from the classes of all observations within a given radius r. In scikit-learn RadiusNeighborsClassifier is very similar to KNeighborsClassifier, with the exception of two parameters. First, in RadiusNeigh borsClassifier we need to specify the radius of the fixed area used to determine if an observation is a neighbor using radius. Unless there is some substantive reason for setting radius to some value, it is best to treat it like any other hyperparameter and tune it during model selection. The second useful parameter is outlier_label, which indicates what label to give an observation that has no observations within the radius—which itself can often be a useful tool for identifying outliers.

## CHAPTER 16

Logistic Regression

16.0 Introduction

Despite being called a regression, logistic regression is actually a widely used supervised classification technique. Logistic regression and its extensions, like multinomial logistic regression, allow us to predict the probability that an observation is of a certain class using a straightforward and well-understood approach. In this chapter, we will cover training a variety of classifiers using scikit-learn.

16.1 Training a Binary Classifier

Problem

You need to train a simple classifier model.

Solution

Train a logistic regression in scikit-learn using `LogisticRegression`:

```
# Load libraries
from sklearn.linear_model import LogisticRegression
from sklearn import datasets
from sklearn.preprocessing import StandardScaler

# Load data with only two classes
iris = datasets.load_iris()
features = iris.data[:100,:]
target = iris.target[:100]

# Standardize features
scaler = StandardScaler()
features_standardized = scaler.fit_transform(features)
```

```
# Create logistic regression object
logistic_regression = LogisticRegression(random_state=0)

# Train model
model = logistic_regression.fit(features_standardized, target)
```

Discussion

Despite having "regression" in its name, a logistic regression is actually a widely used binary classifier (i.e., the target vector can only take two values). In a logistic regression, a linear model (e.g., $\beta_0 + \beta_1 x$) is included in a logistic (also called sigmoid) function, $\frac{1}{1 + e^{-z}}$, such that:

$$P(y_i = 1 \mid X) = \frac{1}{1 + e^{-(\beta_0 + \beta_1 x)}}$$

where $P(y_i = 1 \mid X)$ is the probability of the ith observation's target value, y_i, being class 1, X is the training data, β_0 and β_1 are the parameters to be learned, and e is Euler's number. The effect of the logistic function is to constrain the value of the function's output to between 0 and 1 so that it can be interpreted as a probability. If $P(y_i = 1 \mid X)$ is greater than 0.5, class 1 is predicted; otherwise, class 0 is predicted.

In scikit-learn, we can learn a logistic regression model using `LogisticRegression`. Once it is trained, we can use the model to predict the class of new observations:

```
# Create new observation
new_observation = [[.5, .5, .5, .5]]

# Predict class
model.predict(new_observation)

array([1])
```

In this example, our observation was predicted to be class 1. Additionally, we can see the probability that an observation is a member of each class:

```
# View predicted probabilities
model.predict_proba(new_observation)

array([[ 0.18823041,  0.81176959]])
```

Our observation had an 18.8% chance of being class 0 and 81.1% chance of being class 1.

16.2 Training a Multiclass Classifier

Problem

Given more than two classes, you need to train a classifier model.

Solution

Train a logistic regression in scikit-learn with `LogisticRegression` using one-vs-rest or multinomial methods:

```
# Load libraries
from sklearn.linear_model import LogisticRegression
from sklearn import datasets
from sklearn.preprocessing import StandardScaler

# Load data
iris = datasets.load_iris()
features = iris.data
target = iris.target

# Standardize features
scaler = StandardScaler()
features_standardized = scaler.fit_transform(features)

# Create one-vs-rest logistic regression object
logistic_regression = LogisticRegression(random_state=0, multi_class="ovr")

# Train model
model = logistic_regression.fit(features_standardized, target)
```

Discussion

On their own, logistic regressions are only binary classifiers, meaning they cannot handle target vectors with more than two classes. However, two clever extensions to logistic regression do just that. First, in one-vs-rest logistic regression (OVR) a separate model is trained for each class predicted whether an observation is that class or not (thus making it a binary classification problem). It assumes that each classification problem (e.g., class 0 or not) is independent.

Alternatively, in multinomial logistic regression (MLR) the logistic function we saw in Recipe 15.1 is replaced with a softmax function:

$$P(y_i = k \mid X) = \frac{e^{\beta_k x_i}}{\sum_{j=1}^{K} e^{\beta_j x_i}}$$

where $P(y_i = k \mid X)$ is the probability of the ith observation's target value, y_i, is class k, and K is the total number of classes. One practical advantage of the MLR is that its predicted probabilities using the `predict_proba` method are more reliable (i.e., better calibrated).

When using `LogisticRegression` we can select which of the two techniques we want, with OVR, `ovr`, being the default argument. We can switch to an MNL by setting the argument to `multinomial`.

16.3 Reducing Variance Through Regularization

Problem

You need to reduce the variance of your logistic regression model.

Solution

Tune the regularization strength hyperparameter, C:

```
# Load libraries
from sklearn.linear_model import LogisticRegressionCV
from sklearn import datasets
from sklearn.preprocessing import StandardScaler

# Load data
iris = datasets.load_iris()
features = iris.data
target = iris.target

# Standardize features
scaler = StandardScaler()
features_standardized = scaler.fit_transform(features)

# Create decision tree classifier object
logistic_regression = LogisticRegressionCV(
    penalty='l2', Cs=10, random_state=0, n_jobs=-1)

# Train model
model = logistic_regression.fit(features_standardized, target)
```

Discussion

Regularization is a method of penalizing complex models to reduce their variance. Specifically, a penalty term is added to the loss function we are trying to minimize, typically the L1 and L2 penalties. In the L1 penalty:

$$\alpha \sum_{j=1}^{p} |\hat{\beta}_j|$$

where $\hat{\beta}_j$ is the parameters of the jth of p features being learned and α is a hyperparameter denoting the regularization strength. With the L2 penalty:

$$\alpha \sum_{j=1}^{p} \hat{\beta}_j^2$$

Higher values of α increase the penalty for larger parameter values (i.e., more complex models). scikit-learn follows the common method of using C instead of α where C is the inverse of the regularization strength: $C = \frac{1}{\alpha}$. To reduce variance while using logistic regression, we can treat C as a hyperparameter to be tuned to find the value of C that creates the best model. In scikit-learn we can use the `LogisticRegressionCV` class to efficiently tune C. `LogisticRegressionCV`'s parameter, Cs, can either accept a range of values for C to search over (if a list of floats is supplied as an argument) or if supplied an integer, will generate a list of that many candidate values drawn from a logarithmic scale between –10,000 and 10,000.

Unfortunately, `LogisticRegressionCV` does not allow us to search over different penalty terms. To do this we have to use the less efficient model selection techniques discussed in Chapter 12.

16.4 Training a Classifier on Very Large Data

Problem

You need to train a simple classifier model on a very large set of data.

Solution

Train a logistic regression in scikit-learn with `LogisticRegression` using the stochastic average gradient (SAG) solver:

```
# Load libraries
from sklearn.linear_model import LogisticRegression
from sklearn import datasets
from sklearn.preprocessing import StandardScaler

# Load data
iris = datasets.load_iris()
features = iris.data
target = iris.target
```

```
# Standardize features
scaler = StandardScaler()
features_standardized = scaler.fit_transform(features)

# Create logistic regression object
logistic_regression = LogisticRegression(random_state=0, solver="sag")

# Train model
model = logistic_regression.fit(features_standardized, target)
```

Discussion

scikit-learn's `LogisticRegression` offers a number of techniques for training a logistic regression, called *solvers*. Most of the time scikit-learn will select the best solver automatically for us or warn us that we cannot do something with that solver. However, there is one particular case we should be aware of.

While an exact explanation is beyond the bounds of this book (for more information see Mark Schmidt's slides in "See Also" on page 264), stochastic average gradient descent allows us to train a model much faster than other solvers when our data is very large. However, it is also very sensitive to feature scaling, so standardizing our features is particularly important. We can set our learning algorithm to use this solver by setting `solver='sag'`.

See Also

- Minimizing Finite Sums with the Stochastic Average Gradient Algorithm, Mark Schmidt (*http://bit.ly/2GRrVw0*)

16.5 Handling Imbalanced Classes

Problem

You need to train a simple classifier model.

Solution

Train a logistic regression in scikit-learn using `LogisticRegression`:

```
# Load libraries
import numpy as np
from sklearn.linear_model import LogisticRegression
from sklearn import datasets
from sklearn.preprocessing import StandardScaler

# Load data
```

```
iris = datasets.load_iris()
features = iris.data
target = iris.target

# Make class highly imbalanced by removing first 40 observations
features = features[40:,:]
target = target[40:]

# Create target vector indicating if class 0, otherwise 1
target = np.where((target == 0), 0, 1)

# Standardize features
scaler = StandardScaler()
features_standardized = scaler.fit_transform(features)

# Create decision tree classifier object
logistic_regression = LogisticRegression(random_state=0, class_weight="balanced")

# Train model
model = logistic_regression.fit(features_standardized, target)
```

Discussion

Like many other learning algorithms in scikit-learn, `LogisticRegression` comes with a built-in method of handling imbalanced classes. If we have highly imbalanced classes and have not addressed it during preprocessing, we have the option of using the `class_weight` parameter to weight the classes to make certain we have a balanced mix of each class. Specifically, the `balanced` argument will automatically weigh classes inversely proportional to their frequency:

$$w_j = \frac{n}{kn_j}$$

where w_j is the weight to class j, n is the number of observations, n_j is the number of observations in class j, and k is the total number of classes.

## CHAPTER 17

Support Vector Machines

17.0 Introduction

To understand support vector machines, we must understand hyperplanes. Formally, a hyperplane is an *n – 1* subspace in an *n*-dimensional space. While that sounds complex, it actually is pretty simple. For example, if we wanted to divide a two-dimensional space, we'd use a one-dimensional hyperplane (i.e., a line). If we wanted to divide a three-dimensional space, we'd use a two-dimensional hyperplane (i.e., a flat piece of paper or a bed sheet). A hyperplane is simply a generalization of that concept into *n* dimensions.

Support vector machines classify data by finding the hyperplane that maximizes the margin between the classes in the training data. In a two-dimensional example with two classes, we can think of a hyperplane as the widest straight "band" (i.e., line with margins) that separates the two classes.

In this chapter, we cover training support vector machines in a variety of situations and dive under the hood to look at how we can extend the approach to tackle common problems.

17.1 Training a Linear Classifier

Problem

You need to train a model to classify observations.

Solution

Use a support vector classifier (SVC) to find the hyperplane that maximizes the margins between the classes:

```
# Load libraries
from sklearn.svm import LinearSVC
from sklearn import datasets
from sklearn.preprocessing import StandardScaler
import numpy as np

# Load data with only two classes and two features
iris = datasets.load_iris()
features = iris.data[:100,:2]
target = iris.target[:100]

# Standardize features
scaler = StandardScaler()
features_standardized = scaler.fit_transform(features)

# Create support vector classifier
svc = LinearSVC(C=1.0)

# Train model
model = svc.fit(features_standardized, target)
```

Discussion

scikit-learn's `LinearSVC` implements a simple SVC. To get an intuition behind what an SVC is doing, let us plot out the data and hyperplane. While SVCs work well in high dimensions, in our solution we only loaded two features and took a subset of observations so that the data contains only two classes. This will let us visualize the model. Recall that SVC attempts to find the hyperplane—a line when we only have two dimensions—with the maximum margin between the classes. In the following code we plot the two classes on a two-dimensional space, then draw the hyperplane:

```
# Load library
from matplotlib import pyplot as plt

# Plot data points and color using their class
color = ["black" if c == 0 else "lightgrey" for c in target]
plt.scatter(features_standardized[:,0], features_standardized[:,1], c=color)

# Create the hyperplane
w = svc.coef_[0]
a = -w[0] / w[1]
xx = np.linspace(-2.5, 2.5)
yy = a * xx - (svc.intercept_[0]) / w[1]

# Plot the hyperplane
plt.plot(xx, yy)
plt.axis("off"), plt.show();
```

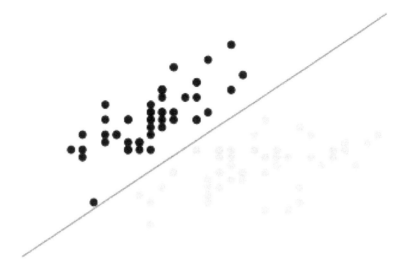

In this visualization, all observations of class 0 are black and observations of class 1 are light gray. The hyperplane is the decision boundary deciding how new observations are classified. Specifically, any observation above the line will by classified as class 0 while any observation below the line will be classified as class 1. We can prove this by creating a new observation in the top-left corner of our visualization, meaning it should be predicted to be class 0:

```
# Create new observation
new_observation = [[ -2,  3]]

# Predict class of new observation
svc.predict(new_observation)

array([0])
```

There are a few things to note about SVCs. First, for the sake of visualization we limited our example to a binary example (e.g., only two classes); however, SVCs can work well with multiple classes. Second, as our visualization shows, the hyperplane is by definition linear (i.e., not curved). This was okay in this example because the data was linearly separable, meaning there was a hyperplane that could perfectly separate the two classes. Unfortunately, in the real world this will rarely be the case.

More typically, we will not be able to perfectly separate classes. In these situations there is a balance between SVC maximizing the margin of the hyperplane and minimizing the misclassification. In SVC, the latter is controlled with the hyperparameter

C, the penalty imposed on errors. C is a parameter of the SVC learner and is the penalty for misclassifying a data point. When C is small, the classifier is okay with misclassified data points (high bias but low variance). When C is large, the classifier is heavily penalized for misclassified data and therefore bends over backwards to avoid any misclassified data points (low bias but high variance).

In scikit-learn, C is determined by the parameter C and defaults to C=1.0. We should treat C has a hyperparameter of our learning algorithm, which we tune using model selection techniques in Chapter 12.

17.2 Handling Linearly Inseparable Classes Using Kernels

Problem

You need to train a support vector classifier, but your classes are linearly inseparable.

Solution

Train an extension of a support vector machine using kernel functions to create nonlinear decision boundaries:

```
# Load libraries
from sklearn.svm import SVC
from sklearn import datasets
from sklearn.preprocessing import StandardScaler
import numpy as np

# Set randomization seed
np.random.seed(0)

# Generate two features
features = np.random.randn(200, 2)

# Use a XOR gate (you don't need to know what this is) to generate
# linearly inseparable classes
target_xor = np.logical_xor(features[:, 0] > 0, features[:, 1] > 0)
target = np.where(target_xor, 0, 1)

# Create a support vector machine with a radial basis function kernel
svc = SVC(kernel="rbf", random_state=0, gamma=1, C=1)

# Train the classifier
model = svc.fit(features, target)
```

Discussion

A full explanation of support vector machines is outside the scope of this book. However, a short explanation is likely beneficial for understanding support vector machines and kernels. For reasons best learned elsewhere, a support vector classifier can be represented as:

$$f(x) = \beta_0 + \sum_{i \in S} \alpha_i K(x_i, x_{i'})$$

where β_0 is the bias, S is the set of all support vector observations, α are the model parameters to be learned, and $(x_i, x_{i'})$ are pairs of two support vector observations, x_i and $x_{i'}$. Most importantly, K is a kernel function that compares the similarity between x_i and $x_{i'}$. Don't worry if you don't understand kernel functions. For our purposes, just realize that K 1) determines the type of hyperplane used to separate our classes and 2) we create different hyperplanes by using different kernels. For example, if we wanted the basic linear hyperplane like the one we created in Recipe 17.1, we can use the linear kernel:

$$K(x_i, x_{i'}) = \sum_{j=1}^{p} x_{ij} x_{i'j}$$

where p is the number of features. However, if we wanted a nonlinear decision boundary, we swap the linear kernel with a polynomial kernel:

$$K(x_i, x_{i'}) = \left(1 + \sum_{j=1}^{p} x_{ij} x_{i'j}\right)^2$$

where d is the degree of the polynomial kernel function. Alternatively, we can use one of the most common kernels in support vectors machines, the radial basis function kernel:

$$K(x_i, x_{i'}) = e^{\left(-\gamma \sum_{j=1}^{p} \left(x_{ij} x_{i'j}\right)^2\right)}$$

where γ is a hyperparameter and must be greater than zero. The main point of the preceding explanation is that if we have linearly inseparable data we can swap out a linear kernel with an alternative kernel to create a nonlinear hyperplane decision boundary.

We can understand the intuition behind kernels by visualizing a simple example. This function, based on one by Sebastian Raschka, plots the observations and decision boundary hyperplane of a two-dimensional space. You do not need to understand how this function works; I have included it here so you can experiment on your own:

```
# Plot observations and decision boundary hyperplane
from matplotlib.colors import ListedColormap
import matplotlib.pyplot as plt

def plot_decision_regions(X, y, classifier):
    cmap = ListedColormap(("red", "blue"))
    xx1, xx2 = np.meshgrid(np.arange(-3, 3, 0.02), np.arange(-3, 3, 0.02))
    Z = classifier.predict(np.array([xx1.ravel(), xx2.ravel()]).T)
    Z = Z.reshape(xx1.shape)
    plt.contourf(xx1, xx2, Z, alpha=0.1, cmap=cmap)

    for idx, cl in enumerate(np.unique(y)):
        plt.scatter(x=X[y == cl, 0], y=X[y == cl, 1],
                    alpha=0.8, c=cmap(idx),
                    marker="+", label=cl)
```

In our solution, we have data containing two features (i.e., two dimensions) and a target vector with the class of each observation. Importantly, the classes are assigned such that they are linearly inseparable. That is, there is no straight line we can draw that will divide the two classes. First, let's create a support vector machine classifier with a linear kernel:

```
# Create support vector classifier with a linear kernel
svc_linear = SVC(kernel="linear", random_state=0, C=1)

# Train model
svc_linear.fit(features, target)

SVC(C=1, cache_size=200, class_weight=None, coef0=0.0,
  decision_function_shape='ovr', degree=3, gamma='auto', kernel='linear',
  max_iter=-1, probability=False, random_state=0, shrinking=True,
  tol=0.001, verbose=False)
```

Next, since we have only two features, we are working in a two-dimensional space and can visualize the observations, their classes, and our model's linear hyperplane:

```
# Plot observations and hyperplane
plot_decision_regions(features, target, classifier=svc_linear)
plt.axis("off"), plt.show();
```

As we can see, our linear hyperplane did very poorly at dividing the two classes! Now, let's swap out the linear kernel with a radial basis function kernel and use it to train a new model:

```
# Create a support vector machine with a radial basis function kernel
svc = SVC(kernel="rbf", random_state=0, gamma=1, C=1)

# Train the classifier
model = svc.fit(features, target)
```

And then visualize the observations and hyperplane:

```
# Plot observations and hyperplane
plot_decision_regions(features, target, classifier=svc)
plt.axis("off"), plt.show();
```

By using the radial basis function kernel we could create a decision boundary able to do a much better job of separating the two classes than the linear kernel. This is the motivation behind using kernels in support vector machines.

In scikit-learn, we can select the kernel we want to use by using the `kernel` parameter. Once we select a kernel, we will need to specify the appropriate kernel options such as the value of d (using the `degree` parameter) in polynomial kernels and γ (using the `gamma` parameter) in radial basis function kernels. We will also need to set the penalty parameter, C. When training the model, in most cases we should treat all of these as hyperparameters and use model selection techniques to identify the combination of their values that produces the model with the best performance.

17.3 Creating Predicted Probabilities

Problem

You need to know the predicted class probabilities for an observation.

Solution

When using scikit-learn's SVC, set `probability=True`, train the model, then use `pre dict_proba` to see the calibrated probabilities:

```
# Load libraries
from sklearn.svm import SVC
from sklearn import datasets
from sklearn.preprocessing import StandardScaler
import numpy as np

# Load data
iris = datasets.load_iris()
features = iris.data
target = iris.target

# Standardize features
scaler = StandardScaler()
features_standardized = scaler.fit_transform(features)

# Create support vector classifier object
svc = SVC(kernel="linear", probability=True, random_state=0)

# Train classifier
model = svc.fit(features_standardized, target)

# Create new observation
new_observation = [[.4, .4, .4, .4]]

# View predicted probabilities
model.predict_proba(new_observation)

array([[ 0.00588822,  0.96874828,  0.0253635 ]])
```

Discussion

Many of the supervised learning algorithms we have covered use probability estimates to predict classes. For example, in k-nearest neighbor, an observation's k neighbor's classes were treated as votes to create a probability that an observation was of
that class. Then the class with the highest probability was predicted. SVC's use of a
hyperplane to create decision regions does not naturally output a probability estimate
that an observation is a member of a certain class. However, we can in fact output
calibrated class probabilities with a few caveats. In an SVC with two classes, Platt scaling can be used, wherein first the SVC is trained, and then a separate cross-validated
logistic regression is trained to map the SVC outputs into probabilities:

$$P(y = 1 \mid x) = \frac{1}{1 + e^{(A * f(x) + B)}}$$

where A and B are parameter vectors and f is the ith observation's signed distance
from the hyperplane. When we have more than two classes, an extension of Platt scaling is used.

In more practical terms, creating predicted probabilities has two major issues. First, because we are training a second model with cross-validation, generating predicted probabilities can significantly increase the time it takes to train our model. Second, because the predicted probabilities are created using cross-validation, they might not always match the predicted classes. That is, an observation might be predicted to be class 1, but have a predicted probability of being class 1 of less than 0.5.

In scikit-learn, the predicted probabilities must be generated when the model is being trained. We can do this by setting SVC's `probability` to True. After the model is trained, we can output the estimated probabilities for each class using `predict_proba`.

17.4 Identifying Support Vectors

Problem

You need to identify which observations are the support vectors of the decision hyperplane.

Solution

Train the model, then use `support_vectors_`:

```
# Load libraries
from sklearn.svm import SVC
from sklearn import datasets
from sklearn.preprocessing import StandardScaler
import numpy as np

#Load data with only two classes
iris = datasets.load_iris()
features = iris.data[:100,:]
target = iris.target[:100]

# Standardize features
scaler = StandardScaler()
features_standardized = scaler.fit_transform(features)

# Create support vector classifier object
svc = SVC(kernel="linear", random_state=0)

# Train classifier
model = svc.fit(features_standardized, target)

# View support vectors
model.support_vectors_

array([[-0.5810659 ,  0.43490123, -0.80621461, -0.50581312],
       [-1.52079513, -1.67626978, -1.08374115, -0.8607697 ],
```

```
       [-0.89430898, -1.46515268,  0.30389157,  0.38157832],
       [-0.5810659 , -1.25403558,  0.09574666,  0.55905661]])
```

Discussion

Support vector machines get their name from the fact that the hyperplane is being determined by a relatively small number of observations, called the support vectors. Intuitively, think of the hyperplane as being "carried" by these support vectors. These support vectors are therefore very important to our model. For example, if we remove an observation that is not a support vector from the data, the model does not change; however, if we remove a support vector, the hyperplane will not have the maximum margin.

After we have trained an SVC, scikit-learn offers us a number of options for identifying the support vector. In our solution, we used `support_vectors_` to output the actual observations' features of the four support vectors in our model. Alternatively, we can view the indices of the support vectors using `support_`:

```
model.support_
```

```
array([23, 41, 57, 98], dtype=int32)
```

Finally, we can use `n_support_` to find the number of support vectors belonging to each class:

```
model.n_support_
```

```
array([2, 2], dtype=int32)
```

17.5 Handling Imbalanced Classes

Problem

You need to train a support vector machine classifier in the presence of imbalanced classes.

Solution

Increase the penalty for misclassifying the smaller class using `class_weight`:

```
# Load libraries
from sklearn.svm import SVC
from sklearn import datasets
from sklearn.preprocessing import StandardScaler
import numpy as np

#Load data with only two classes
iris = datasets.load_iris()
features = iris.data[:100,:]
target = iris.target[:100]
```

```
# Make class highly imbalanced by removing first 40 observations
features = features[40:,:]
target = target[40:]

# Create target vector indicating if class 0, otherwise 1
target = np.where((target == 0), 0, 1)

# Standardize features
scaler = StandardScaler()
features_standardized = scaler.fit_transform(features)

# Create support vector classifier
svc = SVC(kernel="linear", class_weight="balanced", C=1.0, random_state=0)

# Train classifier
model = svc.fit(features_standardized, target)
```

Discussion

In support vector machines, C is a hyperparameter determining the penalty for misclassifying an observation. One method for handling imbalanced classes in support vector machines is to weight C by classes, so that:

$$C_k = C^* w_j$$

where C is the penalty for misclassification, w_j is a weight inversely proportional to class j's frequency, and C_j is the C value for class j. The general idea is to increase the penalty for misclassifying minority classes to prevent them from being "overwhelmed" by the majority class.

In scikit-learn, when using SVC we can set the values for C_j automatically by setting class_weight='balanced'. The balanced argument automatically weighs classes such that:

$$w_j = \frac{n}{kn_j}$$

where w_j is the weight to class j, n is the number of observations, n_j is the number of observations in class j, and k is the total number of classes.

## CHAPTER 18

Naive Bayes

18.0 Introduction

Bayes' theorem is the premier method for understanding the probability of some event, $P(A \mid B)$, given some new information, $P(B \mid A)$, and a prior belief in the probability of the event, $P(A)$:

$$P(A \mid B) = \frac{P(B \mid A)\,P(A)}{P(B)}$$

The Bayesian method's popularity has skyrocketed in the last decade, more and more rivaling traditional frequentist applications in academia, government, and business. In machine learning, one application of Bayes' theorem to classification comes in the form of the naive Bayes classifier. Naive Bayes classifiers combine a number of desirable qualities in practical machine learning into a single classifier. These include:

1. An intuitive approach

2. The ability to work with small data

3. Low computation costs for training and prediction

4. Often solid results in a variety of settings.

Specifically, a naive Bayes classifier is based on:

$$P\!\left(y \mid x_1, \cdots, x_j\right) = \frac{P\!\left(x_1, \cdots x_j \mid y\right)P(y)}{P\!\left(x_1, \cdots, x_j\right)}$$

where:

- $P(y \mid x_1, \cdots, x_j)$ is called the *posterior* and is the probability that an observation is class y given the observation's values for the j features, $x_1, \cdots, x_j$.
- $P(x_1, \ldots x_j \mid y)$ is called likelihood and is the *likelihood* of an observation's values for features, $x_1, \ldots, x_j$, given their class, y.
- $P(y)$ is called the *prior* and is our belief for the probability of class y before looking at the data.
- $P(x_1, \ldots, x_j)$ is called the *marginal probability*.

In naive Bayes, we compare an observation's posterior values for each possible class. Specifically, because the marginal probability is constant across these comparisons, we compare the numerators of the posterior for each class. For each observation, the class with the greatest posterior numerator becomes the predicted class, $\hat{y}$.

There are two important things to note about naive Bayes classifiers. First, for each feature in the data, we have to assume the statistical distribution of the likelihood, $P(x_j \mid y)$. The common distributions are the normal (Gaussian), multinomial, and Bernoulli distributions. The distribution chosen is often determined by the nature of features (continuous, binary, etc.). Second, naive Bayes gets its name because we assume that each feature, and its resulting likelihood, is independent. This "naive" assumption is frequently wrong, yet in practice does little to prevent building high-quality classifiers.

In this chapter we will cover using scikit-learn to train three types of naive Bayes classifiers using three different likelihood distributions.

18.1 Training a Classifier for Continuous Features

Problem

You have only continuous features and you want to train a naive Bayes classifier.

Solution

Use a Gaussian naive Bayes classifier in scikit-learn:

```
# Load libraries
from sklearn import datasets
from sklearn.naive_bayes import GaussianNB

# Load data
iris = datasets.load_iris()
features = iris.data
target = iris.target

# Create Gaussian Naive Bayes object
```

```
classifer = GaussianNB()

# Train model
model = classifer.fit(features, target)
```

Discussion

The most common type of naive Bayes classifier is the Gaussian naive Bayes. In Gaussian naive Bayes, we assume that the likelihood of the feature values, x, given an observation is of class y, follows a normal distribution:

$$p\left(x_j \mid y\right) = \frac{1}{\sqrt{2\pi\sigma_y^2}} e^{-\frac{\left(x_j - \mu_y\right)^2}{2\sigma_y^2}}$$

where σ_y^2 and μ_y are the variance and mean values of feature x_j for class y. Because of the assumption of the normal distribution, Gaussian naive Bayes is best used in cases when all our features are continuous.

In scikit-learn, we train a Gaussian naive Bayes like any other model using fit, and in turn can then make predictions about the class of an observation:

```
# Create new observation
new_observation = [[ 4,  4,  4,  0.4]]

# Predict class
model.predict(new_observation)

array([1])
```

One of the interesting aspects of naive Bayes classifiers is that they allow us to assign a prior belief over the respected target classes. We can do this using GaussianNB's pri ors parameter, which takes in a list of the probabilities assigned to each class of the target vector:

```
# Create Gaussian Naive Bayes object with prior probabilities of each class
clf = GaussianNB(priors=[0.25, 0.25, 0.5])

# Train model
model = classifer.fit(features, target)
```

If we do not add any argument to the priors parameter, the prior is adjusted based on the data.

Finally, note that the raw predicted probabilities from Gaussian naive Bayes (outputted using predict_proba) are not calibrated. That is, they should not be believed. If we want to create useful predicted probabilities, we will need to calibrate them using an isotonic regression or a related method.

See Also

- How the Naive Bayes Classifier Works in Machine Learning, Dataaspirant (*http:// bit.ly/2F6trtt*)

18.2 Training a Classifier for Discrete and Count Features

Problem

Given discrete or count data, you need to train a naive Bayes classifier.

Solution

Use a multinomial naive Bayes classifier:

```
# Load libraries
import numpy as np
from sklearn.naive_bayes import MultinomialNB
from sklearn.feature_extraction.text import CountVectorizer

# Create text
text_data = np.array(['I love Brazil. Brazil!',
                      'Brazil is best',
                      'Germany beats both'])

# Create bag of words
count = CountVectorizer()
bag_of_words = count.fit_transform(text_data)

# Create feature matrix
features = bag_of_words.toarray()

# Create target vector
target = np.array([0,0,1])

# Create multinomial naive Bayes object with prior probabilities of each class
classifer = MultinomialNB(class_prior=[0.25, 0.5])

# Train model
model = classifer.fit(features, target)
```

Discussion

Multinomial naive Bayes works similarly to Gaussian naive Bayes, but the features are assumed to be multinomially distributed. In practice, this means that this classifier is commonly used when we have discrete data (e.g., movie ratings ranging from 1 to 5). One of the most common uses of multinomial naive Bayes is text classification using bags of words or tf-idf approaches (see Recipes 6.8 and 6.9).

In our solution, we created a toy text dataset of three observations, and converted the text strings into a bag-of-words feature matrix and an accompanying target vector. We then used `MultinomialNB` to train a model while defining the prior probabilities for the two classes (pro-`brazil` and pro-`germany`).

`MultinomialNB` works similarly to `GaussianNB`; models are trained using `fit`, and observations can be predicted using `predict`:

```
# Create new observation
new_observation = [[0, 0, 0, 1, 0, 1, 0]]

# Predict new observation's class
model.predict(new_observation)

array([0])
```

If `class_prior` is not specified, prior probabilities are learned using the data. However, if we want a uniform distribution to be used as the prior, we can set `fit_prior=False`.

Finally, `MultinomialNB` contains an additive smoothing hyperparameter, `alpha`, that should be tuned. The default value is `1.0`, with `0.0` meaning no smoothing takes place.

18.3 Training a Naive Bayes Classifier for Binary Features

Problem

You have binary feature data and need to train a naive Bayes classifier.

Solution

Use a Bernoulli naive Bayes classifier:

```
# Load libraries
import numpy as np
from sklearn.naive_bayes import BernoulliNB

# Create three binary features
features = np.random.randint(2, size=(100, 3))

# Create a binary target vector
target = np.random.randint(2, size=(100, 1)).ravel()

# Create Bernoulli Naive Bayes object with prior probabilities of each class
```

```
classifer = BernoulliNB(class_prior=[0.25, 0.5])

# Train model
model = classifer.fit(features, target)
```

Discussion

The Bernoulli naive Bayes classifier assumes that all our features are binary such that they take only two values (e.g., a nominal categorical feature that has been one-hot encoded). Like its multinomial cousin, Bernoulli naive Bayes is often used in text classification, when our feature matrix is simply the presence or absence of a word in a document. Furthermore, like `MultinomialNB`, `BernoulliNB` has an additive smoothing hyperparameter, `alpha`, we will want to tune using model selection techniques. Finally, if we want to use priors we can use the `class_prior` parameter with a list containing the prior probabilities for each class. If we want to specify a uniform prior, we can set `fit_prior=False`:

```
model_uniform_prior = BernoulliNB(class_prior=None, fit_prior=True)
```

18.4 Calibrating Predicted Probabilities

Problem

You want to calibrate the predicted probabilities from naive Bayes classifiers so they are interpretable.

Solution

Use `CalibratedClassifierCV`:

```
# Load libraries
from sklearn import datasets
from sklearn.naive_bayes import GaussianNB
from sklearn.calibration import CalibratedClassifierCV

# Load data
iris = datasets.load_iris()
features = iris.data
target = iris.target

# Create Gaussian Naive Bayes object
classifer = GaussianNB()

# Create calibrated cross-validation with sigmoid calibration
classifer_sigmoid = CalibratedClassifierCV(classifer, cv=2, method='sigmoid')

# Calibrate probabilities
classifer_sigmoid.fit(features, target)
```

```
# Create new observation
new_observation = [[ 2.6,  2.6,  2.6,  0.4]]

# View calibrated probabilities
classifer_sigmoid.predict_proba(new_observation)

array([[ 0.31859969,  0.63663466,  0.04476565]])
```

Discussion

Class probabilities are a common and useful part of machine learning models. In scikit-learn, most learning algortihms allow us to see the predicted probabilities of class membership using predict_proba. This can be extremely useful if, for instance, we want to only predict a certain class if the model predicts the probability that it is that class is over 90%. However, some models, including naive Bayes classifiers, output probabilities that are not based on the real world. That is, predict_proba might predict an observation has a 0.70 chance of being a certain class, when the reality is that it is 0.10 or 0.99. Specifically in naive Bayes, while the ranking of predicted probabilities for the different target classes is valid, the raw predicted probabilities tend to take on extreme values close to 0 and 1.

To obtain meaningful predicted probabilities we need conduct what is called *calibration*. In scikit-learn we can use the CalibratedClassifierCV class to create well-calibrated predicted probabilities using k-fold cross-validation. In CalibratedClassifierCV the training sets are used to train the model and the test set is used to calibrate the predicted probabilities. The returned predicted probabilities are the average of the k-folds.

Using our solution we can see the difference between raw and well-calibrated predicted probabilities. In our solution, we created a Gaussian naive Bayes classifier. If we train that classifier and then predict the class probabilities for a new observation, we can see very extreme probability estimates:

```
# Train a Gaussian naive Bayes then predict class probabilities
classifer.fit(features, target).predict_proba(new_observation)

array([[  2.58229098e-04,   9.99741447e-01,   3.23523643e-07]])
```

However, if after we calibrate the predicted probabilities (which we did in our solution), we get very different results:

```
# View calibrated probabilities
classifer_sigmoid.predict_proba(new_observation)

array([[ 0.31859969,  0.63663466,  0.04476565]])
```

CalibratedClassifierCV offers two calibration methods—Platt's sigmoid model and isotonic regression—defined by the method paramenter. While we don't have the space to go into the specifics, because isotonic regression is nonparametric it tends to overfit when sample sizes are very small (e.g., 100 observations). In our solution we used the Iris dataset with 150 observations and therefore used the Platt's sigmoid model.

## CHAPTER 19

Clustering

19.0 Introduction

In much of this book we have looked at supervised machine learning—where we have access to both the features and the target. This is, unfortunately, not always the case. Frequently, we run into situations where we only know the features. For example, imagine we have records of sales from a grocery store and we want to break up sales by whether or not the shopper is a member of a discount club. This would be impossible using supervised learning because we don't have a target to train and evaluate our models. However, there is another option: unsupervised learning. If the behavior of discount club members and nonmembers in the grocery store is actually disparate, then the average difference in behavior between two members will be smaller than the average difference in behavior between a member and nonmember shopper. Put another way, there will be two clusters of observations.

The goal of clustering algorithms is to identify those latent groupings of observations, which if done well, allow us to predict the class of observations even without a target vector. There are many clustering algorithms and they have a wide variety of approaches to identifying the clusters in data. In this chapter, we will cover a selection of clustering algorithms using scikit-learn and how to use them in practice.

19.1 Clustering Using K-Means

Problem

You want to group observations into k groups.

Solution

Use k-means clustering:

```
# Load libraries
from sklearn import datasets
from sklearn.preprocessing import StandardScaler
from sklearn.cluster import KMeans

# Load data
iris = datasets.load_iris()
features = iris.data

# Standardize features
scaler = StandardScaler()
features_std = scaler.fit_transform(features)

# Create k-mean object
cluster = KMeans(n_clusters=3, random_state=0, n_jobs=-1)

# Train model
model = cluster.fit(features_std)
```

Discussion

k-means clustering is one of the most common clustering techniques. In k-means clustering, the algorithm attempts to group observations into k groups, with each group having roughly equal variance. The number of groups, k, is specified by the user as a hyperparameter. Specifically, in k-means:

1. k cluster "center" points are created at random locations.

2. For each observation:

    a. The distance between each observation and the k center points is calculated.

    b. The observation is assigned to the cluster of the nearest center point.

3. The center points are moved to the means (i.e., centers) of their respective clusters.

4. Steps 2 and 3 are repeated until no observation changes in cluster membership.

At this point the algorithm is considered converged and stops.

It is important to note three things about k-means. First, k-means clustering assumes the clusters are convex shaped (e.g., a circle, a sphere). Second, all features are equally scaled. In our solution, we standardized the features to meet this assumption. Third, the groups are balanced (i.e., have roughly the same number of observations). If we suspect that we cannot meet these assumptions, we might try other clustering approaches.

In scikit-learn, k-means clustering is implemented in the `KMeans` class. The most important parameter is `n_clusters`, which sets the number of clusters *k*. In some situations, the nature of the data will determine the value for *k* (e.g., data on a school's students will have one cluster per grade), but often we don't know the number of clusters. In these cases, we will want to select *k* based on using some criteria. For example, silhouette coefficients (see Recipe 11.9) measure the similarity within clusters compared with the similarity between clusters. Furthermore, because k-means clustering is computationally expensive, we might want to take advantage of all the cores on our computer. We can do this by setting `n_jobs=-1`.

In our solution, we cheated a little and used the Iris flower data, in which we know there are three classes. Therefore, we set *k = 3*. We can use `labels_` to see the predicted classes of each observation:

```
# View predict class
model.labels_

array([1, 1, 1, 1, 1, 1, 1, 1, 1, 1, 1, 1, 1, 1, 1, 1, 1, 1, 1, 1, 1, 1, 1,
       1, 1, 1, 1, 1, 1, 1, 1, 1, 1, 1, 1, 1, 1, 1, 1, 1, 1, 1, 1, 1, 1,
       1, 1, 1, 1, 0, 0, 0, 2, 2, 2, 0, 2, 2, 2, 2, 2, 2, 2, 2, 0, 2, 2, 2,
       2, 0, 2, 2, 2, 2, 0, 0, 0, 2, 2, 2, 2, 2, 2, 2, 0, 0, 2, 2, 2, 2, 2,
       2, 2, 2, 2, 2, 2, 2, 2, 0, 2, 0, 0, 0, 0, 2, 0, 0, 0, 0, 0, 0, 2, 2,
       0, 0, 0, 0, 2, 0, 2, 0, 2, 0, 0, 2, 0, 0, 0, 0, 0, 0, 2, 2, 0, 0, 0,
       2, 0, 0, 0, 2, 0, 0, 0, 2, 0, 0, 2], dtype=int32)
```

If we compare this to the observation's true class we can see that despite the difference in class labels (i.e., 1, 2, and 3), k-means did reasonably well:

```
# View true class
iris.target

array([0, 0, 0, 0, 0, 0, 0, 0, 0, 0, 0, 0, 0, 0, 0, 0, 0, 0, 0, 0, 0, 0, 0, 0,
       0, 0, 0, 0, 0, 0, 0, 0, 0, 0, 0, 0, 0, 0, 0, 0, 0, 0, 0, 0, 0, 0, 0, 0,
       0, 0, 1, 1, 1, 1, 1, 1, 1, 1, 1, 1, 1, 1, 1, 1, 1, 1, 1, 1, 1, 1,
       1, 1, 1, 1, 1, 1, 1, 1, 1, 1, 1, 1, 1, 1, 1, 1, 1, 1, 1, 1, 1, 1,
       1, 1, 1, 1, 1, 1, 1, 1, 2, 2, 2, 2, 2, 2, 2, 2, 2, 2, 2, 2, 2, 2,
       2, 2, 2, 2, 2, 2, 2, 2, 2, 2, 2, 2, 2, 2, 2, 2, 2, 2, 2, 2, 2, 2,
       2, 2, 2, 2, 2, 2, 2, 2, 2, 2, 2, 2])
```

However, as you might imagine, the performance of k-means drops considerably, even critically, if we select the wrong number of clusters.

Finally, as with other scikit-learns we can use the trained cluster to predict the value of new observations:

```
# Create new observation
new_observation = [[0.8, 0.8, 0.8, 0.8]]

# Predict observation's cluster
model.predict(new_observation)

array([0], dtype=int32)
```

The observation is predicted to belong to the cluster whose center point is closest. We can even use `cluster_centers_` to see those center points:

```
# View cluster centers
model.cluster_centers_

array([[ 1.13597027,  0.09659843,  0.996271  ,  1.01717187],
       [-1.01457897,  0.84230679, -1.30487835, -1.25512862],
       [-0.05021989, -0.88029181,  0.34753171,  0.28206327]])
```

See Also

- Introduction to K-means Clustering, DataScience.com (*http://bit.ly/2Hjik1f*)

19.2 Speeding Up K-Means Clustering

Problem

You want to group observations into *k* groups, but k-means takes too long.

Solution

Use mini-batch k-means:

```
# Load libraries
from sklearn import datasets
from sklearn.preprocessing import StandardScaler
from sklearn.cluster import MiniBatchKMeans

# Load data
iris = datasets.load_iris()
features = iris.data

# Standardize features
scaler = StandardScaler()
features_std = scaler.fit_transform(features)

# Create k-mean object
cluster = MiniBatchKMeans(n_clusters=3, random_state=0, batch_size=100)

# Train model
model = cluster.fit(features_std)
```

Discussion

Mini-batch k-means works similarly to the k-means algorithm discussed in Recipe 19.1. Without going into too much detail, the difference is that in mini-batch k-means the most computationally costly step is conducted on only a random sample

---

of observations as opposed to all observations. This approach can significantly reduce the time required for the algorithm to find convergence (i.e., fit the data) with only a small cost in quality.

`MiniBatchKMeans` works similarly to `KMeans`, with one significant difference: the `batch_size` parameter. `batch_size` controls the number of randomly selected observations in each batch. The larger the size of the batch, the more computationally costly the training process.

19.3 Clustering Using Meanshift

Problem

You want to group observations without assuming the number of clusters or their shape.

Solution

Use meanshift clustering:

```
# Load libraries
from sklearn import datasets
from sklearn.preprocessing import StandardScaler
from sklearn.cluster import MeanShift

# Load data
iris = datasets.load_iris()
features = iris.data

# Standardize features
scaler = StandardScaler()
features_std = scaler.fit_transform(features)

# Create meanshift object
cluster = MeanShift(n_jobs=-1)

# Train model
model = cluster.fit(features_std)
```

Discussion

One of the disadvantages of k-means clustering we discussed previously is that we needed to set the number of clusters, *k*, prior to training, and the method made assumptions about the shape of the clusters. One clustering algorithm without these limitations is meanshift.

Meanshift is a simple concept, but somewhat difficult to explain. Therefore, an analogy might be the best approach. Imagine a very foggy football field (i.e., a two-dimensional feature space) with 100 people standing on it (i.e., our observations). Because it is foggy, a person can only see a short distance. Every minute each person looks around and takes a step in the direction of the most people they can see. As time goes on, people start to group up as they repeatedly take steps toward larger and larger crowds. The end result is clusters of people around the field. People are assigned to the clusters in which they end up.

scikit-learn's actual implementation of meanshift, MeanShift, is more complex but follows the same basic logic. MeanShift has two important parameters we should be aware of. First, bandwidth sets the radius of the area (i.e., kernel) an observation uses to determine the direction to shift. In our analogy, bandwidth was how far a person could see through the fog. We can set this parameter manually, but by default a reasonable bandwidth is estimated automatically (with a significant increase in computational cost). Second, sometimes in meanshift there are no other observations within an observation's kernel. That is, a person on our football field cannot see a single other person. By default, MeanShift assigns all these "orphan" observations to the kernel of the nearest observation. However, if we want to leave out these orphans, we can set cluster_all=False wherein orphan observations are given the label of -1.

See Also

- The mean shift clustering algorithm, EFAVDB (*http://efavdb.com/mean-shift/*)

19.4 Clustering Using DBSCAN

Problem

You want to group observations into clusters of high density.

Solution

Use DBSCAN clustering:

```
# Load libraries
from sklearn import datasets
from sklearn.preprocessing import StandardScaler
from sklearn.cluster import DBSCAN

# Load data
iris = datasets.load_iris()
features = iris.data

# Standardize features
scaler = StandardScaler()
features_std = scaler.fit_transform(features)
```

```
# Create meanshift object
cluster = DBSCAN(n_jobs=-1)

# Train model
model = cluster.fit(features_std)
```

Discussion

DBSCAN is motivated by the idea that clusters will be areas where many observations are densely packed together and makes no assumptions of cluster shape. Specifically, in DBSCAN:

1. A random observation, x_i, is chosen.

2. If x_i has a minimum number of close neighbors, we consider it to be part of a cluster.

3. Step 2 is repeated recursively for all of x_i's neighbors, then neighbor's neighbor, and so on. These are the cluster's core observations.

4. Once step 3 runs out of nearby observations, a new random point is chosen (i.e., restarting step 1).

Once this is complete, we have a set of core observations for a number of clusters. Finally, any observation close to a cluster but not a core sample is considered part of a cluster, while any observation not close to the cluster is labeled an outlier.

DBSCAN has three main parameters to set:

eps
  The maximum distance from an observation for another observation to be considered its neighbor.

min_samples
  The minimum number of observations less than eps distance from an observation for it to be considered a core observation.

metric
  The distance metric used by eps—for example, minkowski or euclidean (note that if Minkowski distance is used, the parameter p can be used to set the power of the Minkowski metric).

If we look at the clusters in our training data we can see two clusters have been identified, 0 and 1, while outlier observations are labeled -1:

```
# Show cluster membership
model.labels_
```

```
array([ 0,  0,  0,  0,  0,  0,  0,  0,  0,  0,  0,  0,  0,  0, -1, -1,  0,
        0,  0,  0,  0,  0, -1,  0,  0,  0,  0,  0,  0,  0,  0,  0, -1, -1,
        0,  0,  0,  0,  0,  0,  0, -1,  0,  0,  0,  0,  0,  0,  0,  0,  1,
        1,  1,  1,  1,  1, -1, -1,  1, -1, -1,  1, -1,  1,  1,  1,  1,  1,
       -1,  1,  1,  1, -1,  1,  1,  1,  1,  1,  1,  1,  1,  1,  1,  1,  1,
       -1,  1, -1,  1,  1,  1,  1,  1, -1,  1,  1,  1,  1, -1,  1, -1,  1,
        1,  1,  1, -1, -1, -1, -1, -1,  1,  1,  1,  1, -1,  1,  1, -1, -1,
       -1,  1,  1, -1,  1,  1, -1,  1,  1,  1, -1, -1, -1,  1,  1,  1, -1,
       -1,  1,  1,  1,  1,  1,  1,  1,  1,  1,  1,  1, -1,  1]))
```

See Also

- DBSCAN, Wikipedia (*https://en.wikipedia.org/wiki/DBSCAN*)

19.5 Clustering Using Hierarchical Merging

Problem

You want to group observations using a hierarchy of clusters.

Solution

Use agglomerative clustering:

```
# Load libraries
from sklearn import datasets
from sklearn.preprocessing import StandardScaler
from sklearn.cluster import AgglomerativeClustering

# Load data
iris = datasets.load_iris()
features = iris.data

# Standardize features
scaler = StandardScaler()
features_std = scaler.fit_transform(features)

# Create meanshift object
cluster = AgglomerativeClustering(n_clusters=3)

# Train model
model = cluster.fit(features_std)
```

Discussion

Agglomerative clustering is a powerful, flexible hierarchical clustering algorithm. In agglomerative clustering, all observations start as their own clusters. Next, clusters meeting some criteria are merged together. This process is repeated, growing clusters until some end point is reached. In scikit-learn, `AgglomerativeClustering` uses the `linkage` parameter to determine the merging strategy to minimize the following:

1. Variance of merged clusters (`ward`)

2. Average distance between observations from pairs of clusters (`average`)

3. Maximum distance between observations from pairs of clusters (`complete`)

Two other parameters are useful to know. First, the `affinity` parameter determines the distance metric used for `linkage` (`minkowski`, `euclidean`, etc.). Second, `n_clusters` sets the number of clusters the clustering algorithm will attempt to find. That is, clusters are successively merged until there are only `n_clusters` remaining.

As with other clustering algorithms we have covered, we can use `labels_` to see the cluster in which every observation is assigned:

```
# Show cluster membership
model.labels_
```

```
array([1, 1, 1, 1, 1, 1, 1, 1, 1, 1, 1, 1, 1, 1, 1, 1, 1, 1, 1, 1, 1, 1, 1,
       1, 1, 1, 1, 1, 1, 1, 1, 1, 1, 1, 1, 1, 1, 1, 1, 2, 1, 1, 1, 1,
       1, 1, 1, 1, 0, 0, 0, 2, 0, 2, 0, 2, 0, 2, 2, 0, 2, 0, 2, 0, 2, 2, 2,
       2, 0, 0, 0, 0, 0, 0, 0, 0, 0, 2, 2, 2, 2, 0, 2, 0, 0, 2, 2, 2, 2, 0,
       2, 2, 2, 2, 2, 0, 2, 2, 0, 0, 0, 0, 0, 0, 2, 0, 0, 0, 0, 0, 0, 0, 0,
       0, 0, 0, 0, 2, 0, 0, 0, 0, 0, 0, 0, 0, 0, 0, 0, 0, 0, 0, 0, 0, 0, 0,
       0, 0, 0, 0, 0, 0, 0, 0, 0, 0, 0, 0])
```

## CHAPTER 20

Neural Networks

20.0 Introduction

At the heart of neural networks is the *unit* (also called a *node* or *neuron*). A unit takes in one or more inputs, multiplies each input by a parameter (also called a *weight*), sums the weighted input's values along with some bias value (typically 1), and then feeds the value into an activation function. This output is then sent forward to the other neurals deeper in the neural network (if they exist).

Feedforward neural networks—also called *multilayer perceptron*—are the simplest artificial neural network used in any real-world setting. Neural networks can be visualized as a series of connected layers that form a network connecting an observation's feature values at one end, and the target value (e.g., observation's class) at the other end. The name feedforward comes from the fact that an observation's feature values are fed "forward" through the network, with each layer successively transforming the feature values with the goal that the output at the end is the same as the target's value.

Specifically, feedforward neural networks contain three types of layers of units. At the start of the neural network is an input layer where each unit contains an observation's value for a single feature. For example, if an observation has 100 features, the input layer has 100 nodes. At the end of the neural network is the output layer, which transforms the output of the hidden layers into values useful for the task at hand. For example, if our goal was binary classification, we could use an output layer with a single unit that uses a sigmoid function to scale its own output to between 0 and 1, representing a predicted class probability. Between the input and output layers are the so-called "hidden" layers (which aren't hidden at all). These hidden layers successively transform the feature values from the input layer to something that, once processed by the output layer, resembles the target class. Neural networks with many hidden layers (e.g., 10, 100, 1,000) are considered "deep" networks and their application is called *deep learning*.

Neural networks are typically created with all parameters initialized as small random values from a Gaussian or normal uniform. Once an observation (or more often a set number of observations called a *batch*) is fed through the network, the outputted value is compared with the observation's true value using a loss function. This is called *forward propagation*. Next an algorithm goes "backward" through the network identifying how much each parameter contributed to the error between the predicted and true values, a process called *backpropagation*. At each parameter, the optimization algorithm determines how much each weight should be adjusted to improve the output.

Neural networks learn by repeating this process of forward propagation and backpropagation for every observation in the training data multiple times (each time all observations have been sent through the network is called an *epoch* and training typically consists of multiple epochs), iteratively updating the values of the parameters.

In this chapter, we will use the popular Python library Keras to build, train, and evaluate a variety of neural networks. Keras is a high-level library, using other libraries like TensorFlow and Theano as its "engine." For us the advantage of Keras is that we can focus on network design and training, leaving the specifics of the tensor operations to the other libraries.

Neural networks created using Keras code can be trained using both CPUs (i.e., on your laptop) and GPUs (i.e., on a specialized deep learning computer). In the real world with real data, it is *highly* advisable to train neural networks using GPUs; however, for the sake of learning, all the neural networks in this book are small and simple enough to be trained on your laptop in only a few minutes. Just be aware that when we have larger networks and more training data, training using CPUs is *significantly* slower than training using GPUs.

20.1 Preprocessing Data for Neural Networks

Problem

You want to preprocess data for use in a neural network.

Solution

Standardize each feature using scikit-learn's StandardScaler:

```
# Load libraries
from sklearn import preprocessing
import numpy as np
```

```
# Create feature
features = np.array([[-100.1, 3240.1],
                     [-200.2, -234.1],
                     [5000.5, 150.1],
                     [6000.6, -125.1],
                     [9000.9, -673.1]])

# Create scaler
scaler = preprocessing.StandardScaler()

# Transform the feature
features_standardized = scaler.fit_transform(features)

# Show feature
features_standardized

array([[-1.12541308,  1.96429418],
       [-1.15329466, -0.50068741],
       [ 0.29529406, -0.22809346],
       [ 0.57385917, -0.42335076],
       [ 1.40955451, -0.81216255]])
```

Discussion

While this recipe is very similar to Recipe 4.3, it is worth repeating because of how important it is for neural networks. Typically, a neural network's parameters are initialized (i.e., created) as small random numbers. Neural networks often behave poorly when the feature values are much larger than parameter values. Furthermore, since an observation's feature values are combined as they pass through individual units, it is important that all features have the same scale.

For these reasons, it is best practice (although not always necessary; for example, when we have all binary features) to standardize each feature such that the feature's values have the mean of 0 and the standard deviation of 1. This can be easily accomplished with scikit-learn's StandardScaler.

You can see the effect of the standardization by checking the mean and standard deviation of our first features:

```
# Print mean and standard deviation
print("Mean:", round(features_standardized[:,0].mean()))
print('"Standard deviation:", features_standardized[:,0].std())

Mean: 0.0
Standard deviation: 1.0
```

20.2 Designing a Neural Network

Problem

You want to design a neural network.

Solution

Use Keras' Sequential model:

```
# Load libraries
from keras import models
from keras import layers

# Start neural network
network = models.Sequential()

# Add fully connected layer with a ReLU activation function
network.add(layers.Dense(units=16, activation="relu", input_shape=(10,)))

# Add fully connected layer with a ReLU activation function
network.add(layers.Dense(units=16, activation="relu"))

# Add fully connected layer with a sigmoid activation function
network.add(layers.Dense(units=1, activation="sigmoid"))

# Compile neural network
network.compile(loss="binary_crossentropy", # Cross-entropy
                optimizer="rmsprop", # Root Mean Square Propagation
                metrics=["accuracy"]) # Accuracy performance metric

Using TensorFlow backend.
```

Discussion

Neural networks consist of layers of units. However, there is incredible variety in the types of layers and how they are combined to form the network's architecture. At present, while there are commonly used architecture patterns (which we will cover in this chapter), the truth is that selecting the right architecture is mostly an art and the topic of much research.

To construct a feedforward neural network in Keras, we need to make a number of choices about both the network architecture and training process. Remember that each unit in the hidden layers:

1. Receives a number of inputs.

2. Weights each input by a parameter value.

3. Sums together all weighted inputs along with some bias (typically 1).

---

4. Most often then applies some function (called an *activation function*).

5. Sends the output on to units in the next layer.

First, for each layer in the hidden and output layers we must define the number of units to include in the layer and the activation function. Overall, the more units we have in a layer, the more our network is able to learn complex patterns. However, more units might make our network overfit the training data in a way detrimental to the performance on the test data.

For hidden layers, a popular activation function is the *rectified linear unit* (ReLU):

$$f(z) = \max{(0, z)}$$

where z is the sum of the weighted inputs and bias. As we can see, if z is greater than 0, the activation function returns z; otherwise, the function returns 0. This simple activation function has a number of desirable properties (a discussion of which is beyond the scope of this book) and this has made it a popular choice in neural networks. We should be aware, however, that many dozens of activation functions exist.

Second, we need to define the number of hidden layers to use in the network. More layers allow the network to learn more complex relationships, but with a computational cost.

Third, we have to define the structure of the activation function (if any) of the output layer. The nature of the output function is often determined by the goal of the network. Here are some common output layer patterns:

Binary classification
    One unit with a sigmoid activation function.

Multiclass classification
    k units (where k is the number of target classes) and a softmax activation function.

Regression
    One unit with no activation function.

Fourth, we need to define a loss function (the function that measures how well a predicted value matches the true value); this is again often determined by the problem type:

Binary classification
    Binary cross-entropy.

Multiclass classification
    Categorical cross-entropy.

Regression
 Mean square error.

Fifth, we have to define an optimizer, which intuitively can be thought of as our strategy "walking around" the loss function to find the parameter values that produce the lowest error. Common choices for optimizers are stochastic gradient descent, stochastic gradient descent with momentum, root mean square propagation, and adaptive moment estimation (more information on these optimizers in "See Also" on page 302).

Sixth, we can select one or more metrics to use to evaluate the performance, such as accuracy.

Keras offers two ways for creating neural networks. Keras' sequential model creates neural networks by stacking together layers. An alternative method for creating neural networks is called the functional API, but that is more for researchers rather than practitioners.

In our solution, we created a two-layer neural network (when counting layers we don't include the input layer because it does not have any parameters to learn) using Keras' sequential model. Each layer is "dense" (also called fully connected), meaning that all the units in the previous layer are connected to all the neurals in the next layer. In the first hidden layer we set `units=16`, meaning that layer contains 16 units with ReLU activation functions: `activation='relu'`. In Keras, the first hidden layer of any network has to include an `input_shape` parameter, which is the shape of feature data. For example, `(10,)` tells the first layer to expect each observation to have 10 feature values. Our second layer is the same as the first, without the need for the `input_shape` parameter. This network is designed for binary classification so the output layer contains only one unit with a sigmoid activation function, which constrains the output to between 0 and 1 (representing the probability an observation is class 1).

Finally, before we can train our model, we need to tell Keras how we want our network to learn. We do this using the `compile` method, with our optimization algorithm (`RMSProp`), loss function (`binary_crossentropy`), and one or more performance metrics.

See Also

- Losses, Keras (*https://keras.io/losses/*)
- Loss functions for classification, Wikipedia (*http://bit.ly/2FwpCkM*)
- On Loss Functions for Deep Neural Networks in Classification, Katarzyna Janocha, Wojciech Marian Czarnecki (*https://arxiv.org/abs/1702.05659*)

20.3 Training a Binary Classifier

Problem

You want to train a binary classifier neural network.

Solution

Use Keras to construct a feedforward neural network and train it using the `fit` method:

```python
# Load libraries
import numpy as np
from keras.datasets import imdb
from keras.preprocessing.text import Tokenizer
from keras import models
from keras import layers

# Set random seed
np.random.seed(0)

# Set the number of features we want
number_of_features = 1000

# Load data and target vector from movie review data
(data_train, target_train), (data_test, target_test) = imdb.load_data(
    num_words=number_of_features)

# Convert movie review data to one-hot encoded feature matrix
tokenizer = Tokenizer(num_words=number_of_features)
features_train = tokenizer.sequences_to_matrix(data_train, mode="binary")
features_test = tokenizer.sequences_to_matrix(data_test, mode="binary")

# Start neural network
network = models.Sequential()

# Add fully connected layer with a ReLU activation function
network.add(layers.Dense(units=16, activation="relu", input_shape=(
    number_of_features,)))

# Add fully connected layer with a ReLU activation function
network.add(layers.Dense(units=16, activation="relu"))

# Add fully connected layer with a sigmoid activation function
network.add(layers.Dense(units=1, activation="sigmoid"))

# Compile neural network
network.compile(loss="binary_crossentropy", # Cross-entropy
                optimizer="rmsprop", # Root Mean Square Propagation
                metrics=["accuracy"]) # Accuracy performance metric
```

```
# Train neural network
history = network.fit(features_train, # Features
                      target_train, # Target vector
                      epochs=3, # Number of epochs
                      verbose=1, # Print description after each epoch
                      batch_size=100, # Number of observations per batch
                      validation_data=(features_test, target_test)) # Test data

Using TensorFlow backend.


Train on 25000 samples, validate on 25000 samples
Epoch 1/3
25000/25000 [==============================]
- 1s - loss: 0.4215 - acc: 0.8105 - val_loss: 0.3386 - val_acc: 0.8555
Epoch 2/3
25000/25000 [==============================]
- 1s - loss: 0.3242 - acc: 0.8645 - val_loss: 0.3258 - val_acc: 0.8633
Epoch 3/3
25000/25000 [==============================]
- 1s - loss: 0.3121 - acc: 0.8699 - val_loss: 0.3265 - val_acc: 0.8599
```

Discussion

In Recipe 20.2, we discussed how to construct a neural network using Keras' sequential model. In this recipe we train that neural network using real data. Specifically, we use 50,000 movie reviews (25,000 as training data, 25,000 held out for testing), categorized as positive or negative. We convert the text of the reviews into 5,000 binary features indicating the presence of one of the 1,000 most frequent words. Put more simply, our neural networks will use 25,000 observations, each with 1,000 features, to predict if a movie review is positive or negative.

The neural network we are using is the same as the one in Recipe 20.2 (see there for a detailed explanation). The only addition is that in that recipe we only created the neural network, we didn't train it.

In Keras, we train our neural network using the `fit` method. There are six significant parameters to define. The first two parameters are the features and target vector of the training data. We can view the shape of feature matrix using `shape`:

```
# View shape of feature matrix
features_train.shape

(25000, 1000)
```

The `epochs` parameter defines how many epochs to use when training the data. `ver bose` determines how much information is outputted during the training process, with 0 being no output, 1 outputting a progress bar, and 2 one log line per epoch. `batch_size` sets the number of observations to propagate through the network before updating the parameters.

Finally, we held out a test set of data to use to evaluate the model. These test features and test target vector can be arguments of `validation_data`, which will use them for evaluation. Alternatively, we could have used `validation_split` to define what fraction of the training data we want to hold out for evaluation.

In scikit-learn the `fit` method returned a trained model, but in Keras the `fit` method returns a `History` object containing the loss values and performance metrics at each epoch.

20.4 Training a Multiclass Classifier

Problem

You want to train a multiclass classifier neural network.

Solution

Use Keras to construct a feedforward neural network with an output layer with softmax activation functions:

```
# Load libraries
import numpy as np
from keras.datasets import reuters
from keras.utils.np_utils import to_categorical
from keras.preprocessing.text import Tokenizer
from keras import models
from keras import layers

# Set random seed
np.random.seed(0)

# Set the number of features we want
number_of_features = 5000

# Load feature and target data
data = reuters.load_data(num_words=number_of_features)
(data_train, target_vector_train), (data_test, target_vector_test) = data

# Convert feature data to a one-hot encoded feature matrix
tokenizer = Tokenizer(num_words=number_of_features)
features_train = tokenizer.sequences_to_matrix(data_train, mode="binary")
features_test = tokenizer.sequences_to_matrix(data_test, mode="binary")

# One-hot encode target vector to create a target matrix
target_train = to_categorical(target_vector_train)
target_test = to_categorical(target_vector_test)

# Start neural network
network = models.Sequential()
```

```
# Add fully connected layer with a ReLU activation function
network.add(layers.Dense(units=100,
                         activation="relu",
                         input_shape=(number_of_features,)))

# Add fully connected layer with a ReLU activation function
network.add(layers.Dense(units=100, activation="relu"))

# Add fully connected layer with a softmax activation function
network.add(layers.Dense(units=46, activation="softmax"))

# Compile neural network
network.compile(loss="categorical_crossentropy", # Cross-entropy
                optimizer="rmsprop", # Root Mean Square Propagation
                metrics=["accuracy"]) # Accuracy performance metric

# Train neural network
history = network.fit(features_train, # Features
                      target_train, # Target
                      epochs=3, # Three epochs
                      verbose=0, # No output
                      batch_size=100, # Number of observations per batch
                      validation_data=(features_test, target_test)) # Test data
```

Using TensorFlow backend.

Discussion

In this solution we created a similar neural network to the binary classifier from the last recipe, but with some notable changes. First, our data is 11,228 Reuters newswires. Each newswire is categorized into 46 topics. We prepared our feature data by converting the newswires into 5,000 binary features (denoting the presence of a certain word in the newswires). We prepared the target data by one-hot encoding it so that we obtain a target matrix denoting which of the 46 classes an observation belongs to:

```
# View target matrix
target_train
array([[ 0.,  0.,  0., ...,  0.,  0.,  0.],
       [ 0.,  0.,  0., ...,  0.,  0.,  0.],
       [ 0.,  0.,  0., ...,  0.,  0.,  0.],
       ...,
       [ 0.,  0.,  0., ...,  0.,  0.,  0.],
       [ 0.,  0.,  0., ...,  0.,  0.,  0.],
       [ 0.,  0.,  0., ...,  0.,  0.,  0.]])
```

Second, we increased the number of units in each of the hidden layers to help the neural network represent the more complex relationship between the 46 classes.

Third, since this is a multiclass classification problem, we used an output layer with 46 units (one per class) containing a softmax activation function. The softmax activation function will return an array of 46 values summing to 1. These 46 values represent an observation's probability of being a member of each of the 46 classes.

Fourth, we used a loss function suited to multiclass classification, the categorical cross-entropy loss function, `categorical_crossentropy`.

20.5 Training a Regressor

Problem

You want to train a neural network for regression.

Solution

Use Keras to construct a feedforward neural network with a single output unit and no activation function:

```
# Load libraries
import numpy as np
from keras.preprocessing.text import Tokenizer
from keras import models
from keras import layers
from sklearn.datasets import make_regression
from sklearn.model_selection import train_test_split
from sklearn import preprocessing

# Set random seed
np.random.seed(0)

# Generate features matrix and target vector
features, target = make_regression(n_samples = 10000,
                                   n_features = 3,
                                   n_informative = 3,
                                   n_targets = 1,
                                   noise = 0.0,
                                   random_state = 0)

# Divide our data into training and test sets
features_train, features_test, target_train, target_test = train_test_split(
features, target, test_size=0.33, random_state=0)

# Start neural network
network = models.Sequential()

# Add fully connected layer with a ReLU activation function
network.add(layers.Dense(units=32,
                         activation="relu",
                         input_shape=(features_train.shape[1],)))
```

```
# Add fully connected layer with a ReLU activation function
network.add(layers.Dense(units=32, activation="relu"))

# Add fully connected layer with no activation function
network.add(layers.Dense(units=1))

# Compile neural network
network.compile(loss="mse", # Mean squared error
                optimizer="RMSprop", # Optimization algorithm
                metrics=["mse"]) # Mean squared error

# Train neural network
history = network.fit(features_train, # Features
                      target_train, # Target vector
                      epochs=10, # Number of epochs
                      verbose=0, # No output
                      batch_size=100, # Number of observations per batch
                      validation_data=(features_test, target_test)) # Test data

Using TensorFlow backend.
```

Discussion

It is completely possible to create a neural network to predict continuous values instead of class probabilities. In the case of our binary classifier (Recipe 20.3) we used an output layer with a single unit and a sigmoid activation function to produce a probability that an observation was class 1. Importantly, the sigmoid activation function constrained the outputted value to between 0 and 1. If we remove that constraint by having no activation function, we allow the output to be a continuous value.

Furthermore, because we are training a regression, we should use an appropriate loss function and evaluation metric, in our case the mean square error:

$$\text{MSE} = \frac{1}{n} \sum_{i=1}^{n} \left(\widehat{y}_i - y_i \right)^2$$

where n is the number of observations; y_i is the true value of the target we are trying to predict, y, for observation i; and $\hat{y}_i$ is the model's predicted value for y_i.

Finally, because we are using simulated data using scikit-learn, make_regression, we didn't have to standardize the features. It should be noted, however, that in almost all real-world cases standardization would be necessary.

20.6 Making Predictions

Problem

You want to use a neural network to make predictions.

Solution

Use Keras to construct a feedforward neural network, then make predictions using predict:

```
# Load libraries
import numpy as np
from keras.datasets import imdb
from keras.preprocessing.text import Tokenizer
from keras import models
from keras import layers

# Set random seed
np.random.seed(0)

# Set the number of features we want
number_of_features = 10000

# Load data and target vector from IMDB movie data
(data_train, target_train), (data_test, target_test) = imdb.load_data(
    num_words=number_of_features)

# Convert IMDB data to a one-hot encoded feature matrix
tokenizer = Tokenizer(num_words=number_of_features)
features_train = tokenizer.sequences_to_matrix(data_train, mode="binary")
features_test = tokenizer.sequences_to_matrix(data_test, mode="binary")

# Start neural network
network = models.Sequential()

# Add fully connected layer with a ReLU activation function
network.add(layers.Dense(units=16,
                         activation="relu",
                         input_shape=(number_of_features,)))

# Add fully connected layer with a ReLU activation function
network.add(layers.Dense(units=16, activation="relu"))

# Add fully connected layer with a sigmoid activation function
network.add(layers.Dense(units=1, activation="sigmoid"))

# Compile neural network
network.compile(loss="binary_crossentropy", # Cross-entropy
                optimizer="rmsprop", # Root Mean Square Propagation
                metrics=["accuracy"]) # Accuracy performance metric
```

```
# Train neural network
history = network.fit(features_train, # Features
                      target_train, # Target vector
                      epochs=3, # Number of epochs
                      verbose=0, # No output
                      batch_size=100, # Number of observations per batch
                      validation_data=(features_test, target_test)) # Test data

# Predict classes of test set
predicted_target = network.predict(features_test)

Using TensorFlow backend.
```

Discussion

Making predictions is easy in Keras. Once we have trained our neural network we can use the `predict` method, which takes as an argument a set of features and returns the predicted output for each observation. In our solution our neural network is set up for binary classification so the predicted output is the probability of being class 1. Observations with predicted values very close to 1 are highly likely to be class 1, while observations with predicted values very close to 0 are highly likely to be class 0. For example, this is the predicted probability that the first observation in our test feature matrix is class 1:

```
# View the probability the first observation is class 1
predicted_target[0]

array([ 0.83937484], dtype=float32)
```

20.7 Visualize Training History

Problem

You want to find the "sweet spot" in a neural network's loss and/or accuracy score.

Solution

Use Matplotlib to visualize the loss of the test and training set over each epoch:

```
# Load libraries
import numpy as np
from keras.datasets import imdb
from keras.preprocessing.text import Tokenizer
from keras import models
from keras import layers
import matplotlib.pyplot as plt

# Set random seed
np.random.seed(0)
```

```
# Set the number of features we want
number_of_features = 10000

# Load data and target vector from movie review data
(data_train, target_train), (data_test, target_test) = imdb.load_data(
    num_words=number_of_features)

# Convert movie review data to a one-hot encoded feature matrix
tokenizer = Tokenizer(num_words=number_of_features)
features_train = tokenizer.sequences_to_matrix(data_train, mode="binary")
features_test = tokenizer.sequences_to_matrix(data_test, mode="binary")

# Start neural network
network = models.Sequential()

# Add fully connected layer with a ReLU activation function
network.add(layers.Dense(units=16,
                         activation="relu",
                         input_shape=(number_of_features,)))

# Add fully connected layer with a ReLU activation function
network.add(layers.Dense(units=16, activation="relu"))

# Add fully connected layer with a sigmoid activation function
network.add(layers.Dense(units=1, activation="sigmoid"))

# Compile neural network
network.compile(loss="binary_crossentropy", # Cross-entropy
                optimizer="rmsprop", # Root Mean Square Propagation
                metrics=["accuracy"]) # Accuracy performance metric

# Train neural network
history = network.fit(features_train, # Features
                      target_train, # Target
                      epochs=15, # Number of epochs
                      verbose=0, # No output
                      batch_size=1000, # Number of observations per batch
                      validation_data=(features_test, target_test)) # Test data

# Get training and test loss histories
training_loss = history.history["loss"]
test_loss = history.history["val_loss"]

# Create count of the number of epochs
epoch_count = range(1, len(training_loss) + 1)

# Visualize loss history
plt.plot(epoch_count, training_loss, "r--")
plt.plot(epoch_count, test_loss, "b-")
plt.legend(["Training Loss", "Test Loss"])
plt.xlabel("Epoch")
```

```
plt.ylabel("Loss")
plt.show();

Using TensorFlow backend.
```

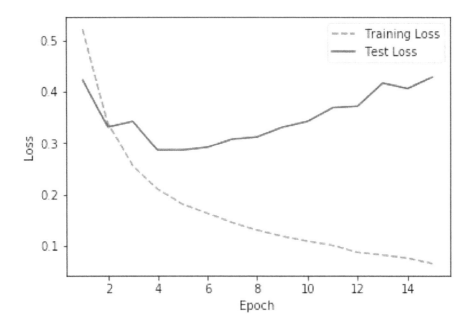

Alternatively, we can use the same approach to visualize the training and test accuracy over each epoch:

```
# Get training and test accuracy histories
training_accuracy = history.history["acc"]
test_accuracy = history.history["val_acc"]
plt.plot(epoch_count, training_accuracy, "r--")
plt.plot(epoch_count, test_accuracy, "b-")

# Visualize accuracy history
plt.legend(["Training Accuracy", "Test Accuracy"])
plt.xlabel("Epoch")
plt.ylabel("Accuracy Score")
plt.show();
```

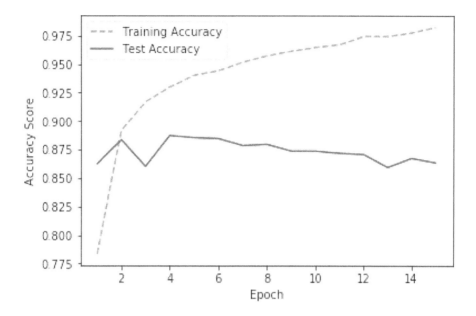

Discussion

When our neural network is new, it will have a poor performance. As the neural network learns on the training data, the model's error on both the training and test set will tend to increase. However, at a certain point the neural network starts "memorizing" the training data, and overfits. When this starts happening, the training error will decrease while the test error will start increasing. Therefore, in many cases there is a "sweet spot" where the test error (which is the error we mainly care about) is at its lowest point. This effect can be plainly seen in the solution where we visualize the training and test loss at each epoch. Note that the test error is lowest around epoch five, after which the training loss continues to increase while the test loss starts increasing. At this point onward, the model is overfitting.

20.8 Reducing Overfitting with Weight Regularization

Problem

You want to reduce overfitting.

Solution

Try penalizing the parameters of the network, also called *weight regularization*:

```
# Load libraries
import numpy as np
from keras.datasets import imdb
from keras.preprocessing.text import Tokenizer
from keras import models
from keras import layers
from keras import regularizers

# Set random seed
np.random.seed(0)

# Set the number of features we want
number_of_features = 1000

# Load data and target vector from movie review data
(data_train, target_train), (data_test, target_test) = imdb.load_data(
    num_words=number_of_features)

# Convert movie review data to a one-hot encoded feature matrix
tokenizer = Tokenizer(num_words=number_of_features)
features_train = tokenizer.sequences_to_matrix(data_train, mode="binary")
features_test = tokenizer.sequences_to_matrix(data_test, mode="binary")

# Start neural network
network = models.Sequential()

# Add fully connected layer with a ReLU activation function
network.add(layers.Dense(units=16,
                         activation="relu",
                         kernel_regularizer=regularizers.l2(0.01),
                         input_shape=(number_of_features,)))

# Add fully connected layer with a ReLU activation function
network.add(layers.Dense(units=16,
                         kernel_regularizer=regularizers.l2(0.01),
                         activation="relu"))

# Add fully connected layer with a sigmoid activation function
network.add(layers.Dense(units=1, activation="sigmoid"))

# Compile neural network
network.compile(loss="binary_crossentropy", # Cross-entropy
                optimizer="rmsprop", # Root Mean Square Propagation
                metrics=["accuracy"]) # Accuracy performance metric

# Train neural network
history = network.fit(features_train, # Features
                      target_train, # Target vector
                      epochs=3, # Number of epochs
                      verbose=0, # No output
                      batch_size=100, # Number of observations per batch
                      validation_data=(features_test, target_test)) # Test data
```

Using TensorFlow backend.

Discussion

One strategy to combat overfitting neural networks is by penalizing the parameters (i.e., weights) of the neural network such that they are driven to be small values—creating a simpler model less prone to overfit. This method is called weight regularization or weight decay. More specifically, in weight regularization a penalty is added to the loss function, such as the L2 norm.

In Keras, we can add a weight regularization by including using `kernel_regular izer=regularizers.l2(0.01)` in a layer's parameters. In this example, `0.01` determines how much we penalize higher parameter values.

20.9 Reducing Overfitting with Early Stopping

Problem

You want to reduce overfitting.

Solution

Try stopping training when the test loss stops decreasing, a strategy called *early stopping*:

```
# Load libraries
import numpy as np
from keras.datasets import imdb
from keras.preprocessing.text import Tokenizer
from keras import models
from keras import layers
from keras.callbacks import EarlyStopping, ModelCheckpoint

# Set random seed
np.random.seed(0)

# Set the number of features we want
number_of_features = 1000

# Load data and target vector from movie review data
(data_train, target_train), (data_test, target_test) = imdb.load_data(
    num_words=number_of_features)

# Convert movie review data to a one-hot encoded feature matrix
tokenizer = Tokenizer(num_words=number_of_features)
features_train = tokenizer.sequences_to_matrix(data_train, mode="binary")
features_test = tokenizer.sequences_to_matrix(data_test, mode="binary")

# Start neural network
```

```
network = models.Sequential()

# Add fully connected layer with a ReLU activation function
network.add(layers.Dense(units=16,
                         activation="relu",
                         input_shape=(number_of_features,)))

# Add fully connected layer with a ReLU activation function
network.add(layers.Dense(units=16, activation="relu"))

# Add fully connected layer with a sigmoid activation function
network.add(layers.Dense(units=1, activation="sigmoid"))

# Compile neural network
network.compile(loss="binary_crossentropy", # Cross-entropy
                optimizer="rmsprop", # Root Mean Square Propagation
                metrics=["accuracy"]) # Accuracy performance metric

# Set callback functions to early stop training and save the best model so far
callbacks = [EarlyStopping(monitor="val_loss", patience=2),
             ModelCheckpoint(filepath="best_model.h5",
                             monitor="val_loss",
                             save_best_only=True)]

# Train neural network
history = network.fit(features_train, # Features
                      target_train, # Target vector
                      epochs=20, # Number of epochs
                      callbacks=callbacks, # Early stopping
                      verbose=0, # Print description after each epoch
                      batch_size=100, # Number of observations per batch
                      validation_data=(features_test, target_test)) # Test data

Using TensorFlow backend.
```

Discussion

As we discussed in Recipe 20.7, typically in the first training epochs both the training and test errors will decrease, but at some point the network will start "memorizing" the training data, causing the training error to continue to decrease even while the test error starts increasing. Because of this phenomenon, one of the most common and very effective methods to counter overfitting is to monitor the training process and stop training when the test error starts to increase. This strategy is called early stopping.

In Keras, we can implement early stopping as a callback function. Callbacks are functions that can be applied at certain stages of the training process, such as at the end of each epoch. Specifically, in our solution, we included EarlyStopping(moni tor='val_loss', patience=2) to define that we wanted to monitor the test (validation) loss at each epoch and after the test loss has not improved after two epochs, training is interrupted. However, since we set `patience=2`, we won't get the best model, but the model two epochs after the best model. Therefore, optionally, we can include a second operation, `ModelCheckpoint`, which saves the model to a file after every checkpoint (which can be useful in case a multiday training session is interrupted for some reason). It would be helpful for us, if we set `save_best_only=True`, because then `ModelCheckpoint` will only save the best model.

20.10 Reducing Overfitting with Dropout

Problem

You want to reduce overfitting.

Solution

Introduce noise into your network's architecture using dropout:

```
# Load libraries
import numpy as np
from keras.datasets import imdb
from keras.preprocessing.text import Tokenizer
from keras import models
from keras import layers

# Set random seed
np.random.seed(0)

# Set the number of features we want
number_of_features = 1000

# Load data and target vector from movie review data
(data_train, target_train), (data_test, target_test) = imdb.load_data(
    num_words=number_of_features)

# Convert movie review data to a one-hot encoded feature matrix
tokenizer = Tokenizer(num_words=number_of_features)
features_train = tokenizer.sequences_to_matrix(data_train, mode="binary")
features_test = tokenizer.sequences_to_matrix(data_test, mode="binary")

# Start neural network
network = models.Sequential()

# Add a dropout layer for input layer
network.add(layers.Dropout(0.2, input_shape=(number_of_features,)))

# Add fully connected layer with a ReLU activation function
network.add(layers.Dense(units=16, activation="relu"))

# Add a dropout layer for previous hidden layer
```

```
network.add(layers.Dropout(0.5))

# Add fully connected layer with a ReLU activation function
network.add(layers.Dense(units=16, activation="relu"))

# Add a dropout layer for previous hidden layer
network.add(layers.Dropout(0.5))

# Add fully connected layer with a sigmoid activation function
network.add(layers.Dense(units=1, activation="sigmoid"))

# Compile neural network
network.compile(loss="binary_crossentropy", # Cross-entropy
                optimizer="rmsprop", # Root Mean Square Propagation
                metrics=["accuracy"]) # Accuracy performance metric

# Train neural network
history = network.fit(features_train, # Features
                      target_train, # Target vector
                      epochs=3, # Number of epochs
                      verbose=0, # No output
                      batch_size=100, # Number of observations per batch
                      validation_data=(features_test, target_test)) # Test data
```

Using TensorFlow backend.

Discussion

Dropout is a popular and powerful method for regularizing neural networks. In dropout, every time a batch of observations is created for training, a proportion of the units in one or more layers is multiplied by zero (i.e., dropped). In this setting, every batch is trained on the same network (e.g., the same parameters), but each batch is confronted by a slightly different version of that network's *architecture*.

Dropout is effective because by constantly and randomly dropping units in each batch, it forces units to learn parameter values able to perform under a wide variety of network architectures. That is, they learn to be robust to disruptions (i.e., noise) in the other hidden units, and this prevents the network from simply memorizing the training data.

It is possible to add dropout to both the hidden and input layers. When an input layer is dropped, its feature value is not introduced into the network for that batch. A common choice for the portion of units to drop is 0.2 for input units and 0.5 for hidden units.

In Keras, we can implement dropout by adding Dropout layers into our network architecture. Each Dropout layer will drop a user-defined hyperparameter of units in the previous layer every batch. Remember in Keras the input layer is assumed to be the first layer and not added using add. Therefore, if we want to add dropout to the input layer, the first layer we add in our network architecture is a dropout layer. This layer contains both the proportion of the input layer's units to drop `0.2` and `input_shape` defining the shape of the observation data. Next, we add a dropout layer with `0.5` after each of the hidden layers.

20.11 Saving Model Training Progress

Problem

Given a neural network that will take a long time to train, you want to save your progress in case the training process is interrupted.

Solution

Use the callback function `ModelCheckpoint` to save the model after every epoch:

```
# Load libraries
import numpy as np
from keras.datasets import imdb
from keras.preprocessing.text import Tokenizer
from keras import models
from keras import layers
from keras.callbacks import ModelCheckpoint

# Set random seed
np.random.seed(0)

# Set the number of features we want
number_of_features = 1000

# Load data and target vector from movie review data
(data_train, target_train), (data_test, target_test) = imdb.load_data(
    num_words=number_of_features)

# Convert movie review data to a one-hot encoded feature matrix
tokenizer = Tokenizer(num_words=number_of_features)
features_train = tokenizer.sequences_to_matrix(data_train, mode="binary")
features_test = tokenizer.sequences_to_matrix(data_test, mode="binary")

# Start neural network
network = models.Sequential()

# Add fully connected layer with a ReLU activation function
network.add(layers.Dense(units=16,
                         activation="relu",
                         input_shape=(number_of_features,)))

# Add fully connected layer with a ReLU activation function
network.add(layers.Dense(units=16, activation="relu"))
```

```
# Add fully connected layer with a sigmoid activation function
network.add(layers.Dense(units=1, activation="sigmoid"))

# Compile neural network
network.compile(loss="binary_crossentropy", # Cross-entropy
                optimizer="rmsprop", # Root Mean Square Propagation
                metrics=["accuracy"]) # Accuracy performance metric

# Set callback functions to early stop training and save the best model so far
checkpoint = [ModelCheckpoint(filepath="models.hdf5")]

# Train neural network
history = network.fit(features_train, # Features
                      target_train, # Target vector
                      epochs=3, # Number of epochs
                      callbacks=checkpoint, # Checkpoint
                      verbose=0, # No output
                      batch_size=100, # Number of observations per batch
                      validation_data=(features_test, target_test)) # Test data
```

Using TensorFlow backend.

Discussion

In Recipe 20.8 we used the callback function ModelCheckpoint in conjunction with
EarlyStopping to end monitoring and end training when the test error stopped
improving. However, there is another, more mundane reason for using ModelCheck
point. In the real world, it is common for neural networks to train for hours or even
days. During that time a lot can go wrong: computers can lose power, servers can
crash, or inconsiderate graduate students can close your laptop.

ModelCheckpoint alleviates this problem by saving the model after every epoch.
Specifically, after every epoch ModelCheckpoint saves a model to the location specified by the filepath parameter. If we include only a filename (e.g., *models.hdf5*) that
file will be overridden with the latest model every epoch. If we only wanted to save
the best model according to the performance of some loss function, we can set
save_best_only=True and monitor='val_loss' to not override a file if the model
has a worse test loss than the previous model. Alternatively, we can save every epoch's
model as its own file by including the epoch number and test loss score into the filename itself. For example, if we set filepath to model_{epoch:02d}_{val_loss:.
2f}.hdf5, the name of the file containing the model saved after the 11th epoch with a
test loss value of 0.33 would be *model_10_0.35.hdf5* (notice that the epoch number is
0-indexed).

20.12 k-Fold Cross-Validating Neural Networks

Problem

You want to evaluate a neural network using k-fold cross-validation.

Solution

Often k-fold cross-validating neural networks is neither necessary nor advisable. However, if it is appropriate: use Keras' scikit-learn wrapper to allow Keras' sequential models to use the scikit-learn API:

```python
# Load libraries
import numpy as np
from keras import models
from keras import layers
from keras.wrappers.scikit_learn import KerasClassifier
from sklearn.model_selection import cross_val_score
from sklearn.datasets import make_classification

# Set random seed
np.random.seed(0)

# Number of features
number_of_features = 100

# Generate features matrix and target vector
features, target = make_classification(n_samples = 10000,
                                       n_features = number_of_features,
                                       n_informative = 3,
                                       n_redundant = 0,
                                       n_classes = 2,
                                       weights = [.5, .5],
                                       random_state = 0)

# Create function returning a compiled network
def create_network():

    # Start neural network
    network = models.Sequential()

    # Add fully connected layer with a ReLU activation function
    network.add(layers.Dense(units=16, activation="relu", input_shape=(
        number_of_features,)))

    # Add fully connected layer with a ReLU activation function
    network.add(layers.Dense(units=16, activation="relu"))

    # Add fully connected layer with a sigmoid activation function
    network.add(layers.Dense(units=1, activation="sigmoid"))
```

```
# Compile neural network
network.compile(loss="binary_crossentropy", # Cross-entropy
                optimizer="rmsprop", # Root Mean Square Propagation
                metrics=["accuracy"]) # Accuracy performance metric

# Return compiled network
return network

# Wrap Keras model so it can be used by scikit-learn
neural_network = KerasClassifier(build_fn=create_network,
                                 epochs=10,
                                 batch_size=100,
                                 verbose=0)

# Evaluate neural network using three-fold cross-validation
cross_val_score(neural_network, features, target, cv=3)

Using TensorFlow backend.

array([ 0.90461907,  0.77437743,  0.87068707])
```

Discussion

Theoretically, there is no reason we cannot use cross-validation to evaluate neural networks. However, neural networks are often used on very large data and can take hours or even days to train. For this reason, if the training time is long, adding the computational expense of k-fold cross-validation is unadvisable. For example, a model normally taking one day to train would take 10 days to evaluate using 10-fold cross-validation. If we have large data, it is often appropriate to simply evaluate the neural network on some test set.

If we have smaller data, k-fold cross-validation can be useful to maximize our ability to evaluate the neural network's performance. This is possible in Keras because we can "wrap" any neural network such that it can use the evaluation features available in scikit-learn, including k-fold cross-validation. To accomplish this, we first have to create a function that returns a compiled neural network. Next we use KerasClassifier (if we have a classifier; if we have a regressor we can use KerasRegressor) to wrap the model so it can be used by scikit-learn. After this, we can use our neural network like any other scikit-learn learning algorithm (e.g., random forests, logistic regression). In our solution, we used cross_val_score to run a three-fold cross-validation on our neural network.

20.13 Tuning Neural Networks

Problem

You want to automatically select the best hyperparameters for your neural network.

Solution

Combine a Keras neural network with scikit-learn's model selection tools like Grid SearchCV:

```python
# Load libraries
import numpy as np
from keras import models
from keras import layers
from keras.wrappers.scikit_learn import KerasClassifier
from sklearn.model_selection import GridSearchCV
from sklearn.datasets import make_classification

# Set random seed
np.random.seed(0)

# Number of features
number_of_features = 100

# Generate features matrix and target vector
features, target = make_classification(n_samples = 10000,
                                       n_features = number_of_features,
                                       n_informative = 3,
                                       n_redundant = 0,
                                       n_classes = 2,
                                       weights = [.5, .5],
                                       random_state = 0)

# Create function returning a compiled network
def create_network(optimizer="rmsprop"):

    # Start neural network
    network = models.Sequential()

    # Add fully connected layer with a ReLU activation function
    network.add(layers.Dense(units=16,
                             activation="relu",
                             input_shape=(number_of_features,)))

    # Add fully connected layer with a ReLU activation function
    network.add(layers.Dense(units=16, activation="relu"))

    # Add fully connected layer with a sigmoid activation function
    network.add(layers.Dense(units=1, activation="sigmoid"))

    # Compile neural network
    network.compile(loss="binary_crossentropy", # Cross-entropy
                    optimizer=optimizer, # Optimizer
                    metrics=["accuracy"]) # Accuracy performance metric

    # Return compiled network
    return network
```

```
# Wrap Keras model so it can be used by scikit-learn
neural_network = KerasClassifier(build_fn=create_network, verbose=0)

# Create hyperparameter space
epochs = [5, 10]
batches = [5, 10, 100]
optimizers = ["rmsprop", "adam"]

# Create hyperparameter options
hyperparameters = dict(optimizer=optimizers, epochs=epochs, batch_size=batches)

# Create grid search
grid = GridSearchCV(estimator=neural_network, param_grid=hyperparameters)

# Fit grid search
grid_result = grid.fit(features, target)

Using TensorFlow backend.
```

Discussion

In Recipes 12.1 and 12.2, we covered using scikit-learn's model selection techniques to identify the best hyperparameters of a scikit-learn model. In Recipe 20.12 we learned that we can wrap our neural network so it can use the scikit-learn API. In this recipe we combine these two techniques to identify the best hyperparameters of a neural network.

The hyperparameters of a model *are* important and should be selected with care. However, before we get it into our heads that model selection strategies like grid search are a good idea, we must realize that if our model would normally have taken 12 hours or a day to train, this grid search process could take a week or more. Therefore, automatic hyperparameter tuning of neural networks is not the silver bullet, but it is a useful tool to have in certain circumstances.

In our solution we conducted a cross-validated grid search over a number of options for the optimization algorithm, number of epochs, and batch size. Even this toy example took a few minutes to run, but once it is done we can use best_params_ to view the hyperparameters of the neural network with the best results:

```
# View hyperparameters of best neural network
grid_result.best_params_
```

```
{'batch_size': 10, 'epochs': 5, 'optimizer': 'adam'}
```

20.14 Visualizing Neural Networks

Problem

You want to quickly visualize a neural network's architecture.

Solution

Use Keras' model_to_dot or plot_model:

```
# Load libraries
from keras import models
from keras import layers
from IPython.display import SVG
from keras.utils.vis_utils import model_to_dot
from keras.utils import plot_model

# Start neural network
network = models.Sequential()

# Add fully connected layer with a ReLU activation function
network.add(layers.Dense(units=16, activation="relu", input_shape=(10,)))

# Add fully connected layer with a ReLU activation function
network.add(layers.Dense(units=16, activation="relu"))

# Add fully connected layer with a sigmoid activation function
network.add(layers.Dense(units=1, activation="sigmoid"))

# Visualize network architecture
SVG(model_to_dot(network, show_shapes=True).create(prog="dot", format="svg"))

Using TensorFlow backend.
```

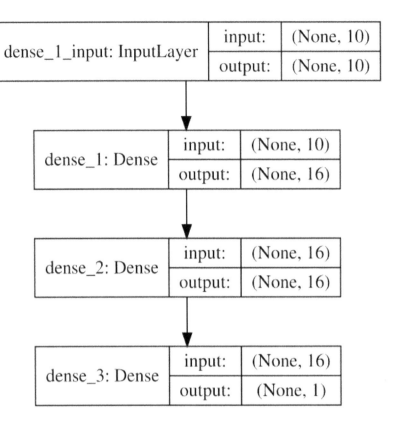

Alternatively, if we want to save the visualization as a file, we can use plot_model:

```
# Save the visualization as a file
plot_model(network, show_shapes=True, to_file="network.png")
```

Discussion

Keras provides utility functions to quickly visualize neural networks. If we wish to display a neural network in a Jupyter Notebook, we can use model_to_dot. The show_shapes parameter shows the shape of the inputs and outputs and can help with debugging. For a simpler model, we can set show_shapes=True:

```
# Visualize network architecture
SVG(model_to_dot(network, show_shapes=False).create(prog="dot", format="svg"))
```

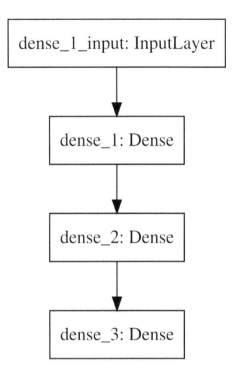

20.15 Classifying Images

Problem

You want to classify images using a convolutional neural network.

Solution

Use Keras to create a neural network with at least one convolutional layer:

```
import numpy as np
from keras.datasets import mnist
from keras.models import Sequential
from keras.layers import Dense, Dropout, Flatten
from keras.layers.convolutional import Conv2D, MaxPooling2D
from keras.utils import np_utils
from keras import backend as K

# Set that the color channel value will be first
K.set_image_data_format("channels_first")

# Set seed
np.random.seed(0)
```

```
# Set image information
channels = 1
height = 28
width = 28

# Load data and target from MNIST data
(data_train, target_train), (data_test, target_test) = mnist.load_data()

# Reshape training image data into features
data_train = data_train.reshape(data_train.shape[0], channels, height, width)

# Reshape test image data into features
data_test = data_test.reshape(data_test.shape[0], channels, height, width)

# Rescale pixel intensity to between 0 and 1
features_train = data_train / 255
features_test = data_test / 255

# One-hot encode target
target_train = np_utils.to_categorical(target_train)
target_test = np_utils.to_categorical(target_test)
number_of_classes = target_test.shape[1]

# Start neural network
network = Sequential()

# Add convolutional layer with 64 filters, a 5x5 window, and ReLU activation function
network.add(Conv2D(filters=64,
                   kernel_size=(5, 5),
                   input_shape=(channels, width, height),
                   activation='relu'))

# Add max pooling layer with a 2x2 window
network.add(MaxPooling2D(pool_size=(2, 2)))

# Add dropout layer
network.add(Dropout(0.5))

# Add layer to flatten input
network.add(Flatten())

# # Add fully connected layer of 128 units with a ReLU activation function
network.add(Dense(128, activation="relu"))

# Add dropout layer
network.add(Dropout(0.5))

# Add fully connected layer with a softmax activation function
network.add(Dense(number_of_classes, activation="softmax"))

# Compile neural network
```

```
network.compile(loss="categorical_crossentropy", # Cross-entropy
                optimizer="rmsprop", # Root Mean Square Propagation
                metrics=["accuracy"]) # Accuracy performance metric

# Train neural network
network.fit(features_train, # Features
            target_train, # Target
            epochs=2, # Number of epochs
            verbose=0, # Don't print description after each epoch
            batch_size=1000, # Number of observations per batch
            validation_data=(features_test, target_test)) # Data for evaluation

Using TensorFlow backend.

<keras.callbacks.History at 0x133f37e80>
```

Discussion

Convolutional neural networks (also called ConvNets) are a popular type of network that has proven very effective at computer vision (e.g., recognizing cats, dogs, planes, and even hot dogs). It is completely possible to use feedforward neural networks on images, where each pixel is a feature. However, when doing so we run into two major problems. First, feedforward neural networks do not take into account the spatial structure of the pixels. For example, in a 10 × 10 pixel image we might convert it into a vector of 100 pixel features, and in this case feedforward would consider the first feature (e.g., pixel value) to have the same relationship with the 10th feature as the 11th feature. However, in reality the 10th feature represents a pixel on the far side of the image as the first feature, while the 11th feature represents the pixel immediately below the first pixel. Second, and relatedly, feedforward neural networks learn global relationships in the features instead of local patterns. In more practical terms, this means that feedforward neural networks are not able to detect an object regardless of where it appears in an image. For example, imagine we are training a neural network to recognize faces, and these faces might appear anywhere in the image from the upper right to the middle to the lower left.

The power of convolutional neural networks is their ability handle both of these issues (and others). A complete explanation of convolutional neural networks is well beyond the scope of this book, but a brief explanation will be useful. The data of an individual image contains two or three dimensions: height, width, and depth. The first two should be obvious, but the last deserves explanation. The depth is the color of a pixel. In grayscale images the depth is only one (the intensity of the pixel) and therefore the image is a matrix. However, in color images a pixel's color is represented by multiple values. For example, in an RGB image a pixel's color is represented by three values representing red, green, and blue. Therefore, the data for an image can be imagined to be a three-dimensional tensor: *width* × *height* × *depth* (called *feature maps*). In convolutional neural networks, a convolution (don't worry if you don't know what that means) can be imagined to slide a window over the pixels of an image, looking at both the individual pixel and also its neighbors. It then transforms the raw image data into a new three-dimensional tensor where the first two dimensions are approximately width and height, while the third dimension (which contained the color values) now represents the patterns—called *filters*—(for example, a sharp corner or sweeping gradient) to which that pixel "belongs."

The second important concept for our purposes is that of pooling layers. Pooling layers move a window over our data (though usually they only look at every nth pixel, called *striding*) downsizing our data by summarizing the window in some way. The most common method is max pooling where the maximum value in each window is sent to the next layer. One reason for max pooling is merely practical; the convolutional process creates many more parameters to learn, which can get ungainly very quickly. Second, more intuitively, max pooling can be thought of as "zooming out" of an image.

An example might be useful here. Imagine we have an image containing a dog's face. The first convolutional layer might find patterns like shape edges. Then we use a max pool layer to "zoom out," and a second convolutional layer to find patterns like dog ears. Finally we use another max pooling layer to zoom out again and a final convolutional layer to find patterns like dogs' faces.

Finally, fully connected layers are often used at the end of the network to do the actual classification.

While our solution might look like a lot of lines of code, it is actually very similar to our binary classifier from earlier in this chapter. In this solution we used the famous MNIST dataset, which is a de facto benchmark dataset in machine learning. The MNIST dataset contains 70,000 small images (28 × 28) of handwritten digits from 0 to 9. This dataset is labeled so that we know the actual digit (i.e., class) for each small image. The standard training-test split is to use 60,000 images for training and 10,000 for testing.

We reorganized the data into the format expected by a convolutional network. Specifically, we used `reshape` to convert the observation data such that it is the shape Keras expects. Next, we rescaled the values to be between 0 and 1, since training performance can suffer if an observation's values are much greater than the network's parameters (which are initialized as small numbers). Finally, we one-hot encoded the target data so that every observation's target has 10 classes, representing the digits 0–9.

With the image data process we can build our convolutional network. First, we add a convolutional layer and specify the number of filters and other characteristics. The size of the window is a hyperparameter; however, 3 × 3 is standard practice for most images, while larger windows are often used in larger images. Second, we add a max pooling layer, summarizing the nearby pixels. Third, we add a dropout layer to reduce the chances of overfitting. Fourth, we add a flatten layer to convert the convolutionary inputs into a format able to be used by a fully connected layer. Finally, we add the fully connected layers and an output layer to do the actual classification. Notice that because this is a multiclass classification problem, we use the softmax activation function in the output layer.

It should be noted that this is a pretty simple convolutional neural network. It is common to see a much deeper network with many more convolutional and max pooling layers stacked together.

20.16 Improving Performance with Image Augmentation

Problem

You want to improve the performance of your convolutional neural network.

Solution

For better results, preprocess the images and augment the data beforehand using `ImageDataGenerator`:

```
# Load library
from keras.preprocessing.image import ImageDataGenerator

# Create image augmentation
augmentation = ImageDataGenerator(featurewise_center=True, # Apply ZCA whitening
                                  zoom_range=0.3, # Randomly zoom in on images
                                  width_shift_range=0.2, # Randomly shift images
                                  horizontal_flip=True, # Randomly flip images
                                  rotation_range=90) # Randomly rotate

# Process all images from the directory 'raw/images'
augment_images = augmentation.flow_from_directory("raw/images", # Image folder
                                                  batch_size=32, # Batch size
                                                  class_mode="binary", # Classes
                                                  save_to_dir="processed/images")

Using TensorFlow backend.


Found 12665 images belonging to 2 classes.
```

Discussion

First an apology—this solution's code will not immediately run for you because you do not have the required folders of images. However, since the most common situation is having a directory of images, I wanted to include it. The technique should easily translate to your own images.

One way to improve the performance of a convolutional neural network is to preprocess the images. We discussed a number of techniques in Chapter 8; however, it is worth noting that Keras' `ImageDataGenerator` contains a number of basic preprocessing techniques. For example, in our solution we used `featurewise_center=True` to standardize the pixels across the entire data.

A second technique to improve performance is to add noise. An interesting feature of neural networks is that, counterintuitively, their performance often improves when noise is added to the data. The reason is that the additional noise can make the neural networks more robust in the face of real-world noise and prevents them from overfitting the data.

When training convolutional neural networks for images, we can add noise to our observations by randomly transforming images in various ways, such as flipping images or zooming in on images. Even small changes can significantly improve model performance. We can use the same `ImageDataGenerator` class to conduct these transformations. The Keras documentation (referenced in "See Also" on page 333) specifies the full list of available transformations; however, our example contains a sample of them are, including random zooming, shifting, flipping, and rotation.

It is important to note that the output of `flow_from_directory` is a Python generator object. This is because in most cases we will want to process the images on-demand as they are sent to the neural network for training. If we wanted to process all the images prior to training, we could simply iterate over the generator.

Finally, since `augment_images` is a generator, when training our neural network we will have to use `fit_generator` instead of `fit`. For example:

```
# Train neural network
network.fit_generator(augment_images,
                      #Number of times to call the generator for each epoch
                      steps_per_epoch=2000,
                      # Number of epochs
                      epochs=5,
                      # Test data generator
                      validation_data=augment_images_test,
                      # Number of items to call the generator
                      # for each test epoch
                      validation_steps=800)
```

Note all the raw images used in this recipe are available on GitHub (*http://bit.ly/ 2FvrVVq*).

See Also

- Image Preprocessing, Keras (*https://keras.io/preprocessing/image/*)

20.17 Classifying Text

Problem

You want to classify text data.

Solution

Use a long short-term memory recurrent neural network:

```
# Load libraries
import numpy as np
from keras.datasets import imdb
from keras.preprocessing import sequence
from keras import models
from keras import layers

# Set random seed
np.random.seed(0)

# Set the number of features we want
number_of_features = 1000

# Load data and target vector from movie review data
(data_train, target_train), (data_test, target_test) = imdb.load_data(
    num_words=number_of_features)

# Use padding or truncation to make each observation have 400 features
features_train = sequence.pad_sequences(data_train, maxlen=400)
features_test = sequence.pad_sequences(data_test, maxlen=400)

# Start neural network
network = models.Sequential()

# Add an embedding layer
network.add(layers.Embedding(input_dim=number_of_features, output_dim=128))

# Add a long short-term memory layer with 128 units
network.add(layers.LSTM(units=128))

# Add fully connected layer with a sigmoid activation function
network.add(layers.Dense(units=1, activation="sigmoid"))

# Compile neural network
network.compile(loss="binary_crossentropy", # Cross-entropy
```

```
                    optimizer="Adam", # Adam optimization
                    metrics=["accuracy"]) # Accuracy performance metric

# Train neural network
history = network.fit(features_train, # Features
                      target_train, # Target
                      epochs=3, # Number of epochs
                      verbose=0, # Do not print description after each epoch
                      batch_size=1000, # Number of observations per batch
                      validation_data=(features_test, target_test)) # Test data

Using TensorFlow backend.
```

Discussion

Oftentimes we have text data that we want to classify. While it is possible to use a type of convolutional network, we are going to focus on a more popular option: the recurrent neural network. The key feature of recurrent neural networks is that information loops back in the network. This gives recurrent neural networks a type of memory they can use to better understand sequential data. A popular type of recurrent neural network is the long short-term memory (LSTM) network, which allows for information to loop backward in the network. For a more detailed explanation, see the additional resources.

In this solution, we have our movie review data from Recipe 20.3 and we want to train an LSTM network to predict if these reviews are positive or negative. Before we can train our network, a little data processing is needed. Our text data comes in the form of a list of integers:

```
# View first observation
print(data_train[0])
```

```
[1, 14, 22, 16, 43, 530, 973, 2, 2, 65, 458, 2, 66, 2, 4, 173, 36, 256, 5, 25,
    100, 43, 838, 112, 50, 670, 2, 9, 35, 480, 284, 5, 150, 4, 172, 112, 167, 2,
    336, 385, 39, 4, 172, 2, 2, 17, 546, 38, 13, 447, 4, 192, 50, 16, 6, 147, 2,
    19, 14, 22, 4, 2, 2, 469, 4, 22, 71, 87, 12, 16, 43, 530, 38, 76, 15, 13, 2,
    4, 22, 17, 515, 17, 12, 16, 626, 18, 2, 5, 62, 386, 12, 8, 316, 8, 106, 5, 4,
    2, 2, 16, 480, 66, 2, 33, 4, 130, 12, 16, 38, 619, 5, 25, 124, 51, 36, 135,
    48, 25, 2, 33, 6, 22, 12, 215, 28, 77, 52, 5, 14, 407, 16, 82, 2, 8, 4, 107,
    117, 2, 15, 256, 4, 2, 7, 2, 5, 723, 36, 71, 43, 530, 476, 26, 400, 317, 46,
    7, 4, 2, 2, 13, 104, 88, 4, 381, 15, 297, 98, 32, 2, 56, 26, 141, 6, 194, 2,
    18, 4, 226, 22, 21, 134, 476, 26, 480, 5, 144, 30, 2, 18, 51, 36, 28, 224,
    92, 25, 104, 4, 226, 65, 16, 38, 2, 88, 12, 16, 283, 5, 16, 2, 113, 103, 32,
    15, 16, 2, 19, 178, 32]
```

Each integer in this list corresponds to some word. However, because each review does not contain the same number of words, each observation is not the same length. Therefore, before we can input this data into our neural network, we need to make all the observations the same length. We can do this using pad_sequences. pad_sequen ces pads each observation's data so that they are all the same size. We can see this if we look at our first observation after it is processed by pad_sequences:

```
# View first observation
print(features_test[0])
```

```
[  0   0   0   0   0   0   0   0   0   0   0   0   0   0   0   0   0   0
   0   0   0   0   0   0   0   0   0   0   0   0   0   0   0   0   0   0
   0   0   0   0   0   0   0   0   0   0   0   0   0   0   0   0   0   0
   0   0   0   0   0   0   0   0   0   0   0   0   0   0   0   0   0   0
   0   0   0   0   0   0   0   0   0   0   0   0   0   0   0   0   0   0
   0   0   0   0   0   0   0   0   0   0   0   0   0   0   0   0   0   0
   0   0   0   0   0   0   0   0   0   0   0   0   0   0   0   0   0   0
   0   0   0   0   0   0   0   0   0   0   0   0   0   0   0   0   0   0
   0   0   0   0   0   0   0   0   0   0   0   0   0   0   0   0   0   0
   0   0   0   0   0   0   0   0   0   0   0   0   0   0   0   0   0   0
   0   0   0   0   0   0   0   0   0   0   0   0   0   0   0   0   0   0
   0   0   0   0   0   0   0   0   0   0   0   0   0   0   0   0   0   0
   0   0   0   0   0   0   0   0   0   0   0   0   0   0   0   0   0   0
   0   0   0   0   0   0   0   0   0   0   0   0   0   0   0   0   0   0
   0   0   0   0   0   0   0   0   0   0   0   0   0   0   0   0   0   0
   0   0   0   0   0   0   0   0   0   0   0   0   0   0   0   0   0   0
   0   0   0   0   0   0   0   0   0   0   0   0   0   0   0   0   0   0
   0   0   0   0   0   0   0   0   0   0   0   0   0   0   0   0   0   0
   0   0   0   0   1  89  27   2   2  17 199 132   5   2  16   2  24   8
 760   4   2   7   4  22   2   2  16   2  17   2   7   2   2   9   4   2
   8  14 991  13 877  38  19  27 239  13 100 235  61 483   2   4   7   4
  20 131   2  72   8  14 251  27   2   7 308  16 735   2  17  29 144  28
  77   2  18  12]
```

Next, we use one of the most promising techniques in natural language processing: word embeddings. In our binary classifier from Recipe 20.3, we one-hot encoded the observations and used that as inputs to the neural network. However, this time we will represent each word as a vector in a multidimensional space, and allow the distance between two vectors to represent the similarity between words. In Keras we can do this by adding an Embedding layer. For each value sent to the Embedding layer, it will output a vector representing that word. The following layer is our LSTM layer with 128 units, which allows for information from earlier inputs to be used in futures, directly addressing the sequential nature of the data. Finally, because this is a binary classification problem (each review is positive or negative), we add a fully connected output layer with one unit and a sigmoid activation function.

It is worth noting that LSTMs are a very broad topic and the focus of much research. This recipe, while hopefully useful, is far from the last word on the implementation of LSTMs.

## CHAPTER 21

Saving and Loading Trained Models

21.0 Introduction

In the last 20 chapters and around 200 recipes, we have covered how to take raw data and use machine learning to create well-performing predictive models. However, for all our work to be worthwhile we eventually need to *do something* with our model, such as integrating it with an existing software application. To accomplish this goal, we need to be able to both save our models after training and load them when they are needed by an application. That is the focus of our final chapter together.

21.1 Saving and Loading a scikit-learn Model

Problem

You have a trained scikit-learn model and want to save it and load it elsewhere.

Solution

Save the model as a pickle file:

```
# Load libraries
from sklearn.ensemble import RandomForestClassifier
from sklearn import datasets
from sklearn.externals import joblib

# Load data
iris = datasets.load_iris()
features = iris.data
target = iris.target

# Create decision tree classifer object
classifer = RandomForestClassifier()
```

```
# Train model
model = classifer.fit(features, target)

# Save model as pickle file
joblib.dump(model, "model.pkl")

['model.pkl']
```

Once the model is saved we can use scikit-learn in our destination application (e.g., web application) to load the model:

```
# Load model from file
classifer = joblib.load("model.pkl")
```

And use it make predictions:

```
# Create new observation
new_observation = [[ 5.2,  3.2,  1.1,  0.1]]

# Predict observation's class
classifer.predict(new_observation)

array([0])
```

Discussion

The first step in using a model in production is to save that model as a file that can be loaded by another application or workflow. We can accomplish this by saving the model as a pickle file, a Python-specific data format. Specifically, to save the model we use joblib, which is a library extending pickle for cases when we have large NumPy arrays—a common occurrence for trained models in scikit-learn.

When saving scikit-learn models, be aware that saved models might not be compatible between versions of scikit-learn; therefore, it can be helpful to include the version of scikit-learn used in the model in the filename:

```
# Import library
import sklearn

# Get scikit-learn version
scikit_version = joblib.__version__

# Save model as pickle file
joblib.dump(model, "model_{version}.pkl".format(version=scikit_version))

['model_0.11.pkl']
```

21.2 Saving and Loading a Keras Model

Problem

You have a trained Keras model and want to save it and load it elsewhere.

Solution

Save the model as HDF5:

```
# Load libraries
import numpy as np
from keras.datasets import imdb
from keras.preprocessing.text import Tokenizer
from keras import models
from keras import layers
from keras.models import load_model

# Set random seed
np.random.seed(0)

# Set the number of features we want
number_of_features = 1000

# Load data and target vector from movie review data
(train_data, train_target), (test_data, test_target) = imdb.load_data(
    num_words=number_of_features)

# Convert movie review data to a one-hot encoded feature matrix
tokenizer = Tokenizer(num_words=number_of_features)
train_features = tokenizer.sequences_to_matrix(train_data, mode="binary")
test_features = tokenizer.sequences_to_matrix(test_data, mode="binary")

# Start neural network
network = models.Sequential()

# Add fully connected layer with a ReLU activation function
network.add(layers.Dense(units=16,
                         activation="relu",
                         input_shape=(number_of_features,)))

# Add fully connected layer with a sigmoid activation function
network.add(layers.Dense(units=1, activation="sigmoid"))

# Compile neural network
network.compile(loss="binary_crossentropy", # Cross-entropy
                optimizer="rmsprop", # Root Mean Square Propagation
                metrics=["accuracy"]) # Accuracy performance metric

# Train neural network
history = network.fit(train_features, # Features
```

```
                    train_target, # Target vector
                    epochs=3, # Number of epochs
                    verbose=0, # No output
                    batch_size=100, # Number of observations per batch
                    validation_data=(test_features, test_target)) # Test data
```

```
# Save neural network
network.save("model.h5")
```

```
Using TensorFlow backend.
```

We can then load the model either in another application or for additional training:

```
# Load neural network
network = load_model("model.h5")
```

Discussion

Unlike scikit-learn, Keras does not recommend you save models using pickle. Instead, models are saved as an HDF5 file. The HDF5 file contains everything you need to not only load the model to make predictions (i.e., architecture and trained parameters), but also to restart training (i.e., loss and optimizer settings and the current state).

Index

A

accuracy, 186-188
AdaBoostClassifier, 247-249
AdaBoostRegressor, 247-249
adaptiveThreshold, 137-140
affinity, 295
Agglomerative clustering, 294-295
algorithm, 255
algorithms for faster model selection, 219-220
ANOVA F-value statistic, 174, 176
append, 56
apply, 54, 55
area under the ROC curve (AUCROC), 192
arrays
    descriptive statistics about, 8
    max and min methods, 7
    one-dimensional, 1
    reshaping, 9-10
    slicing, 126-128
    two-dimensional, 2
augment_images, 332
average, 8, 42
axis, 8, 55, 56

B

back-filling, 120
backpropagation, 298
Bag of Words model, 104-106
balanced, 245, 265
bandwidth, 292
baseline classification model, 184-186
baseline regression model, 183-184
base_estimator, 248
batch_size, 291, 304

Bayes' theorem, 279-286
    (see also naive Bayes classifiers)
Beautiful Soup, 97
Bernoulli naive Bayes, 283-284
best_estimator_, 215
best_params, 324
BigramTagger, 103
Binarizer, 73
binarizing images, 137-140
binary classifier thresholds, 189-192
binary classifiers, 259-260, 301, 303-305
binary feature variance thresholding, 171
bins, 74
blurring images, 128-130
boolean conditions, 112
bootstrap, 240, 241
Brown Corpus text tagger, 103

C

C, 210
calibrating predicted probabilities, 284-286
callbacks, 316, 319
Canny edge detector, 144-146
categorical data, 81-94
    dictionary encoding, 86-88
    imbalanced classes, 90-94
    imputing missing values, 89-90
    nominal features encoding, 82-84
    nominal versus ordinal, 81
    ordinal features encoding, 84-86
chi-squared statistics, 174-176
class separability maximization, 162-164
classes, 102
classification_report, 203

make_classification, 25-27
make_regression, 25-26
make_scorer, 200-201
Manhattan distance, 253
Matplotlib, 122, 310-313
matrices
    adding/subtracting, 17
    calculating trace, 14
    compressed sparse row (CSR), 4
    confusion matrix, 194-196
    creating, 2-4
    describing, 6
    determinants, 12
    diagonal elements, 13
    factorization, 165-166
    finding Eigenvalues/Eigenvectors, 15
    flattening, 12
    inverting, 19
    multiplying, 18
    rank, 12
    selecting elements in, 4
        m1sei, 5
    sparse, 3, 105
max pooling, 330
maximum/minimum values, 7, 42
max_depth, 247
max_features, 239, 241
max_output_value, 139
mean, 42
mean color as feature, 152
mean squared error (MSE), 196-198
meanshift clustering, 291
median, 43
merge, 57-60
metric, 253, 255, 293
mini-batch k-means clustering, 290
Minkowski distance, 253
MinMaxScaler, 61-62
min_impurity_split, 247
min_samples, 293
Missing At Random (MAR), 77
Missing Completely At Random (MCAR), 77
missing data, 76-79
missing data in time series, 118-120
Missing Not At Random (MNAR), 77
mode, 43
model evaluation, 179-207
    baseline classification model, 184-186
    baseline regression model, 183-184

binary classifier prediction evaluation,
    186-188
binary classifier thresholds, 189-192
classification report, 203
classifier performance visualization,
    194-196
clustering models, 198-199
cross-validation (CV), 179
custom evaluation metric, 199-201
hyperparameter value effects, 205-207
multiclass classifier predictions, 192-194
regression models, 196-198
training set size visualization, 201-203
model selection, 209-222
    algorithm-specific methods for speed,
        219-220
    exhaustive search, 210-211
    from multiple learning algorithms, 214-215
    parallelization for speed, 217-218
    post-selection performance evaluation,
        220-222
    preprocessing during, 215-217
    randomized search, 212-213
model.pkl, 338, 338
ModelCheckpoint, 317, 319-320
models, xiii
model_to_dot, 325-326
moving time windows, 117-118
multiclass classifier predictions, 192-194
multiclass classifiers, 301, 305-307
multinomial logistic regression (MLR), 261-262
multinomial naive Bayes, 282-283

N

n-grams, 105
naive Bayes classifiers, 279-286
    Bernoulli, 283-284
    calibrating predicted probabilities, 284-286
    Gaussian, 280-282
    multinomial, 282-283
Natural Language Toolkit (NLTK), 99
    PorterStemmer, 100
    pre-trained parts of speech tagger, 101-103
    stopwords, 99
    word_tokenize, 98
neg_mean_squared_error, 197
nested cross-validation (CV), 220-222
neural networks, 297-335
    binary classification, 303-305

calculating dot products, 16
creating, 1
selecting elements in, 4-5
verbose, 211, 304
visualization of classifier performance, 194-196

weight regularization, 313-315
weights, 255
whiten=True, 159
word embeddings, 335
word tokenization, 98

W
weekday_name, 115

About the Author

Chris Albon is a data scientist and political scientist with a decade of experience applying statistical learning, artificial intelligence, and software engineering to political, social, and humanitarian efforts—from election monitoring to disaster relief. Currently, Chris is the Chief Data Scientist at BRCK, a Kenyan startup building a rugged network for frontier market internet users.

Colophon

The animal on the cover of *Machine Learning with Python Cookbook* is the Narina trogon (*Apaloderma narina*), which is named for the mistress of French ornithologist François Levaillant, who derived the name from a Khoikhoi word for "flower", as his mistress's name was difficult to pronounce. The Narina trogon is largely found in Africa, inhabiting both low and highlands, and tropical and temperate climates, usually nesting in the hollows of trees. Its diverse range of habitats makes it a species of least conservation concern.

The Narina trogon eats mostly insects and small invertebrates as well as small rodents and reptiles. Males, which are more brightly colored, give off a grating, low, repeated hoot to defend territory and attract mates. Both sexes have green upper plumage and metallic blue-green tail feathers. Female faces and chest plumages are brown, while males have bright red undersides. Immature birds have similar coloring to females with distinct white tips to their inner wings.

Many of the animals on O'Reilly covers are endangered; all of them are important to the world. To learn more about how you can help, go to *animals.oreilly.com*.

The cover image is from *Wood's Animate Creation*. The cover fonts are URW Typewriter and Guardian Sans. The text font is Adobe Minion Pro; the heading font is Adobe Myriad Condensed; and the code font is Dalton Maag's Ubuntu Mono.

Learn from experts.
Find the answers you need.

Sign up for a **10-day free trial** to get **unlimited access** to all of the content on Safari, including Learning Paths, interactive tutorials, and curated playlists that draw from thousands of ebooks and training videos on a wide range of topics, including data, design, DevOps, management, business—and much more.

Start your free trial at:
oreilly.com/safari

(No credit card required)

Lightning Source UK Ltd.
Milton Keynes UK
UKHW03f0103140518
322475UK00003B/4/P